The Illustrated

AT THE FIRESIDE

TRUE SOUTHERN AFRICAN STORIES

Roger Webster

SPEARHEAD

Published by Spearhead
An imprint of New Africa Books (Pty) Ltd.
99 Garfield Road
Claremont
7700

(021) 674 4136
info@newafricabooks.co.za

First edition 2003

ISBN 0-86486-558-9

Cover design by Toby Newsome
Editing by Sue Ollerhead
Artwork by Robert Hichens
Design by Fresh Identity
Typesetting by Charlene Bate
Photographs courtesy of the National Library of South Africa, the Knysna Museum
and the Adelaide Dutch Reformed Church
Reproduction by House of Colours
Printed and bound by Clyson Printers, 11th Avenue, Maitland

CONTENTS

FOREWORD

There is Big History, about dates and battles and people with epaulettes. We learn it at school. It skids into hibernation at noon on the day of the matric exam, henceforth to muster on average one heartbeat per five years under the tutorship of a Mel Gibson or a Charlton Heston. Big History, properly viewed, is interesting, not to say riveting, but it labours under the misfortune of being linked in our minds to (a) battling to stay awake until the break bell rings, and (b) the propaganda of winning sides.

Then there is little history, about people you've never heard of whose dates scarcely matter. Extremely few people ever deliberately *learn* little history, anywhere or ever. Instead, the fortunate among us may find that it sneaks up and smites us with a soft 'cosh', like sand in a sock, so we don't know what hit us. We just think someone has told us a story, an adventure story or a poignant story or a romance story – a story that touches us.

Roger tells us stories. Yo, doesn't he just! He tells us stories of triumphs and of disappointments, of pain and of joy, of brutality and of horror but also, and especially, of love and faith and trust and sincerity. It's a surprise, when we come round and wonder what hit us, to realise that these are more than stories; these are our past, our background; part of where our society came from and what informed its thinking; our history.

How Roger digs these things up, heaven knows. His knack of keeping eyes and ears extremely wide open must help. His unchained spirit must help – no rules or themes for Roger; any story of any kind of person from any corner of the land and any quarter of the human spectrum; as long as it's a story. But the extent of the search, taking him from the archives of the Cape to the gogos of Limpopo and everywhere between … no-one has half this widely, half this eclectically, traversed South Africa's time, South Africa's space.

I particularly appreciate Roger's bent towards the uplifting. I have a similar outlook – find the truth, whether it's a happy truth or the other kind, but when the truth you find speaks of the beauty of the human soul … aah, revel! There are times we South Africans almost persuade ourselves that the entire past was a long round of aggro and brutality. Thanks, Roger, for miraculously hunting down so many examples of the human nobility that makes us wiser and stronger, and humbled.

May this special edition of already successful books be followed by more of the same. Better, may it be followed by sequel. That's the thing about little history: once you get the taste, you're hooked. Roger, bring out the magnifying glass, unleash the bloodhound, and keep hunting.

Khotso! Sterkte!

Denis Beckett

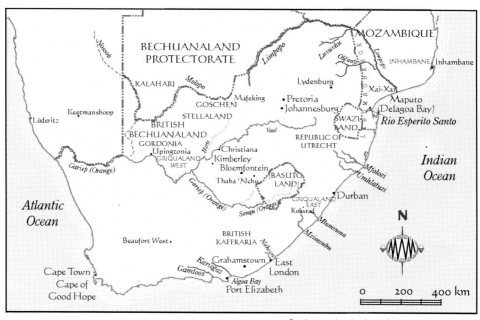

Settlers and colonisers frequently changed
country and area boundaries of South Africa
until an agreement on provincial boundaries
was formed in 1910

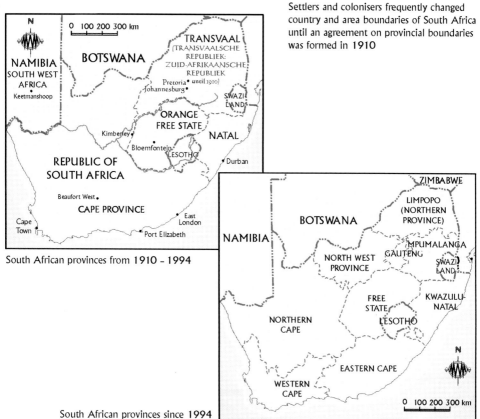

South African provinces from 1910 – 1994

South African provinces since 1994

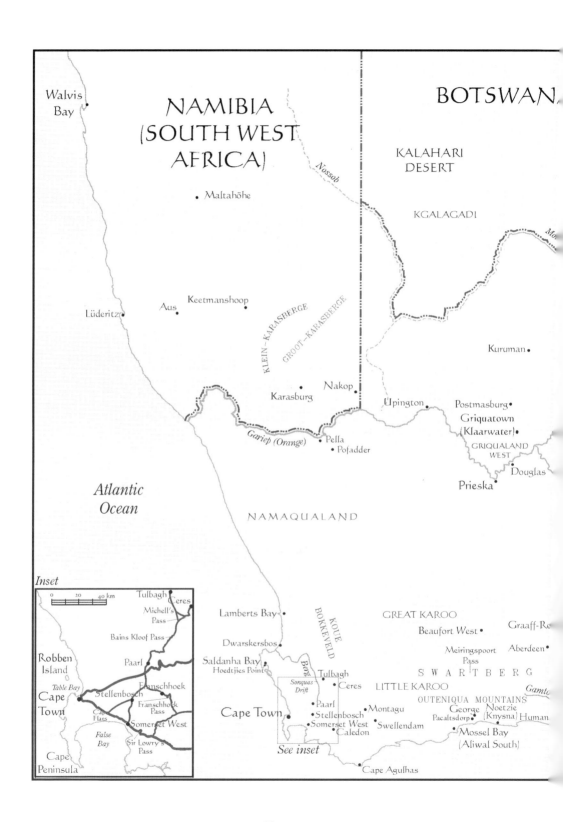

NAMIBIA (SOUTH WEST AFRICA)

BOTSWAN...

Walvis Bay

Maltahöhe

Nossob

KALAHARI DESERT

KGALAGADI

Mo...

Lüderitz

Aus

Keetmanshoop

KLEIN-KARASBERGE

GROOT-KARASBERGE

Kuruman

Karasburg

Nakop

Upington

Postmasburg

Griquatown (Klaarwater)

GRIQUALAND WEST

Gariep (Orange)

Pella

Pofadder

Prieska

Douglas

Atlantic Ocean

NAMAQUALAND

Inset

0   20   40 km

Tulbagh

Ceres

Michell's Pass

Bains Kloof Pass

Robben Island

Table Bay

Cape Town

Paarl

Stellenbosch

Franschhoek Pass

Franschhoek

Cape Flats

False Bay

Somerset West

Sir Lowry's Pass

Cape Peninsula

Lamberts Bay

KOUE BOKKEVELD

Dwarskersbos

Saldanha Bay

Hoedtjies Point

Berg

Sonquas Drift

Tulbagh

Ceres

Cape Town

Paarl

Stellenbosch

Montagu

Somerset West

Caledon

Swellendam

See inset

Cape Agulhas

GREAT KAROO

Beaufort West

Graaff-Re...

Meiringspoort Pass

Aberdeen

SWARTBERG

LITTLE KAROO

OUTENIQUA MOUNTAINS

Gamto...

George

Noetzie

Pacaltsdorp

(Knysna)

Human...

Mossel Bay (Aliwal South)

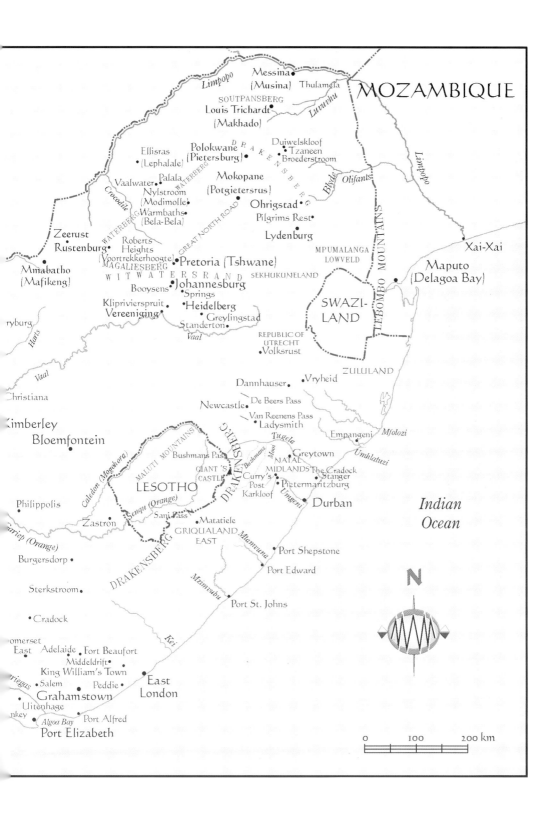

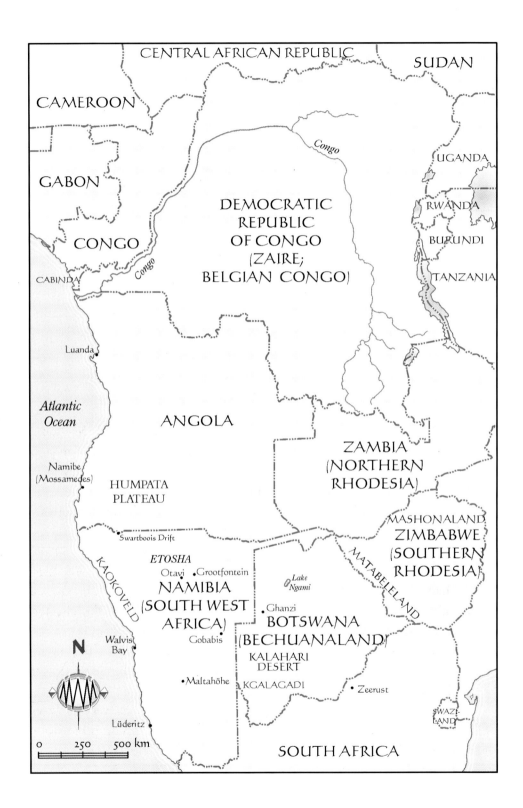

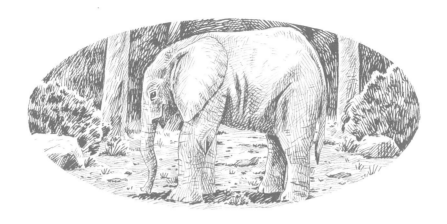

Jabulani of
Kapama

I t's not often in one's life that you meet someone who stands head and
shoulders above the crowd; someone whose very spirit, passion and
indomitable drive sets them apart. I'm fortunate enough to have met
such a person – her name is Lente Roode.

In 1949, Lente's father and his three brothers bought the farm Kapama,
which borders on Timbavati and the Kruger National Park in Mpumalanga.
Gradually, her father bought out his brothers, one by one. In 1985, Lente,
who was now married to Johan Roode, bought the farm adjacent to Kapama.

She had always longed to keep cheetahs, having reared a cheetah cub as a
young girl. Her lifelong wish was to become a reality when the cheetah
research station at Loskop Dam near Middelburg ran into financial difficulties. Johan surprised her and bought the station's 35 cheetahs – thus Lente
began her cheetah rehabilitation project on the farm. On the death of her
father, Lente inherited Kapama and merged the two farms.

One morning, a Phalaborwa vet phoned the Roode's farm vet, Dr Peter
Rodgers, saying that conservationists had found a three-month-old baby
elephant dying in a pool of mud. They had purposefully left it, hoping that the
mother would return. She didn't. The Roodes rescued the young bull elephant

and named him Jabulani, an isiZulu word meaning 'to be happy'. He was injured, frightened, and very close to death.

Knowing very little about elephants, Lente frantically gathered as much information as she could from experts around the country. She was told that she shouldn't assign only one human to work with Jabulani, as this would result in him bonding strongly with that person. Were this person to be absent later, Jabulani would pine terribly, and eventually die. Following these orders, and applying consistent, loving care, the young elephant started to pull through.

A hand-raised sheep was introduced into Jabulani's enclosure, to keep him company at night. Soon, Jabulani and Skaap became inseparable. It became a familiar sight – the baby elephant and sheep wandering around the farm together.

Then, disaster struck. Skaap was found dead in the sleeping enclosure – it was thought that Jabulani had accidentally rolled on his little friend during the night. The Roodes had other wild elephants on the farm, and they decided that it was time to introduce them to Jabulani. The wild elephants did not take to this 'human' elephant. They began to intimidate him, and it soon became clear that they would kill him.

Lente was forced to advertise for an elephant nurse. A young, local lad called Flippie Botha, who had grown up with wildlife, pleaded for the job. Flippie is still with Jabulani. So Jabulani lived on in captivity, with Lente fully aware that, in time to come, a captive bull would become a problem. They started looking for a new home for him.

One day, out of the blue, Lente received a phone call from Rory Hensman, a Zimbabwean farmer from Chinhoyi, a district northwest of Harare. Robert Mugabe's so-called war veterans had invaded his farm, which was home to twelve tame elephants used for elephant-riding safaris at Victoria Falls. He wanted to know whether the Roodes could take them on, before the farm fell completely into the hands of the invaders. The Roodes consulted experts to find out if this type of practice was acceptable, and were delighted when they realised that it was. This type of activity would suit Jabulani down to the ground. Being 'half-human', Jabulani would thrive on people – he was already used to people on his back.

But the tame elephants were on Rory's farm at Chinhoyi, and with the farm now swarming with war veterans, the only safe haven for the elephants was the river. Rory had a valid export permit, but Lente had no import permit. To obtain one is no easy task, but, with the help of Limpopo Premier, Ngoako Ramatlodi, Lente was finally granted the necessary permit. Lente remains deeply grateful to him, as timing was to prove crucial.

Eventually, with the permits secured, the elephants, along with their twelve trainers, crossed over the border into South Africa, two days prior to the Zimbabwe elections. The costs had been enormous, the transport, the watering, the stockading on the farm all added up to well over one million rand, money that Lente had borrowed from her husband and a very close friend.

In due course, the elephants arrived at Kapama. They were placed in a separate enclosure, far away from Jabulani. Rory Hensman went back to his beautiful farm in Chinhoyi, only to find that it had been completely taken over by the war veterans, who shot at him and his wife as they tried to enter through the farm gates. They fled to South Africa, with only the clothes on their backs. Had the elephants not been moved, they surely would have been history.

Lente Roode with Jabulani

Back at Kapama, in the enclosure, the tame elephants were left to acclimatise to their new surroundings.

Eventually the time came for the meeting of the half-human, five-year-old Jabulani and the new herd from Zimbabwe. Lente couldn't sleep for days. She prayed constantly, knowing that little Jabulani's fate hung in the balance. If he were rejected, he would have to go.

They walked Jabulani down the road towards the herd. There were some very tense moments of sniffing and grunting, when everybody held their breath. The matriarch pushed to the front and faced little Jabulani square-on. The moment had come. She gently lifted her trunk, sniffing his surrounding air, and then softly laid it around the neck of the little bull elephant. Acceptance was immediate. Upon seeing this, Lente Roode sunk to her knees and, with her head in her hands, wept openly. Her lonely little Jabulani had eventually found a family.

Lente has since built a lodge called Camp Jabulani. Visitors are allocated their own elephant for the duration of their stay, so that they can experience all aspects of these gentle giants, from elephant-back safaris, to feeding and watering them, and even swimming with them.

For Lente, this undertaking is about passion, not money. It is the very essence of her life. Tragically, her beloved husband of over 30 years passed away shortly after the elephants had been relocated.

This is a tribute to a woman of immense heart and soul, a true South African.

THE EARLY
HOTTENTOTS

For many years now, I have been fascinated by the Native Americans – their numerous different tribes, belief systems, social structures, dress and behavioural patterns, as well as the myriad festivals and dances celebrated by these mostly misunderstood people.

What strikes me most forcibly is the fact that right here, in our very own country, we had races of people who were just as diverse and colourful as the Native Americans, if not more so. These people performed spirit dances, fertility rituals, moon dances and general festivities to encourage the rainy season, the season of harvesting and the hunting season.

Why is it that we stand in awe of other people's cultures, but largely ignore our own? It is unfortunate that we generally do not realise what a great and diverse nation we are growing into, and what a diverse and rich history we have.When you tell the average South African that the Magaliesberg range is the second oldest mountain range on the planet, you are greeted with looks of utter amazement, usually followed by the next question, 'Where's the oldest?' The answer is the Lebombos, also in South Africa. When you say that the cradle of mankind is euphemistic, for it is actually the area where the very first forms of Life commenced on planet

Earth, people are left gasping. But let's get back to our people.

Today's Zulu Nation was welded together from many different tribal groups, as were the Xhosas, who consisted mainly of the Gqunukhwebe, the Gcaleka, the Pondo, the Fingo, and numerous other splinter groups that go into making up what we roughly call the Xhosa nation today.

One grouping of people that has always intrigued me is the Hottentots. This group of people derived their name from the Dutch words *hut en tut*, which literally mean 'to stammer or stutter whilst speaking'. Some of their dialects consisted of a series of complicated and delicate clicks using palate and tongue, very much like the Masarwa or Bushmen use today. So, to the largely uneducated Dutch peasants who came out to the Cape during the seventeenth century, anybody who spoke with a click and was not fair of skin was called a Hottentot.

Nothing could have been further from the truth. Let's go back to my original example. Amongst the Native Americans we find the Cherokee, Seneca, Cheyenne, Pawnee, Commanche, Sioux, Cree, Mohawk and so on. Here in South Africa, under the broad heading of Hottentots, we too find numerous tribes. Starting at the northwest coast and Namaqualand, going down to the Cape of Good Hope, and then, turning eastwards and stopping at the Kei River, you find the Namaquas, Hensaquas, Gurigriquas, Chainauquas, Hossas, Kochoquas, Goringhaikonas, Attaquas, Ayunnquas, Autiniquas, Hankumquas, Sonquas and the Kabonas.

The first three tribes to occupy the area around Table Bay and False Bay, were the Goringhaiquas, whom the Dutch called 'Cape Men', the Goringhaikonas, who were known as 'the Water Men' and the Gorachouquas, alias the 'Tobacco Thieves'.

None of these people ever cultivated the soil. They were essentially a semi-nomadic, pastoral people, with herds of long-horned cattle and fat-tailed sheep. Their main diet was milk. Women did the milking, whilst the men performed general pasturing and herding duties. Supplements to the diet were wild fruits, berries and tubers of various kinds. Meat was a luxury and was obtained by hunting – a task for the men. Domestic animals were never slaughtered, save for festive or ceremonial occasions.

These nomadic tribes would range in size from a couple of hundred up to several thousand people, and each tribe had its own territory. Land was exploited on equal terms, by all sub-groups of the tribe. No individual ever owned land, nor did it ever belong to the chief. Land was regarded as inalienable. In the old records of the Cape, several instances of land being 'sold' to the colonists by chiefs are not strictly correct. Those transactions would have been looked upon, not as alienation, but as the granting of usufruct, and the purchase price would be the tribute paid for that usage.

This vast difference in belief structure between the Hottentots and the Dutch immediately set the stage for a conflict of interest. On the one hand, there were people to whom ownership of land was part of their culture, and on the other hand were those who believed that land could never be owned, but merely shared.

Another salient difference was the fact that the Hottentots did not till the soil. The European element saw this as pure laziness on their behalf, but according to the Hottentots, tilling of the soil was an absolute no-no. And here's the reason why.

In line with ancient Greek language, everything was either male or female. The Earth, as in pagan belief, was female, and was akin to the female ova. When it rained, the millions of raindrops that would fall onto the Earth's surface were likened to male sperm penetrating the ova. With the help of the male Sun's warmth, which was likened to love, the female Earth would grow, and her people would live off the proceeds. For a man to interfere with this highly feminine ritual of birth and growth, would have been regarded with great disdain by the tribe.

The 'Water Men' were a small group of about 60, including women and children, and occupied a total of about six huts. They were the breakaway tribe of the Goringhaikonas, and were mentioned in the records as Strandlopers or 'beach rangers'. This tribe possessed no cattle at all, and eked out a living by fishing and collecting creatures from the sea. They were noted as the only permanent inhabitants of the peninsula at the time of the arrival of the Dutch settlers in 1652. They were the poorest of the three tribes, and supplemented their income by selling part-time labour to the settlers.

In the early years of this settlement, the Strandlopers were under the leadership of X'hore or 'Herry', as the Dutch called him. This was the now well-known leader who had been taken to England long before the arrival of the Dutch. He had been taught to speak English, then returned to his people at the Cape, and, when the Dutch arrived, to their utter amazement, he greeted them in English. 'Herry die Strandloper' or X'hore, died in 1663 and was succeeded by Khaik Ana Makouka.

The Gorachouquas or 'Tobacco Thieves' are now generally believed to be the ancestors of the Koranna, a division of the Hottentots. These people adapted their name from the chief Kora, and their tribal name Koranna hence means 'men of Kora'. This tribe consisted of 400 men capable of bearing arms, and got their Dutch name from the fact that their men once stole all the tobacco plants from a free farmer in the region. The area that they occupied was east of where Cape Town stands today. They were pastoralists who owned long-horned cattle and fat-tailed sheep.

The last of these three tribes was the Goringhaiquas or 'Cape Men', thus called because they occupied the area where the Dutch settled, and always maintained that this was their ancestral land. Their chief, Gogosoa, had two sons named Osinghaikanna and Otegnoa, who constantly vied for the chieftainship, the younger always trying to do away with the elder.

Of the Cape Men, Jan van Riebeeck had said, 'They are a bad lot, as they do not respect their chief.' Altogether, they were a tribe of about 1 000 men. In 1659, a mere seven years after the settlement came into being, the first local war in the area broke out. The Goringhaiquas linked up with the Gorachouquas and attempted to expel the farmers from the area, saying that this had been their land from time immemorial. They attacked the Dutch farmers, killing, burning and looting the cattle, and successfully drove them away. A clever tactic they had developed was to hold off the attack until it started raining. This, of course, rendered the Dutch flintlocks utterly useless, and they were not very good at hand-to-hand combat.

One morning, in June 1659, after three months of skirmishes, five Hottentot men were surrounded after driving off cattle, and one Eyakamma, who had been badly wounded, was taken back to the Fort for questioning. When asked why his people had attacked the Dutch by killing, plundering and burning, he replied by asking why the Dutch had ploughed over the lands of the Hottentots, and sought to take the bread out of their very mouths by sowing corn on the very lands to which they had to drive their cattle to pasture. He stated that the reason for the attacks was nothing other than revenge for harm and injustice done to them. Not only were they commanded to keep away from certain grazing grounds, which they had always possessed, but they had seen their lands being divided up without their consent and boundaries had been put up within which they could not pasture. Finally, his people had noticed how the fortifications and bulwarks were being erected on a daily basis, which could have no other object than to bring their people under Dutch authority and domination. Never a truer sentence was spoken, for, when the Hottentots came to the Fort to sue for peace, they pressed this land issue very hard.

This is how the Dutch replied: 'In consequence of the war you waged against us, you have completely forfeited your right to the land, and we will not restore it. The land now belongs to the Company by the sword and by the rights of war.'

Eyakamma was captured on 19 July and he died in the Fort on Tuesday, 12 August 1659. And so the scene was set for South African conflict, for years to come.

Hottentots in South West Africa in the early 1900s

Up in the hills and valleys around Saldanha Bay, you will find the Kochoquas or Saldanhars, as the Dutch called them. They were all settled in sixteen villages about a quarter of a mile apart. They were pastoralists and possessed over 100 000 oxen and 200 000 sheep. Their physical features were finely chiselled and their hair was longer and less woolly than the other Hottentot tribes.

Along with the Kochoquas lived the great and the little Karichuriquas – kari meaning 'small', and hurib meaning 'sea'. This interesting group of people quickly interbred with whites. As the pressure of farmers and settlers grew, in the middle of the eighteenth century they moved away to the north and established themselves at Kamiesberg in the little Namaqualand, under the leadership of Adam Kok. It was here that they were joined by various other groups of half-breed Hottentots or 'Basters'.

From the Kamiesberg they again shifted northwards, this time on to Pella on the lower Orange River, just northwest of the town of Pofadder. Here, in 1813, they were found by the missionary John Campbell, who managed to persuade them to resume their old, mostly forgotten name. They became the Griquas – Griquatown is named after them. Under a succession of able leaders, they played a significant role in the political history of South Africa (see 'Adam Kok's Trek' in *At the Fireside*).

Eighteenth-century etching of a Griqua woman

Going in the opposite direction, eastward from the peninsula, far past the Attaquas, and the Autiniquas, dwelt a reputedly savage race of people, who were very dark in colour, with hair so long that it flowed down their backs and hung on the ground. They were said to be cannibals, for if they caught a Hottentot or any other person, they would roast them alive and eat them. They were called the Kabonas. The local Hottentots were terrified of these people. In reality, if we read Van Riebeeck's dispatches, the Kabonas are not Hottentots at all. This is merely the name by which the Hottentots referred to the amaXhosa.

Van Riebeeck heard of this race of people from the well-known Hottentot girl Eva, who told him a marvellous tale of an emperor or king who was called Chobona, who lived far inland and was rich in gold. The gold was taken out of the sand, and the coins that they made were bigger than the palm of a grown man's hand. They lived in large houses of stone and beams, sowing rice and vegetables and speaking a language unlike any heard by the Hottentots in the Cape.

Jan van Riebeeck, haunted by the thought of their vast wealth, sent out several expeditions in search of them. They found no gold and no Chobona, but plenty of Nama and an abundance of copper.

The next tribe is the Sonquas, who dwelt in the mountainous regions of the country. They numbered several thousand and were very small in stature, keeping no cattle and subsisting mainly on dassies. These of course are the Bushmen, who occupied vast areas of land in the central regions and the Drakensberg at that time. The Bushmen gained a very bad name amongst the Hottentots as well as other settlers, for they believed that not only did the land belong to everyone, but so did all the animals. This of course included the cattle and sheep, which they would hunt with impunity from both the Hottentots and the local farmers. There is no doubt that this belief led to them being hunted down and exterminated mercilessly by other people, to the very brink of extinction.

The last to be mentioned are the Namaquas, whose name was mentioned to the commander Van Riebeeck by Eva in 1657. However, the Dutch did not come into contact with them until 1661, when they were encountered by the Cruythoff expedition. In later years, the Dutch learned to differentiate between the Little Namaquas, living in what is now Namaqualand South, and the Greater Namaquas, living north of the Orange River. When they encountered them, they were welcomed with open arms and a group of about 100 musicians. Each with a hollow reed of a different length, they stood in a circle and, by blowing upon the reeds, produced a very pleasant harmony. This musical performance lasted for two hours and the chief then entertained his guests with roasted lamb and milk. In turn, the expedition presented the chief with copper, red beads, brandy and tobacco. Neither the chief nor his people had ever smoked or drunk brandy. This they learned in a very short time and, as is the case for the Inuits of Greenland, both of these activities were destined to become the scourge of their people.

Bushmen women in the Kalahari Desert, 1920

Just before departing this fascinating subject, the Hottentot girl, Eva, is worth a mention. She was the niece of the famous Chief Herry, and the sister-in-law of the Kochoqua chief, Oedasoa. Her real name was Krotoa. She began service with the Van Riebeeck family soon after their arrival at the Cape, and was so good at the Dutch language that she became an interpreter. In 1657 she was fifteen years old, and with the coming of Commander Wagenaar in 1662, she was baptised 'Eva'.

In June 1664 she was married to the Dutch explorer, Pieter van Meerhoff. She bore him three children. When he died in Madagascar, she slipped into a life of debauchery and was sent to Robben Island where, although she could obtain no drink, she abandoned herself to immorality. She was returned to Cape Town and died on 29 July 1674. The archive entry for the following day reads as follows:

'The body of the deceased Hottentot, Eva, was, notwithstanding her un-Christian life, buried today according to Christian usage, in the Church grounds of the New Castle.'

I think that this account is rather biased, for later research has shown that Eva actually accumulated wealth and property in Cape Town, and was an accepted member of Cape society. Such is the bias that has been put into our history.

PERCEPTIONS IN
PEOPLE'S HISTORY

In examining the ancient beliefs and perceptions of people from different continents, it is fascinating to see what guided certain peoples to draw their conclusions about 'the other'. Let us start with what the Europeans in the Dark and Middle Ages wrote when they began to think about Africa.

Ranulf Higden, a Benedictine monk who drew a map of the world in 1350, claimed that Africa was home to one-eyed people who used their feet to cover their heads! Remember that in those times, the Church's word was considered to be absolute. In the next century, an eminent geographer announced that the continent held people with one leg, three faces and the heads of lions.

As late as 1459, Italian monk Frere Mauro declared Africa the home of the roc, a bird so enormous that it could carry an elephant through the air. During the Middle Ages, the sailors knew that if you dared to sail down the African coastline and past the Canary Islands, you would be in Mare Tenebroso, the 'Sea of Darkness'. In the medieval imagination, this was a region of utmost dread – where the heavens flung down liquid sheets of flame, and the waters boiled; where rocks of serpents and islands of ogres lay in wait for the mariner, and the giant hand of Satan would reach up from the fathomless depths to seize him; where he would be burnt black in the face and body as a mark of God's vengeance for the insolence of his prying into this forbidden mystery.

And, even if he should survive all these ghastly perils and manage somehow to sail through, he would arrive at the 'Sea of Obscurity' and be lost forever in the vapours and slime at the very edge of the world.

With all this in mind, it is not surprising that in 1482, when Portuguese mariner Diego Cão landed at the mouth of the Congo River and initiated the first ever sustained encounter with a black African nation, prejudices were already ingrained in their belief system.

To achieve a balance, let us look at the historical perspective of how the Pende people viewed the arrival of the white man on their shores back in 1482. First, they saw the three masts growing out of the water. Then, they saw a monster of wood rising slowly from the sea. Here's how a twentieth century oral historian of the Pende people, Mukunzo Kioko, described the arrival of the Portuguese:

> Our fathers were living comfortably. They had cattle and crops, they had salt marshes and banana trees. Suddenly, they saw a big boat rising out of the ocean. This boat had wings all of white, sparkling like knives. White-coloured men came out of the waters, and spoke words that nobody could understand.
>
> Our ancestors took fright; they said that they were the Vumbi, spirits returned from the dead. They pushed them back into the ocean with volleys of arrows, but the Vumbi spat fire with the noise of thunder, and many of our ancestors were killed. The chiefs and the wise men said that these Vumbi were the former possessors of the land, and from that day forward, the whites have brought nothing but wars and misery!

As the years passed and slave trading took its fatal grip, various stories were told to explain mysterious events. When the ships departed their shores, carrying their local peoples to a life of slavery on foreign shores, the Pende believed that their brethren were being taken to the 'Land of the Dead', beneath the sea. After all, they would watch the ship disappearing into the great waters.

Just as Europe would long be obsessed with the practice of cannibalism in Africa, Africans imagined Europeans to be engaging in the same practice. The white man was thought to turn his captive's flesh into salted meat, his brain into cheese, and his blood into the red wine that he was so fond of drinking. His bones would be burned into grey ash and used as gunpowder, and the huge smoking copper pots on board the ship was where this transformation would begin.

The Africans believed that the various goods that were carried off the ships did not come from the vessels themselves, but that the captain would go below, to a hole in the middle of the vessel. Here he would ring a bell, and the gods of the dead would bring these mysterious things he required.

Such were the perceptions of 'the other' from the heart of the African continent.

THE DORSLAND
TREKKERS

O ne of the most fascinating, yet tragic, periods for the Afrikaner was the Dorsland or 'Thirst Land' Trek. There were four separate Dorsland Treks, undertaken between 1875 and 1905. The reasons for these treks were many and varied, and to truly understand them all, one has to look deep into the psyche of the Boers.

They harboured a real and almost palpable hatred of the British, who had emancipated their slaves and told them to fetch their compensation in London, resulting in the Boers first trekking away from them in 1835. They trekked away from them again in 1843 when the British colonised Natal, thus destroying the little Boer republic of Natalia. The Free State Boers trekked away from them in 1848, when the territory between the Orange River and the Vaal was proclaimed British.

To make matters worse, an Afrikaner named Thomas Francois Burgers, who was elected President of the Transvaal Republic, married a Scottish woman by the name of Mary Bryson. If that was not enough of an insult to the Afrikaner nation, he had the temerity to buy a piano and place it in his home! This was the ultimate slight to the 'volk', as these highly conservative, Calvinistic folk believed that music and dancing were instruments of the devil.

Also of relevance was the fact that the financial affairs of the Transvaal Republic were in a terrible state and there was a very real threat that the British would invade the Transvaal. Significantly, the occupation of the Transvaal by the British took place in 1876, and the first Dorsland Trek took place only one year before, in 1875.

But perhaps the overriding motivation behind these ill-fated journeys was what is called 'trekfees', an Afrikaans word that captures the Boers' spirit of restlessness, and their desire to know what lay over the horizon. Couple this with their deep-seated biblical belief that they, too, would be granted their Promised Land, add to it the threat of a British invasion and stir in a president whom they perceived as a heretic, and you have the end result – a trek to a better place, a Promised Land, where the Boers would be free to live and rule themselves as they saw fit.

They sold their farms and spent a year preparing for their expedition. Gert Alberts was elected head of the trek. They could not have made a better choice, as he was a born leader of men. His chief advisor was Johannes van der Merwe, an 82-year-old Voortrekker, who longed to trek again. Herein lies the enigma of the psyche: Van der Merwe was a wealthy farmer who owned the illustrious farm Rusfontein, just outside Pretoria. He had a special wagon built for the trek, which was more like a caravan, and, with a most competent cook named 'Plaatjierol', he completed the journey and lived to the ripe old age of 92!

In February 1875, ten families, sixteen wagons and 1 400 heads of cattle were seen slowly making their way in a northwesterly direction up the Crocodile River. Gert Alberts was an astute leader – he split the trek into three groups, at intervals of two days, so that the rare waterholes along the journey would not be overcrowded. There were only three families that turned back prior to entering the Kgalagadi Desert, and only a handful of cattle were lost on the last three waterless trek days, before arriving at Lake Ngami, 'the land of many vleis'.

There the trek waited, while the leaders went to negotiate with Lambert, the chief of the Hottentots, for land at Gobabis. Lambert was the leader of the very same people that the settlers had relentlessly driven northward into this almost inhospitable land, and now they had come to ask his permission to settle there. Lambert suggested that they settle around the lovely spring at Rietfontein, southwest of Ghanzi, whilst he negotiated with the other chiefs about a permanent place to settle.

They stayed at Rietfontein for a year, and today you will still find four graves there – three unmarked, and another belonging to Aletta van der Merwe, 'born 1817 – died 1877'.

Then came the call for help – the second party of Dorsland Trekkers were in terrible trouble.

Jan Greyling, who had hunted in the Kgalagadi before, had been appointed to lead the second trek. It was a disastrous decision. The trek was far too big, comprising nearly 500 men, women and children in 128 wagons, more than 7 000 oxen and cows, 500 horses, 1 000 sheep and goats, 200 dogs and hundreds of chickens, ducks and geese. The desert was not designed to support such numbers. By the third day, the cattle became hard to handle, and the waterhole they had reached yielded water only by the spoonful. They pushed on hurriedly, both day and night for two more days, to reach the waterhole at Haakdoorn Pan.

By this time, the cattle were almost out of control, and when they smelt the sweet smell of water, they went berserk. They stormed the shallow water of the pan and turned it into a mud bath. Hundreds of oxen sank into the mud and died, and those that were in front were trampled by the stampeding herd from behind. All that was left for the people was a foul mud. They scooped it up into their shirts, wringing out the water drop by drop.

On they trekked, fathers crying as they watched the distress of their wives and children. They opened the stomachs of the animals that had fallen, in the hope of drinking the liquid. They drank the blood of sheep and neat brandy mixed with vinegar, anything to slake their maddening thirsts. The cattle would approach anything that was shiny and lick it, in the vain hope that it was liquid. They would come into the campfires at night and lick the flames. Many cattle went blind from thirst, as wagon after wagon struggled onwards through the inhospitable sands of the Kalahari. As the cattle became weaker, so treasured furniture was dumped along the route, followed by sacks of mielies and other provisions.

The trekkers learned a trick from the Bushmen. The blowing sands of the Magalagadi tended to hollow out flat rock surfaces over a long period of time, after which the migrating sands covered the rocks. When it rained, the water seeped through the sand and collected in little dams under the surface in the rock depressions. If they were able to find these, they could dig into beautiful clear little dams of filtered water.

A missionary, Reverend J.D. Hepburn, who was visiting King Khama in Bechuanaland, heard of the plight of the trekkers, and sent a wagon loaded with barrels of water. Their ordeal continued until they reached Lake Ngami. By this stage, however, there were not enough oxen to bring the wagons into South West Africa.

When a local trader named Axel Eriksson came upon across the disastrous second Dorsland Trek that crossed the Kalahari, he decided to write to the Cape newspapers to appeal for help. 'It is a bitter and hard-rending story,' he wrote. 'Many have neither dog nor fowl left. Many children driven by hunger eat earth and die almost immediately.' He visited wagon after wagon and found only women and children, abandoned and without help, awaiting their inevitable fate with courage. Theirs were lonely graves out there in the wilderness, hundreds of miles away from any trade routes. Those graves are still there to this day. It was traders like Eriksson, and another splendid fellow named William Worthington Jordaan that saved these people. In February 1878, the remnants of that second Dorsland Trek linked with the main body at Leeupan, and they all trekked on to Etosha.

The famous Dr William Coates-Palgrave advised these settlers to settle in no-man's land in the Kaokoveld, which they did. It was then that two schooners, sent by the people of the Cape with provisions, landed at Walvis Bay, and their situation was saved. Afraid that the British would commandeer the Kaokoveld, they led a deputation, under Commandant Jacobus Botha, through Swartboois Drift and up into Angola, to negotiate for land with the Portuguese. The Portuguese offered these settlers two hectares of land per family, freedom of religion and no taxation for the first ten years. They would, however, have to submit to the laws of Portugal, although they would be free to use their own language. In 1880, they trekked through the Swartboois Drift and up into Angola.

On 4 January 1881, they eventually arrived at the Humpata Plateau, which is about 160 km from the Portuguese coastal town of Mossamedes, and they laid out their village at Humpata. Looking back, they determined that they had lost about 300 men, women and children on the journey from Transvaal to Angola, most of them as a result of fever.

There were grievances at Humpata, and the settlers wrote a letter to President Kruger. His reply was, 'If you go and stay amongst the Portuguese community, your children will become Portuguese and practise Roman Catholicism.' They were also exposed to bands of robbers there and often had to fight for their lives.

William Worthington Jordaan knew of their plight, and had secured land in the lovely Rehoboth district. He also secured land from the Ovambo chief around Grootfontein and Otavi. He went to see the settlers and offered to give them his land. Upon receiving encouragement and support from the Prime Minister of Upington in the Cape Colony, the settlers named this little republic Upingtonia.

There were internecine wars between the Ovambo and the Herero, who were also not too fond of the white settlers. William Worthington Jordaan was on his way to Chief Maharero to settle a dispute, when a petty chief by the name of Kambonde approached him. As he came around the side of his wagon, Kambonde's men attacked him and killed him. William Worthington Jordaan, the saviour of the trekkers, the man who was the offspring of a white Capetonian and a coloured slave girl, the man who had given his huge farm for the establishment of Upingtonia, lay dead. The trekkers had lost their best friend.

In 1893, the third trek made up of 40 wagons crossed the southern Kalahari safely. They reached the spring at Rietfontein and rested. The last of the Dorsland Treks to Angola took place in 1905, and consisted of those people who did not want to remain in the Transvaal after the Boer War. Right up until 1915, the Boers and Ovambos engaged in battle after battle. Although the Portuguese were often defeated, the Boers never lost a battle. After nearly 50 years in Angola, they trekked back to South West Africa. Thus it was, that for the first 20 years of German occupation, the population consisted of more Afrikaners than Germans.

In October 1950, the 75th anniversary of the departure of the first Dorsland Trek was celebrated. More than 600 descendants gathered to stand beside the ruins at Rusplaas in the Kaokoveld, to pay tribute to their embattled and brave ancestors.

THE BOER REPUBLICS OF
STELLALAND AND GOSHEN

Among the numerous independent republics started by the Boers in the latter part of the nineteenth century, were Gordonia, Upingtonia and the Republic of Utrecht in Natal.

The reasons behind the formation of the liveliest republics ever formed by the Boers, Stellaland and Goshen, were twofold. Firstly, Keate's award of the diamond fields to Nicholas Waterboer and his subsequent handing over of them to the British, who controlled the Cape, stank of British deceit and connivance. Secondly, Sir Theopholis Shepstone's takeover of the Transvaal in April 1877, without firing a single shot, had hurt the Boer people deeply. These two events led to the Boers wanting to trek away from the British again, leading to what became known as the 'Dorsland Treks'.

A proposal was made in the British House of Commons that the local chiefs in the Griqualand West District, namely Mankoroane and Montsioa, should be compensated for the effects of the Keate award, in the form of either land or money. At this stage, the Griqualand chiefs were quite willing to live under the jurisdiction of what was termed 'civilised government'.

The advice of Sir William Owen Lanyon (who was later besieged by Hendrik Schoeman in the Siege of Pretoria during the First Boer War of

1881), Sir Theopholis Shepstone (who, along with Rider Haggard, had annexed the Transvaal in 1877), and Sir Charles Warren, was ignored by Sir Michael Hicks Beach, leading to the unfolding of the following events.

The Transvaal Republic changed its name to the Zuid-Afrikaansche Republiek. This, to the British, was a clear indication that the Boers had their own imperial ideas. The entire western border of the Zuid-Afrikaansche Republiek was a filibuster and freebooter's paradise, with internecine wars between the tribes and cattle rustling being the sport of the day.

In July 1882, these filibusters banded together under Gerard Jacob van Niekerk as mercenaries, and backed Chief Montsioa in a war against his rival Mankoroane. In compensation, they were granted 416 farms of 3 000 morgen each, and the Republic of Stellaland came into being. It was named after a comet that was visible in the skies during this time, and its flag was a brilliant white star upon a green background. Its capital was Vryburg, which remains to this day.

The Republic of Goshen was formed in exactly the same way in the area called Rooigrond, a little dorp just south of Mafikeng. It was founded by Nicklaas Gey van Pittius in October 1882, on land ceded by the Bechuana chief. The little town of Geysdorp, just northeast of Vryburg, still bears his name to this day.

The British, in the meantime, had annexed the Western Cape and the Eastern Cape, followed by Natal and Zululand in 1879, and the Transvaal in 1877. One can distinctly see that imperial colonisation of the entire Southern Africa region was their aim. At this time Rhodes, having made money in the diamond fields, had made his first foray into politics in the Cape. The Republics of Stellaland and Goshen straddled the road to the North, then called the Missionary Road, and this did not suit Rhodes' ambitions in the slightest.

Paul Kruger then made a fatal error. He placed the two small republics on the western border under the protection of the Zuid-Afrikaansche Republiek. Britain was up in arms. In the meantime, lawlessness and crime had reached such a pitch on the western border of the Transvaal, that, by mutual agreement, a British and a Transvaal Commissioner were appointed to keep law and order. Here, the British made a similar mistake by nominating the Reverend John MacKenzie to the post. He arrived in Vryburg and instead of carrying out his work, took the following actions. He accepted Chief Montsioa as a British subject, hauled down the flag of Stellaland and hoisted up the Union Jack in its place. (A bit like Theopholis Shepstone's annexure of the Transvaal.)

The freebooters were furious, and if it hadn't been for the small police detachment, MacKenzie would have been physically thrown out of Stellaland. John MacKenzie's action caused tremendous resentment in the Transvaal and he was recalled and replaced by none other than Cecil John Rhodes. This, I think, was another calculated move on behalf of the British.

Rhodes met for talks with Lang Jan de la Rey and Gert van Niekerk. Being the shrewd person that he was, he arrived carrying the flag of Stellaland, and ceremoniously handed it back to them. They were moved. De la Rey did not like Rhodes, and when he arrived, he intoned, 'Blood must flow, blood must flow.' But Rhodes was equal to the occasion. 'Nonsense,' he said. 'I am hungry, give me my breakfast first, and then we can talk about blood.'

This appeal to Boer hospitality did the trick, and during the course of the meal their aggression and suspicion started to fall away. Rhodes stayed in the camp for a week and upon leaving, he became godfather to De la Ray's grandchild. A settlement had been reached. The freebooters were guaranteed the possession of their farms and cattle and in return they agreed to accept British rule. Meanwhile, in Goshen to the north, Montsioa had been forced to surrender his lands to the freebooters under Gey van Pittius. The next day, Paul Kruger boldly annexed Goshen to the Zuid- Afrikaansche Republiek.

As a direct consequence, in a surge of patriotism, Sir Charles Warren set out from the Cape with a large expeditionary force for Bechuanaland. There was no fighting along the way, and when he arrived in Vryburg in 1885, he was greeted with tremendous excitement. He moved on towards Goshen, and all that happened was that the freebooters and diamond smugglers left, seeking sanctuary across the Transvaal border in the little town of Christiana.

And so it was that the short-lived inglorious rule of the freebooters and filibuster, came to an unspectacular end. The southern part of Bechuanaland, including Goshen and Stellaland, became a crown colony, whilst the northern section was proclaimed a British protectorate. It remained as such until the independence of Botswana under Sir Seretse Khama.

THE LIFE OF
MARGARETHA PIETERSEN

During the early 1900s on the farm Helpmekaar, in the district of Uitenhage in the Cape Province, lived the Pietersen family. Gideon Pietersen was a tall blonde farmer of Dutch origins and his wife Margaretha was of Huguenot descent, whose female ancestors, since arrival in Africa in 1685, had all been voluntary midwives.

The year was 1918. Their eight-year-old daughter, Charlotte, told her father that the deaths the previous night had not been that heavy. Four people, she continued, had died, two fewer than the night before. It was the year of the great influenza epidemic and the Tembu people, distinguished by their traditional vivid red cloth and beads, were dying in great numbers. Margaretha was performing the role of doctor and nurse on their own farm as well as on the adjoining four farms, which together comprised an area of some 6 000 acres.

Some time after this father and daughter arrived at a little mud hut, they dismounted and entered. Bending over a farm labourer, they found the tireless Margaretha. The son of the labourer was assisting her in wrapping the man in a blanket. 'He died about half and hour ago,' she said. 'We have work to do and Daniel will help you dig the graves. He is the fourth one.'

Her husband responded, 'You're looking tired. You should get some rest.' 'A rest,' she protested. 'Whatever for? My people are dying and they cry out for my assistance. I will go on working and, besides, someone has to look after the sick and bury the dead.'

Nobody really knows just how many people died in the epidemic. Mrs Pietersen made a list of those they buried, which she sent to the local Justice of the Peace. And later, when she in turn became J.P., she kept the records. She spared neither herself nor her daughter. They nursed all day and most times far into the night, riding from place to place, administering pills and herb potions to the delirious patients.

An even worse epidemic in which Mrs Pietersen became involved, with heart and soul, was the outbreak of bubonic plague in 1925. At 3h00 one morning she was awakened by crying outside the house. She went to investigate and found a man who told her that his whole family had suddenly become sick and he was afraid that they were all going to die. She woke her daughter and they set out on their horses. Occasionally a dark form plunged across the narrow track in front of them, with a low growl, but these were hardened farming folk and the odd leopard did not scare them. After examining the wife, Margaretha's worst fears were confirmed. She found the knobbly tell-tale signs in the woman's armpits and in her groin. Dr Byrne, the district surgeon, would have to be informed immediately and the area placed under quarantine.

The following day, after examining the patients, Dr Byrne was heard to remark, 'We're in for a bad time, everyone in the area must be quarantined or we will have a plague on our hands in no time. As you know, the disease is carried by fleas from infected rats, and spreads like wildfire. The best we can do, seeing that we have no hospital, is to segregate the sick ones as far as possible and then, when they have recovered or died, to burn down the hut. He said to Margaretha, 'I know how devoted you are to these people, but I cannot blame you if you now keep away. You have your family to consider. God knows we need somebody to nurse but I must tell you that the disease is fatal. On other farms where there are cases of the plague, the farmers won't have anything to do with the sick. They are just staying at home and, quite frankly, I cannot blame them.'

Margaretha Pietersen placed her hands on her hips and looked the doctor squarely in the eyes. 'These are my people and I will not desert them in their time of greatest need. Charlotte and I will nurse them.' She turned to her daughter and said, 'God knows we have work to do. Go into the kitchen, get a jar of paraffin and rub it all over you, in your hair, and on every inch of your body. This will prevent the fleas from biting you and if the fleas don't bite, you won't become infected.'

The number of cases rose to over 70 and many of the people died. Dr Byrne himself fell victim, leaving the full responsibility of doctoring and burying to the 45-year-old Mrs Pietersen. The night sky was often lit up with the glow of burning huts. The local people called her Noyeza, the Medicine Woman, as she and her daughter rode from household to household, heedless of the danger to which they were exposing themselves.

It was only when Margaretha turned 80 that her family was able to convince her to give up her vocation. By that time she had delivered over 3 000 babies. As Mrs Charlotte Searle, Margaretha's daughter became the Director of the South African College of Nursing and was the first South African nurse whose research led to the award of a Doctorate. Doctor Searle's monumental thesis, 'A socio-historical survey of the development of nursing in South Africa from 1652 to 1960', remains the only complete history of nursing in this country. And her mother, Margaretha Pietersen, or Noyeza, was truly our South African Lady of the Lamp. We salute you both.

SHIPWRECKS AND THE
SOUTH AFRICAN COASTLINE

During one of Vasco da Gama's many voyages, which led to him opening up the sea route in 1498, he discovered that the sun moved from rising on his left, to rising straight in front of him, and then, within a few days, rising on his right-hand side.

Throughout this period the land was to his left. This can only mean that he had rounded one of the Capes. But even Herodotus, who recorded the event, was sceptical.

The only possible evidence discovered to support his account was some very ancient timber, discovered on a building excavation site on the Cape Flats. The relevant experts from the University of Cape Town were notified, but, alas, when they arrived the following morning, there was no trace of it. The night watchman had used the ancient timber to make a fire to warm himself through the cold winter night.

The first officially recorded wreck on our coastline was in 1505, when a heavily armed Portuguese sailing vessel, loaded with pepper, went down one night with its captain, Pedro de Mendonca, and his entire crew. No trace of this vessel has ever been found.

Since then, there have been over 950 shipwrecks on the South African coast. Malcolm Turner's wonderfully researched book, *Shipwrecks and Salvage in South Africa*, (Struik, Cape Town 1988), provides a comprehensive and chronological list of them all.

But let us look in more detail at one of the most famous wrecks in South African history, *De Jonge Thomas*. In the eighteenth century, outward-bound vessels were of particular concern to the Dutch East Indian Company, as they were laden with valuable chests of spices, to pay for trade goods in the East. These, of course, were of particular interest to the plunderers and pirates of the time. Far less attention was paid on the return-bound vessels, as they normally carried very little money.

On 20 October 1772, *De Jonge Thomas*, commanded by Barend de la Maire, left Texel on a voyage to Batavia. She arrived in Table Bay on 29 March 1773, reporting 70 deaths and 41 sick, who were sent to hospital. Two months later, on 1 June 1773, her anchor cables parted during a northwesterly gale, and she ran aground near Woodstock Beach. This was a time when little store was put by human life. The Company was far more concerned about the money in its holds, and immediately set up a salvage company to recover any cargo that was washed ashore. There was very little attempt made to save the sailors from the now rapidly disintegrating vessel.

A depiction of Wolraad Woltemade and De Jonge Thomas

Early one morning, an elderly German gentleman named Wolraad Woltemade, who was a dairy farmer in the employ of the Company, set out on his horse to the site of the wreck. He was going to deliver a bottle of wine and a loaf of bread to his son, who was a corporal on duty at the salvage site.

Upon arrival, he was so deeply moved and upset by the cries for help emerging from the defeated vessel, that he rode his horse into the surf, towards the back line, and started to bring the men back to the shore, two at a time. Seven times he and his horse swam back and forth through the rough surf, saving a total of fourteen men. By their eighth rescue attempt, the vessel was disintegrating very quickly. The men on board panicked and jumped into the water, clutching onto the exhausted horse and rider. They clung to the bridle, saddle, flanks and tail of the animal. The weight proved to be too much – they were all dragged under.

Woltemade's body, and that of his courageous horse, was washed up on the beach the following day, but his selfless act of bravery earned him a hero's status in South African folk history, which has not diminished in 400 years.

Immediately after this event, an edict was issued stating that anybody coming near the wreck would be hanged, and a gibbet was erected on the beach opposite the wreck. This stopped anybody from trying to save the remaining souls on board, and 138 people eventually perished in that ice-cold surf.

The Dutch East India Company, upon receiving the report of his heroic deed, gave his widow and sons a substantial reward, and later named a vessel after him. It was the 1 150 ton East Indiaman *Helt Woltemade*. Ironically, it was the *Helt Woltemade* that unwittingly betrayed the position of the Dutch merchant fleet at Saldanha Bay to the British warship the *Active*, thus resulting in the Battle of Saldanha Bay, which was a disaster for the Dutch.

Perhaps this was fitting retribution for a great trading company that valued boxes of money above human life.

THE BATTLE OF
SALDANHA BAY

Should you stand on the beach at Saldanha Bay when the wind is not blowing, and gaze out at the tranquillity and quietness of the sea, you would be hard-put to visualise a time long ago when, on this very site, men in beleaguered ships struggled hopelessly for their very lives.

Early on in the year of 1781, Baron Joachim van Plettenberg received dispatches from Europe, stating that Holland, along with France, Spain and the newly founded Colonies of America, was at war with Britain. Realising that the Cape of Good Hope was very vulnerable to attack from Britain, he requested immediate military reinforcements. He then ordered that the entire fleet of homeward-bound merchantmen at anchor in Table Bay, laden with goods from the East, lift anchor and proceed to the anchorage in Saldanha Bay, where they could hide and avoid British capture.

The East Indiaman fleet, commandeered by Captain Gerrit Harmeyer, comprised five vessels: *Middelberg, Honkoop, Pare, Dankbaarheid* and the *Hoogkarspel*. They set sail for Saldanha with the following instructions: 'If your vessel is about to be captured by the British, you are to set fire to it and sink it.' The captain of the *Middelberg*, one Van Gennep and his first mate Abraham de Smidt, seemed to be the only ones to make adequate preparations in this regard.

For the next couple of weeks, the fleet lay at anchor in the calm waters of Saldanha Bay. They were supposed to be on the alert, but instead they relaxed, passing their time hunting and fishing. Also in the bay was the vessel *Helt Woltemade*, carrying the famous naturalist Francois le Vaillant, and his priceless collection of South African fauna and flora.

In June of that year, the French Admiral, Pierre André de Suffren, arrived at the Cape with the necessary reinforcements, and then sailed on to India to engage the British, satisfied that the Cape was now secure from attack. Dispatches were sent to Harmeyer to inform him of the developments, and to await an escort before proceeding homeward.

On 28 June 1781, the *Helt Woltemade* sailed out of the bay, and continued her journey to Ceylon. A few days later, she encountered a frigate flying the French flag, which signalled her for information. The unsuspecting Dutch officers told the captain all about the Dutch fleet lying at anchor in Saldanha Bay, and then watched in absolute horror, as the French flag was hauled down and a British flag raised in its place! The vessel was a British man o'war, the *Active*, commanded by Captain McKenzie, and the Dutch ship had to surrender under the threat of a primed British canon. The East Indiaman and her cargo were eventually taken to Plymouth as a prize of war.

The *Active* then rejoined the British task force, under the command of Commodore George Johnstone and, on 21 July 1781, the British fleet, once again flying French flags, sailed into Saldanha Bay. The bored Dutch sailors were delighted at the sight. They thought that the long-awaited naval escort had eventually arrived to take them back home. As the fleet passed Marcus Island, the French flags were hauled down and the British flags hauled up. Led by the *Romney*, British canon balls ripped into the totally unprepared Dutch fleet. There was pandemonium, with masts falling and canons firing. The only difference between this battle and the previous one was the fact that the Dutch were totally unprepared. The Dutch sailors could not carry out their emergency orders, and it was only the *Middelberg* that succeeded in carrying out the required drill. Blazing furiously, she was towed by the British towards Hoedtjies Point, where her crew abandoned ship. Once the fire reached her powder store, she blew up and sank like a stone. Mission accomplished.

The British sailors were able to extinguish all the fires on the remaining fleet, which were taken as war prizes by Commodore Johnstone. But the

Middelberg, along with her valuable homeward-bound cargo, was destined to lie buried beneath the soft sands of Saldanha Bay. The loss of six vessels was financially very serious, and contributed to the eventual bankruptcy of the Dutch East India Company.

There were many treasure-hunting and salvage expeditions looking for that cargo between 1788 and 1906, but the best documented one occurred in 1969, when Billy and Reggie Dodds of Cape Town salvaged 198 pieces of Ch'ien Lung china – a healthy reward indeed. More recently, a new breakwater has been built out from Hoedtjies Point. This changed the currents and caused a beach to build up and form over the wreck site.

So today, at low tide, one can walk over her final resting place – just smooth sand, belying the dramatic history of a blazing ship being abandoned to the fates of the gods of the foam.

HMS
BIRKENHEAD

I t was a proud Captain Robert Salmond who stood on the bridge of HMS *Birkenhead*, watching the young recruits boarding the first iron vessel in the service of Her Majesty's Royal Navy. Mere lads, they had looked splendid marching down from the barracks to the quayside, dressed in the scarlet and blue of England and the tartans of the Scottish regiments. Women and girls had lined the streets and cheered them on as a fife and drum band led the men. The swagger of the kilts and the cheering of the crowd certainly made it a day to remember. But then that's how it is when men go off to war – often great excitement followed by even greater sadness.

It was January 1852 and the *Birkenhead*, docked in Cork, was loading the new recruits, mostly Irish lads. They had joined the British forces as a way of escaping the devastating effects of the potato blight of the 1840s, which had resulted in thousands starving to death, leaving the economy of Ireland in tatters.

The men were destined for South Africa, to bolster the troops Sir Harry Smith had requested for purposes of fighting another frontier war against the Xhosa. Lieutenant-Colonel Alexander Seton was the Commanding Officer. Aboard there were: 25 women; 31 children; one naval surgeon; seventeen ship's officers; twelve military officers; three military surgeons; 125 crew and 479 soldiers and other ranks. This was a total of 693 personnel.

The cargo included 350 double-barrelled carbine rifles and gold bullion to the value of £250 000 for payment to the troops on active service in the Eastern Cape. The journey southwards was not a pleasant one. They hit enormous storms, the hatches were battened down and for a whole ten days rain lashed the ship as it tumbled and ploughed through the roughest seas imaginable. So bad was the trip that six women went into premature labour. Most of the women on board were accompanying their husbands or were intending to visit their loved ones in South Africa. They were housed in the stern.

Anne Chapman, whose husband Bill was one of the ranks, was going out to South Africa for the first time. While on leave her husband had returned to England to fetch her. She was pregnant with their first child and they intended to settle in the Eastern Cape.

On the night of 26 February, the *Birkenhead*, having left Simon's Town, was steaming along the coast in the calmest of waters. The night was perfect. She was just short of Danger Point, about two miles off the coast. 'Fifteen fathoms' came the voice from the night watch forrard, 'What's our course?' the night officer Davies enquired. 'S.S.E. by E. Sir,' came the reply from the helmsman. 'Twelve fathoms,' the watchman said. Davies frowned, 'We must be on shelving. Probably sand'. 'Eight fathoms.' There was a tone of alarm in the lookout's voice. Mr Davies reached for the speaking tube but in vain. The submerged rocks ripped into the *Birkenhead*. The troops on the lower deck stood no chance. In the engine room the men were cut down by scalding steam and as the great paddles slowed down, the screams of the women and children aft could be heard. The *Birkenhead* had struck a reef and she was breaking up.

'Get all the women and children up on deck,' commanded Lieutenant-Colonel Seton. 'Davies, lower the starboard paddle boat.'

The mate looked at the Captain, his face ashen. 'The gig has staved in, Sir. They can't loosen the big boat amidships.' 'Then take all the women and children to the two little cutters, and load them immediately,' Captain Salmond instructed Lieutenant-Colonel Seton. 'I'll expect your men to stand on parade until the women and children are clear of the vessel.' With the blast of a bugle and the roll of a drum, the men were formed into their regiments.

Just then Anne Chapman came across to the Captain. 'Please, let me go to my man,' she pleaded. 'No, he is on parade,' Seton replied. 'But you don't understand I am with child,' she begged. 'All the more reason for you to get into the boat,' the Captain gently encouraged. 'It would be the way your husband would have wanted it.' Anne Chapman was taken away and the two cutters soon lowered into the sea.

As the women and children pulled away, they heard singing, initially quite softly and then gathering in volume. It was the hymn 'Abide by me'. The women sobbed and wailed and then slowly became quiet. Watching the men standing to attention on the deck of the stricken vessel, the women joined in the song. Together they sang their final farewell.

The ship lurched in a swell, broke apart and then sank. Some of the men managed to cling to bits of flotsam and debris in the water but very soon the sharks arrived and a feeding frenzy started. Later, the cutter *Lioness* arrived and picked up 116 survivors from the wreck. In total 445 lives were lost that night. Only 193 persons survived.

I am told that there are certain regiments that continue to hold a formal dinner on 26 February, where they sing 'Abide with me' as a tribute to the men of the *Birkenhead* who established and gave such perfect form to the heroic maritime practice, 'Women and children first'.

There is a plaque at Danger Point commemorating the bravery of those courageous and steadfast men who did not rush the little boats, for fear of swamping them. I suggest you go and see it sometime.

HMS Birkenhead

TABLE BAY AND
ITS TREASURES

Somebody said a long long time ago while studying charts of the sea, 'These charts – I think the fairies have the making of them, for they bewitch even sober-minded men.' It was Sir Walter Raleigh who spoke these words; and never was a truer thing said. From time immemorial man has been drawn to the sea and the treasures it holds.

Our own Table Bay off Cape Town is literally littered with wrecks. From the sandy beaches of Bloubergstrand to rocky Camps Bay, lie the remains of Portuguese caravels, Dutch and English East Indiamen, galleons, schooners, steamers and liners. And Chinese porcelain almost paves several areas of the seabed.

Table Bay dredgers usually dig up these fragments of forgotten treasures. As they move tons of sand, they bring up shapeless masses of barnacles, sometimes containing a corroded Mauser rifle with the trigger mechanism intact, brass candle snuffers, quaint old bottles and hundreds of cannon balls.

Amongst the valuable artefacts found have been handsome George IV silver coins in almost mint condition and gold 'spade' guineas of George III that made the dredger crew on board stop in their tracks and wonder what treasure chest they had just passed over.

John Lethbridge from Devon in England was the first professional salvor to dive on these wrecks. The Dutch East India Company (VOC) brought him to the Cape in 1727. Finding this field of enterprise untouched in Table Bay, he proceeded to dive on the wrecks in the shallower waters. He made several rich hauls, including 200 bars of silver weighing 800 lbs and a chest of silver ducatoons with a salvage worth then of £20 000 – a fortune in today's terms.

Records of salvage diving off the Cape appear again only much later. In 1881 a Cape Town jeweller named John Courtenay employed an experienced harbour diver, Jan Steyn, to explore two famous wrecks. The *Haarlem* and *De Jonge Thomas* were both Dutch East India Company ships driven ashore by a northwesterly gale during the eighteenth century near the Salt River mouth. A primitive submarine eye was used to survey the seabed and two dark shapes were located and buoys placed to mark the location.

Jan Steyn went to work. First of all there emerged porcelain cups and saucers and then the real success, a large quantity of coins. The auction of these goods was advertised as follows: 'A lot of coins, some Chinese frivolities, a very curious bottle of Japanese-ware, and a conglomerate of rare China, iron, rust and sand. Items that would be of interest to the British Museum.'

The Dutch fleet in Table Bay, 1779

There is no doubt that many more valuable items would have been salvaged on that occasion had a gale force wind not come up and washed the marker buoys away and a huge sea not broken into the bay from the northwest, covering the wrecks with sand. The wrecks have never been seen since.

Shipwrecks were a common occurrence in Table Bay, particularly before 1860 when the breakwater was built by convict labour. As there was no protection until then, shipwrecks occurred every couple of weeks during the winter months. On those nights the bell in the Castle would ring, summoning Company servants for rescue. Near the beach stood the solitary gallows that was a grim reminder of the penalty for looting stranded cargo. On the night of 17 June 1722, for instance, there were ten wrecks. Some 660 lives were lost, together with cargoes of spices, tortoiseshell, sugar, saltpetre and silks to the value of £250 000.

Eighteen years later, the Dutch ship *De Visch* was observed drifting towards the shore, dragging her anchor. On board were 20 chests of gold and silver which were destined as pay for the Company's servants. 'I'll give two months' wages to every man who goes out to save that cargo,' shouted Governor Tulbagh in great desperation. And the result, of course, was that the whole cargo was saved!

There are still many money chests in Table Bay awaiting recovery and the archives are full of accounts of wrecks and the treasures that they hold. One such wreck was the *Huijs te Craijenstein* which ran onto the rocks off Camps Bay on a foggy night in 1698. Bars of metal bearing the Company's coat of arms have been recovered, confirming her identity. Near the same spot the Portuguese slave ship *San Jose* floundered, with 500 slaves in chains held in her hatches. The fortunate ones managed to remove their chains in time. But 200 drowned as the ship went down.

On 5 November 1799 a blood red sun rose and gave warning of terror to come. Remember the lines of the old saying of the sea:

A red sky in the morning is a Sailor's warning
A red sky at night, is a Shepherd's delight.

The Captain of the *Sceptre* ordered the striking of the topmast as the gale burst upon them with a roar. The ship's cables soon parted and she struck a reef. During that day many men were swept overboard and that night the entire poop deck was torn off with the men clinging to it for their very lives. Alas, as the survivors were nearing the shore, a great wave capsized the deck and all perished. There were 411 officers, men and marines on the vessel, and only 42 survived.

So when we stand and gaze out over the calm waters of Table Bay, it is well to remember the tumultuous and often bloody history of those waters. Its moods run deep in our country's history.

WITWATERSRAND GOLD

The story of the discovery of Witwatersrand gold reads like a fairy story, a fable, you could say, of riches yielded from the depths of the earth, in amounts that boggle the mind.

In 1853 Pieter Jacob Marais panned for and found gold in the Jukskei and Crocodile rivers, north of Johannesburg. He was the first official gold prospector in the South African Republic. How cruel was fate to Marais! He turned his gaze to the north and, in so doing, he turned his back on the territories where rich deposits of gold lay waiting. On reading his journals, you find that he devoted his main attention to riverbeds. Time and time again, he returned to the Jukskei and every time he did so he crossed the 'Ridge of White Waters' or the Witwatersrand. It is almost as if the Fates had decided against him.

In 1874 Henry Lewis was fossicking around in the hills of the Magaliesberg when he discovered gold in both alluvial and quartz forms on the farm Blaaubank, owned by an 1820 Settler named Jennings. In 1875 the Nil Desperandum Co-operative Quartz Mine Company was floated, credited with the distinction of being the first company to carry out exploitation near the Witwatersrand.

The South African Republic was keen to locate and develop goldfields. An inspector was appointed and two prospecting parties financed by the government. The men scoured the area, but to no avail. Nevertheless, such processes served to heighten awareness of the search for gold. Soon people everywhere were talking of the probable fortune their farms held.

After an interruption caused by the First Boer War, the search soon resumed. In 1881 J.B. Bantjies was prospecting at Kromdraai (or Mogale City to give it its new name), north of Krugersdorp. In 1885 payable gold was found on the farm of Stephanus Johannes Minnaar and in December of that year the farm was proclaimed a public digging. The rush was on and every manner of people started arriving, driven and fired by the God called Gold.

On a nearby farm called Wilgespruit the Struben brothers stumbled on 'The Confidence Reef' and by December 1885 a five-stamp battery had begun crushing. Still, the giant, the mother of all gold, remained hidden. In late 1885 George Walker and George Harrison, two down-and-out prospectors, arrived on the Witwatersrand on their way to Barberton. The Strubens gave Walker employment and Harrison was contracted to build a house for the Oosthuizen family on the farm, Langlaagte.

History records that it was Harrison who, in the course of construction of the house on Langlaagte, found the main reef. It was he indeed who received the discoverer's claim. However, Walker, in his old age, claimed that he, and not Harrison, had stumbled on the reef while taking a stroll one Sunday morning in February 1886. He recognised it as a conglomerate and found it to be rich in gold.

Whatever the truth, and most people tend to believe Harrison's version of events, neither of the men, nor indeed the Oosthuizens, became rich as a result of the discovery at Langlaagte. The true worth of the find was only established later.

Soon after this Bantjies traced the main reef to the farm Vogelstruis-fontein, and Henry Norse, to Doornfontein. It was also found at Turffontein by Geldenhuis and by the Strubens in the Germiston area. The finds ignited the entire world as the true size of the discovery at last began to sink into people's minds.

From every conceivable corner of our globe, people came in their droves. They begged lifts on the transport wagons and then walked after leaving the rail head. They rode bicycles along the rough tracks and faced the danger of wild animals both by day and night, driven ever onwards by that deadly form of obsessive madness known as gold fever.

People from every walk of life came to that dusty shantytown – beggars, priests, prostitutes, cardsharps, entrepreneurs, financiers, peasant farmers, workers, fortune seekers, hoteliers, dance-hall girls. They came from the Barberton area where the gold was running out and business was not all that brisk. Whiskey-sellers, traders, mechanics and miners flowed into the area and together they built the city of Johannesburg.

Johannesburg in the Gold Rush of the 1880s

Having read about the origins of the city, it is not difficult to understand why Johannesburgers to this day live on the knife edge. Being conscious of the possibility of change at any time, they also have the biggest of all hearts in times of disaster. A sense of *joie de vivre* pumps deep in their veins. Like many of their ancestors, they know what it was like to be wealthy one day and down and out the next.

By September 1886, just months after the discovery of Langlaagte, a total of nine farms had been proclaimed public diggings. All the way from

Germiston to Roodepoort lay priceless tracts of land, which, until a few months previously, were open treeless plains, only good for cattle. The names are legendary – Driefontein, Rietfontein, Elandsfontein, Turffontein, Randjeslaagte, Langlaagte, Paardekraal, Vogelstruisfontein and Roodepoort.

Once mining began many sorts of trades followed in its wake. Bars, brothels, shoemakers, saddlers, seamstresses, sirens and songsters were all in demand, as the town leapt into life. Work and play were plentiful. The new town of Johannesburg founded on the farm, Randjeslaagte, burgeoned. Large-scale industries followed in the area that was destined to become the modern, financial hub of our entire country.

This was the El Dorado that had been dreamed of. Along with the influx of people came entrepreneurs and capitalists like Joseph Robinson, William Knight, George Goch, Barney Barnato, Cecil John Rhodes and Charles Rudd and local lads like Colonel Ignatius Ferreira and Messrs Wemmer, Wolhuter, Fox and Rimer. Much of the early capital on the Rand originated from the diamond fields of Kimberley.

The latter half of 1886 and first half of 1887 saw a massive scramble for gold-bearing farms, which changed hands at unbelievable prices mostly in cash and shares. The farmers of the area, very conservative in upbringing, referred to the new society as the Sodom and Gomorrah of the highveld. In these developing tensions were to lie the origins of a deep distrust between two very distinct cultures that would flare up into a conflagration in the not too distant future.

The first company to be formed was the Witwatersrand Gold Mining Company. It was established by William Knight and was registered in Kimberley in September 1886. By the end of 1887 there were no fewer than 68 companies with a nominal capital of over £3 million.

Another early starter was the Wemmer Gold Mining Company that by February 1888 was paying an 82,5% dividend a year! The company's £1 shares were valued at £8 and the party seemed as if it would go on forever! The gold mines were literally spewing out wealth and millionaires rose from the hot, dry highveld dust overnight.

Then came a whispering, from one mineworker to another, and then a rumble. The mines were going deeper and deeper and the nature and composition of the ore was changing. Iron pyrites had begun to appear and it gobbled up the mercury used in the extraction process of the gold.

The news of the problem spread like a highveld fire running before a strong wind and within a couple of days the share market prices had plummeted. People lost their entire fortunes overnight and others were plunged into debt. Wave after wave of financial terror gripped the community and the realisation dawned that the glorious El Dorado had come to an end, like every other gold rush the world had experienced.

Fleeings and suicides became common as people who were worth a fortune the day before were unable to obtain one penny's credit in town. Shops and all manner of business closed down. Speculators left to seek fortunes elsewhere as the boom turned into a crash.

There are always some people, for whatever reason, who see beyond the panic. When everybody else believed that there was no way around the problem, these men had the chutzpah to buy the worthless shares in companies that could no longer extract gold. Believing in an imminent solution, they took the risk. The rest fled the scene in their droves.

When all seemed totally lost, a team of Scottish chemists came forward with a process of gold extraction by means of cyanide known as the MacArthur-Forrest process. It was introduced on the Robinson Mine in 1890 and by the end of the following year all the other mines had adopted this new, revolutionary process. Johannesburg rose like a phoenix from the ashes. South African gold production doubled from 1889 to 1891. By 1897 the Transvaal was producing 27% of the total world's gold production.

From these social and economic processes emerged the Randlords, a very wealthy group of people who had persisted and not run. They had the guts, perhaps even madness, to believe that the situation would come right. They were the ones who really made it big! And the nice thing is that there is a lot of their blood floating around in the veins of the people in our country to this day.

This is my take on things. It's not the time now to turn our backs and run away from our lovely land, for perhaps the cycle of history is about to repeat itself.

WALKING HOME –
A LONG JOURNEY

I t took just thirteen years, from 1886 to 1899, to change Johannesburg from a dustbowl into the richest goldfields the world has ever seen. Gold reserves then were estimated at £700 million, and by 1899 there were 97 800 black mineworkers on the Rand, many of them from Zululand.

There was talk of war, and in 1895 came the disastrous Jameson Raid. There was more talk of war. In January 1899, many British 'uitlanders' gave up their jobs, boarded up their homes and headed for the safety of Natal and the Cape, which were both British colonies. En masse, the Zuid-Afrikaansche Republiek (ZAR) burgers joined the commandos, and on 11 October, the Boers gave the British Empire an ultimatum: 'Withdraw your troop build-ups from the borders, or face war.'

With the mines closed down and the employees having fled just before the onset of war, there were thousands of black people stranded on the Witwatersrand. The ZAR had commandeered the trains for the movement of troops to the various fronts. The Witwatersrand mineworkers were trapped.

A young 25-year-old from Natal, one John Sidney Marwick, who was employed as a native recruitment officer on the Rand, took his job very seriously. Realising the plight of his Zulu recruits, he requested the termination of their contracts from the mines so that they would not be seen to be absconding. This was granted. He requested rail transport from the government to take them home. He was given the run-around.

Realising that time was running out, he sent word to the mines. All the men from Zululand and Natal were to gather in Johannesburg. He achieved this unbelievable feat in the space of just ten days. He had received the written blessing of the Transvaal President for his quest. Commandant of the armed forces, Piet Joubert, knew that he was coming down the road to Natal, and wished him well.

On 5 October 1899, a crowd of over 7 000 Zulus gathered in Johannesburg for their long walk home. They had been joined by two emissaries from the King of the Zulus, one Peka ka Dinizulu, a member of the Royal Household, and also one Hlobeni Buthelezi, from the Buthelezi family, both of whom had been Prime Ministers to the Zulu Kings. They were the ancestors of our very own honourable Gatsha Mangosuthu Buthelezi.

The people were told to obey their leader, Sid Marwick. They were also warned that, if they were attacked from either side during the journey, they were not to retaliate. They were to retreat and when the threat had passed they were to tend to their wounded, and to bury their dead. Only then could they continue on their journey homewards.

The discipline and obedience of the Zulus is already legendary in our country, and they conducted themselves impeccably throughout. They had to endure suffering, hardship, hunger, thirst and heavy rains. Whenever they came across hostile Boer commandoes, it was Marwick who said 'Stay back, my people, let me talk.' He faced the wrath of the Afrikaner, which was exacerbated by the fact that he was English! The scattered storekeepers along the route were delighted with the chance to supply some 7 000 people who had money on them, with goods and foods. Most of the local farmers sold them chickens and fresh vegetables.

When they came upon the British, they were thought to be invading spies, and it took a lot of persuasion to appease the officers on the front. However, it is no easy task to walk some 500 km and to supervise and nurture about 7 000 people at one time. At various stations along the way, the railways allowed the old and sick free passage. Yet, when they eventually crossed over into Natal, the British made everyone boarding the trains pay their full fare.

The Zulus were never to forget how Marwick placed the sick upon his horse, and walked alongside them calling them 'my people'. Or how, when there was a shortage of rations, he also went without.

On 15 October 1899, ten days after setting out, they reached the safety of Natal. The route they walked went like this: Johannesburg, Kliprivierspruit, Heidelberg, Greylingstad, Standerton, Platrand, Perdekop, Volksrust, Charlestown, Laingsnek, Ingogo, Newcastle, and then Dannhauser. During the last day, the march started to split up. Some 3 000 took the road that turned off to Zululand, about 2 000 took the Ladysmith road, and others managed to reach their homes in the Newcastle district. The remaining people reached Hattingsspruit rail-siding, where they boarded trains for various destinations. Marwick himself went to Pietermaritzburg, where he received a hero's welcome. He was lauded by the Prime Minister of Natal, as well as the British press.

Young Zulu mineworkers on the Rand

John Sidney Marwick, who never liked to talk about his heroic journey, eventually died in Pietermaritzburg in 1958. He was given a Christian funeral. The Zulus, as is their custom, sat patiently on the hillside in respect, waiting their chance. Peka ka Dinizulu, the nephew of Cetshwayo and a lifelong friend, was dressed in Royal leopard skins, carrying his spear and the huge shield of the Royal Regiment. He stepped forward to give the 'izibongo' (praise song) to his friend, on behalf of the grateful Zulus. The white people stepped back.

Here is the last verse of that magnificent piece of praise-singing poetry, dedicated to John Sidney Marwick.

Long may you live Muhle,

And may the Great Spirit preserve you

There was never a courtier so without blemish,

helper of the needy and orphans

Even the penniless will hail you as a hero

Only the dead are appreciated, not the living

It is indeed incidents like these that make us realise why we love our country so –

and show just how inseparable we all really are. Hamba kahle, Muhle!

SAMMY MARKS

Despite escaping conscription into the army, the young Sammy Marks was left with an abiding hatred of Tsarist Russia. In 1861 before he turned eighteen, Sammy had left Russia and set sail for Hull, with a consignment of Russian horses, bound for the industrial city of Sheffield in northern England.

Sheffield society was undergoing radical change and expansion as it developed into the cradle of the English steel industry. The town was attracting thousands of newcomers. Sammy was welcomed to his new refuge by a kinsman who ran a jewellery shop and readily supplied him with the seed money to set up a peddler's business. At the same time Sammy found lodgings with a prominent member of the Jewish community, Tobias Guttmann, a jeweller, hawker and cutler, who became the young man's mentor.

Guttmann advised the young man to sail for South Africa to try his luck on those distant shores. He agreed to pay for Sammy's passage to Cape Town and also presented him with a large case of knives, the sum total of the young man's capital. Perhaps it was his youthful experiences in industrial England that later provided Sammy Marks with the inspiration to establish, among a host of other companies, a Transvaal version of Sheffield, viz. the large steel-works at Vereeniging. Who knows?

Marks arrived at the Cape which was also undergoing important historical change. The year before, in 1867, a large diamond, the 'Eureka', had been discovered on a remote farm in the northern area of the colony and this was followed within a year by the discovery of the 'Star of South Africa' diamond. These events led to the beginnings of a mineral industry that was to revolutionise the sub-continent.

Marks stayed initially in Cape Town. He hawked his stock of knives around Cape Town and made a pleasant profit, reinvesting the profit in goods, which he again peddled in the suburbs of Cape Town. His cousin, Isaac Lewis, joined him, and the partnership prospered. Soon they had accumulated sufficient cash to buy a horse and cart and then another. With goods obtained on credit from Cape Town's wholesale merchants, they extended their 'smousing' into the Boland, Cape Town's then rural hinterland.

In July 1871 news came of a discovery of a major diamond pipe and this set off a frenzied rush. The partners loaded their two carts with goods and immediately set off. But long before they had reached their destination, they had sold every article to the poorly equipped hopefuls making their way to the diamond fields. They turned back to Cape Town, restocked the carts, taking with them this time a prefabricated wooden shop. Arriving at the diggings, they sold off a cart and a horse and opened shop. Goods were in short supply and they made a handsome profit. Payments were made mostly in diamonds and Lewis and Marks soon found that dealing in diamonds was more profitable than trading in general goods.

Lewis and Marks rapidly established a reputation for square dealing which placed them head and shoulders above the dubious types known as 'kopje wallopers' and the petty diamond buyers, who scuttled around the claims, gulling credulous diggers.

Within a very short space of time, Lewis and Marks, along with a handful of diamond merchants, came to dominate the local trade, acting as intermediaries between Kimberley and the great diamond centres of Europe. In a little corrugated iron office, situated in the new main street between the Albion Bar and the Diggers Arms, stones were brought in for sale. Here the partners made their selections to ship off to merchants in London, Amsterdam and elsewhere. Such were the humble beginnings of Sammy Mark's enormously successful career.

Anthony Trollope, a novelist visiting Kimberley in October 1877, found the area 'a most detestable place'. He complained: 'Temperatures soared to 50° in the sun, the landscape was drought stricken and totally bare. I don't think there was a tree to be seen within five miles of the town.' He continued: 'I doubt whether there was a blade of grass for twenty miles, and everything was a drab brown colour where one gagged on an atmosphere of dust and flies. The dust is so thick that the sufferer fears to remove it lest the raising of it may aggravate the evil, and flies are so numerous that one hardly dares to slaughter them by the ordinary means least the bodies should be noisome.'

But the Marks-Lewis partnership endured those terrible climes and they began to invest heavily in diamond mining, buying their first claims in 1872. The restriction limiting the purchase of claims was removed in 1874 and this opened the way for substantial capital investment. Claim holders fell from 1 600 to just 300 by 1877. Fewer than twenty claim holders controlled over half of the claims, while four businesses, the Lewis and Marks partnership, the Paddon brothers, Jules Porges and J. B. Robinson owned a quarter of the entire mine between them.

The partners, the Paddon brothers and a few others, combined their claims to form the Kimberley Mining Company, one of the earliest mining companies on the fields. By 1879, its capital had increased to £200 000, of which Lewis and Marks held half, and the venture was soon giving a return on capital of over 25%. It was then that Lewis went to England to negotiate their company's merger with claims held by Jules Porges; and a new combined company was floated in Paris, Compagnie Française des Mines du Diamantes du Cap.

A joint stock company with a capital of 14 million francs or £560 000, it was the largest mining concern in Africa, representing nearly one quarter of the richest diamond mine on the Cape diamond fields. This was the first South African diamond mining company to be placed before the investing public in Europe and its floatation was an enormous success. By mid-1880 its shares were trading freely at a very high premium.

When Sammy Marks noticed the tensions building up after the Jameson Raid by British-aligned forces, he decided to become active on the diplomatic front. He ran between the two parties trying desperately to avert the ever-growing spectre of war in the Transvaal. He pleaded with President Kruger for a change in attitude and stated on numerous occasions that war with Britain would destroy not only the Transvaal and Orange Free State, but also the very core of the Boer nation. Unfortunately, these wise sentiments fell on deaf ears. The inevitable happened.

After the fall of Bloemfontein, Johannesburg and Pretoria to the British, Sammy Marks desperately tried to convince the Boer generals that it was useless to continue the war. In a letter addressed to Louis Botha and other Boer Generals, he pleaded:

> I ask you and my other friends, if 10 000 men can possibly hope to prevail against a mighty power like England, backed by her colonies and dependencies, which has at her command almost unlimited funds and numberless men. It is not necessary for me to point to the number of widows and orphans as a result of the war, and to tell you that the number is rapidly increasing, and what will be the end? It is all very well for our brave leaders and men in the field to talk about fighting to the bitter end, but you must not forget the thousands of prisoners who are exiled from their country and have been for months. The longer the war lasts the greater will be the destruction wrought and the consequences will be that when the prisoners are brought back to the country, they will have no houses to receive them. Do you not think as a Man, a General, a Husband, and a Father, you should determine to make the best of things, and prevail upon others to do the same?

Such was the passion that Sammy had for the Boer people and for his country. But his appeals were in vain. The letter was sent to General Botha's camp, personally delivered to him by the widow of the late General Piet Joubert. And the result – the Boers were incensed!

As the commandos grew increasingly desperate, they attacked Marks's home at Zwartkoppies and stole a number of horses. His wife Bertha was at home, alone and was terrorised by the commando until four in the morning. The incident angered Sammy deeply. Yet he continued to do what he could for the Boers and their cause. Indeed, he initiated the talks on 19 May, which culminated in the Peace of Vereeniging being signed on 31 May 1902.

Sammy also put aside money to get the Boer generals back on their feet. One day as he came out of the bank in Pretoria, he met Koos de la Rey going in. 'What's that large envelope under your arm?' he asked. 'I have business with the bank,' came the reply. 'Please come with me to my office,' Sammy requested. He shut the door and asked to see the contents of De la Rey's envelope. Inside were the title deeds of De la Rey's farms. 'You were going to mortgage them?' Sammy asked. 'I have no choice, it is for my children's education,' came the soft reply. 'Don't be a fool, you will be ruined in a couple of years. I will lend you all that you require, and you can repay me when you can afford it.' This was the kind of generosity Sammy Marks was capable of.

Sammy Marks

In the post-war boom Marks and Lewis invested heavily in property in the western Transvaal and the Cape. They floated an enormously powerful company, The African & European Investment Company. In 1912 Marks formed the Vereeniging Power Station and then went on to found the South African Iron and Steel Corporation, which was the culmination of a 37-year dream. Although the furnace was small and of an experimental nature, it marked the beginning of steel production made from local highveld ore.

Sammy Marks died of a stomach ailment in Johannesburg on 18 February 1920 at the age of 75. Shops and businesses closed to show their respect. Friends, colleagues and luminaries, including the Prime Minister of South Africa, Jan Smuts, who had been a long-time friend, were present at the graveside in Pretoria. South Africa had lost a visionary and pioneer, and one of its most influential industrialists. A 'haimishe mensch' indeed!

NAME CHANGES IN SOUTH AFRICA

The changing of place names in any country can be a hugely emotive issue. Nevertheless, examples of this have abounded in our own country since the majority of the South African population received the democratic vote and brought their own government to power in 1994. To understand why these changes were made, one has to understand how history was biased and skewed to portray the glory of various interested parties.

There is a little place just outside Swellendam, in the Western Cape, which the ancient Attaqua tribe named Xairu – 'the place of beauty'. Then came the Dutch, and they renamed it Zuurbraak, because of the poor quality of its waters. Not many people are aware that Mossel Bay was first called Aliwal South, by that dubious hero Sir Harry Smith. Having defeated the Sikhs at Aliwal in the Indian Campaign, he lauded himself with the names Aliwal South, Aliwal North and Juanasburg, which he named after his wife. Another dubious English character in our history, Lord Charles Somerset, lives on in the place names Somerset East and Somerset West.

But be that as it may, let us look at some of the historical reasons for the changing of place names. The Great North Road starts from Pretoria, referred to now unofficially as Tshwane. Next you get Bela-Bela, the old Warmbaths. Nylstroom is now Modimolle, Potgietersrus has become Mokopane, Ellisras has been changed to Lephalale and Pietersburg is now Polokwane. Further north, Louis Trichardt has beome Makhado, and finally, Messina has become Musina, the local name for 'the place of copper'.

Modimolle, or 'place of the sacred spirits', is a very holy place for the local people. Along came the Voortrekkers, who named it Kranskop – the toll road bears this name to this day. Upon seeing this strange hill, the 'Jerusalem-gangers', who were a band of extremely religious Voortrekkers that had set out to find the Promised Land, mistook this strange hill to be an Egyptian pyramid. Under the leadership of Commandant Jan Viljoen and the preacher Adam Enslin, they renamed the river they found there Nylstroom, under the misconception that this was the source of the Nile River. The river already had an ancient name – the Mahalakwena River – 'the river of the fierce crocodiles'.

It seems that our country is undergoing a gradual return to the original names given to various rivers and places, prior to the arrival of the Dutch Voortrekkers, the British Colonists and then, of course, the Afrikaner Nationalists. A good example of this was when Lord Roberts put up an army camp just outside Lyttleton, named after Lord Lyttleton. The English called it Roberts Heights, but with the onset of Afrikaner Nationalism in 1948, its name changed to Voortrekkerhoogte.

But let us concentrate on the name change concerning Potgietersrus, now aptly renamed Mokopane. To begin to understand the source of this change, we have to look back to the 1850s. The conditions in the northern part of our country at this time were hardly conducive to peace. Hendrik Potgieter had been in the area for at least fifteen years, and settlers and frontiersmen had systematically encroached upon the land.

In August 1854, Field Cornet Hermanus Potgieter, the brother of the recently deceased Hendrik Potgieter and uncle of the newly elected Commandant-General Piet Potgieter, visited the home of the local chief, Mokopane, seeking concessions for trading in ivory and general hunting rights. Significantly, at that time the Volksraad of the Transvaal had passed a law prohibiting barter with the local people, under a penalty of £37.10. The object of this law was to keep the peace. Hermanus Potgieter, an official who should have known better, was clearly breaking the law. A rough frontiers-man, he was prone to bouts of violence. A quarrel broke out and one of Mokopane's sons mocked him. Being of an excitable and calvanistic disposition, he turned and shot the young boy dead on the spot.

It was this incident, and a few others of a similar intolerant nature, that led to the Potgieter party, totalling 23 and including wives and children, to be set upon by Mokopane's warriors. They were murdered by the Makatees at the place now known as Moorddrift. The horror of this massacre penetrated deep into the hearts of the Afrikaner people, heightened by the fact that Hermanus Potgieter was pinned to the ground, flayed alive, and his skin made into a karos.

Six other clans joined the Makatees and began systematically pillaging the neighbourhood, from lonely outpost farms in the southern Soutpansberg and the Waterberg, to as far south as Rustenberg. The people started fleeing southwards, and retribution became the call of the day. The first to take the field was Commandant Piet Potgieter. Together with 150 men, he marched on the kraal of Mokopane, which was situated near the future town of Potgi-etersrus, just north of Mahalakwena Drift, which became Moorddrift.

With the assistance of Marthinus Wessels Pretorius, the combined commando swelled to 550 men. Even Englishmen like William Hartley from the Magaliesberg and Dr Way from Smithfield in the Free State, joined up. The Makatees were eventually forced into a narrow valley, where they sought refuge in a series of caves. The Voortrekkers could not get in. They decided to dynamite the tops of the hills to block the entrances, and bury the Makatees under the ruins. This attempt failed. They decided to starve them out. Any man who showed his face at any entrance was immediately shot. Fires were lit during the night and all entrances patrolled 24 hours a day.

Several shots from the caverns also found their mark, and on 6 November 1854, a musket ball from a cavern struck Commandant Piet Potgieter as he was standing alongside Paul Kruger. He died instantly. The people's reaction was to drag 1 500 trees to block off all the entrances. At last, after many days, it became too much for the starving people, and the women and children, half mad with thirst, started crawling through the entrances. Every man who showed his face was shot immediately. The stench from inside the cave had become unbearable, and over 1 000 men were shot dead as they crawled out of the caves. It was a grim punishment that was meted on Mokopane's people, and it destroyed most of the tribes in and around that area under Mokopane – hence the name 'Mokopaan se Gat'.

The Voortrekkers have had their time to call it the resting place of the Potgieters. Now it is time to honour the vanquished Mokopane.

MIRAGES IN
THE SANDS

I f you should ever find yourself in the heart of karakul-ranching area of southern Namibia, you would be forgiven for thinking you were witnessing a mirage on catching your first glimpse of Schloss Duwisib, a curious baroque structure 70 km southwest of Maltahöhe.

It was built by Baron Hans Heinrich von Wolf, an eccentric aristocratic German artillery officer. He had come out to South West Africa during the war against the Hottentots, and, at a remote outpost in the Maltahöhe District, he had lost all his field guns and provisions to a superior Hottentot opposition. He was in disgrace. (Incidentally, disgrace was not unknown to the reputation of that military family, for in the Franco-Prussian war of 1870, the Baron's father had lost a complete battery of guns.) The Baron and the survivors of the garrison rode for their lives, and reached Maltahöhe Village.

After this disaster, the Baron was allowed to resign his commission and return to Germany, where most people would have disappeared into obscurity, but not this man.

His blonde, petite wife Jayta, was from a wealthy family of New York homeopathic medicine manufacturers. She was born in New Jersey in 1881, and when her father died, her mother married an Irish-American lawyer named Gaffney, who was a close friend of Kaiser Wilhelm II. Gaffney became the American Consul-General in Dresden, where Jayta met and married Hans Heinrich von Wolf.

It wasn't many years later that the Baron and his pretty wife returned to the scene of his war defeat, where he purchased the farm Duwisib (a Hottentot word meaning 'the place of white chalk with no water'), 80 km west of Maltahöhe. The farm measured 56 000 hectares and cost the princely sum of £700.

From then on, every ship that travelled from Germany to Lüderitz brought building materials, steel girders, antique furniture and paintings. An Afrikaner named Adriaan Esterhuizen had full-time employment with 20 ox-wagons, hauling this freight through the desert to the new farm. It took him two full years to complete the task. He covered 700 km on every round trip. In the meantime, the artisans had arrived – along with Italian stonemasons and Swedish carpenters. There was an army of labourers quarrying stone from the cliffs at Duwisib. Whilst this castle was being built, the Baron and his wife lived in a hut close by. The chalky sandstone of the area usually indicates the presence of water, but the Baron had to hand drill a full 300 m before he found usable water, which supplies the farm to this day.

Schloss Duwisib was eventually finished at the end of 1909. The outer walls were one-and-a-half metres thick and turreted with loopholes, with iron barred windows in the front. In the centre there was a massive tower, and within the huge stone-flagged hall hung old duelling pistols, swords and sabres. Should you stand in the gallery today, you would look down on glass chandeliers, fireplaces and chairs, all bearing the Von Wolf crest. You can almost see the Baron and his petite blonde wife handing out champagne, and mingling with the guests. Some would be German officers who had come to buy horses, others would be bearded Afrikaans transport drivers. The Administrator of the Maltahöhe District would be there, and the Baron, being a democratic nobleman, would tell you that you were quite free to leave if you didn't like his friends. The wine cellar would be full of Piesporter and Riesling, Berncastler, Liebfraumilch, Nierstiner and Zeltingen, with casks of beer and cases of whisky stacked to the roof. The Baron was a fine pianist and a good singer to boot, and his fine entertaining evenings were legendary.

Even Kaiser Wilhelm II's wife Ellen, who was the Baron's sister, spent a year at Duwisib, during which she taught the local Hottentot women how to knit. It is said that after the Second World War, she died a peasant in East Prussia.

The Baron certainly knew how to spend his fortune. Once a month, he would ride in a carriage drawn by six horses to Maltahöhe, and upon his arrival, the procedure was always the same. He would enter the hotel bar, pull out his revolver, shoot five bottles off the shelves, with the the sixth shot always reserved for the lamp. The hotel proprietor would jot down the value of each hit, and if the amounts were correct, the Baron cheerfully paid up. He was a good-humoured man, and there were only two things that would make him lose his temper – firstly, if he was swindled, and secondly, if somebody drank his beer.

He was elected to represent the Maltahöhe District in the Legislative Assembly at Windhoek, and became very popular, chiefly because he never 'played the Baron'. However, he was far too outspoken for the German officials and Governor Seitz totally disapproved of him, forcing the Baron to go his own eccentric way.

In 1908, Von Wolf went in search of diamonds. Now, Duwisib is more than 160 km inland from the Diamond Coast. This did not pose a problem to the Baron and his comrades – together, they covered the first 100 km by camel, and when the shifting sands became too loose, they sent the camels back to the farm and tramped the rest of the distance on foot to Meob on the coast. Here, they refilled their water bottles with brackish water, pegged a few claims at Sylvia's Hill, then plodded southwards to Lüderitz, almost 200 km south. Upon their arrival, they say that Von Wolf sat down, consumed a bottle of the finest champagne and gambled at cards for the entire night.

The Baron had one of the first karakul herds in the country, and it is certain that if not for the advent of the First World War in 1914, he would have made a fortune. Sensing the clouds of war looming, and not wanting to be stuck in what was a German colony, Von Wolf and his young wife packed up and left for Germany. This move afforded the Baron an opportunity to regain his lost status. Germany forgave their son his misdemeanourrs, and he was appointed a Major in the Artillery.

In September 1916, Major von Wolf was killed in action in France. He had fought valiantly in the battle that resulted in his death, and his name was restored. On searching his body, a French Officer recovered letters from his devoted wife, Jayta. These, along with his personal possessions, were forwarded to her through the Red Cross.

The Von Wolfs had placed a personal friend, Count Max von Lettichau, in charge of Schloss Duwisib just before the War. Sadly the estate was soon declared bankrupt and auctioned off, along with its enormous treasures of priceless antiques, paintings, Persian carpets, silver and crockery, for £7 050.

The new owners of the castle were a Swedish couple named Murmann. Shortly after they took over, Mr Murmann died at Duwisib. Their son, who had recently learned to fly, joined the South African Airforce, and was killed in action during the Second World War. The castle and the farm were once again sold, this time to a company, for £25 000.

Meanwhile, Jayta had remarried between the First and Second World Wars. Her new husband was Eric Schlemmer, the Consul-General for Siam, based in Munich.

Schloss Duwisib lost some valuable treasures during the First World War, including a very expensive carpet worth over £10 000. The Baroness put in a claim for the silver after the War, but not one piece could be found. Fortunately, the furniture was far too heavy to be moved, and the looters were not interested in the works of art. That being said, the company that purchased Schloss Duwisib after the Murmanns can be credited with maintaining it the way it was during the time of the Baron's occupation.

If you should stand at the window of the dining room and look out over the plains, you will see a mountain peak in the distance. Its name? 'Wolfsberg'. The Baron has left his name on the map, forever.

Why did this Baron choose to return to this desolate spot with his wife? They had money, they could easily have lived in Dresden, where they could have enjoyed the readily available amenities that civilisation offers. Instead, they chose to settle on the very edge of the world, in a desolate area of devil-winds, cold winters, and the scorching African sun.

Facts are so often stranger than fiction. Jayta Humphreys, prior to her marriage to Von Wolf, was an avid follower of the eminent psychologist Sigmund Freud. When her husband returned to Germany in disgrace after the Hottentot campaign, she realised that he was a broken man. He had not only lost his army career; but had also disgraced the family name. There was nothing that anybody could tell him that would make him realise that that incident was merely a small part of a complete life. It had swamped him completely. She watched the man she so dearly loved, slowly, day by day, destroying himself.

One day, the answer came to her. 'We must go back to the place where you lost yourself,' she said. 'Only then will you see that it is merely a small part of your life. We will face the people together, we will build a magnificent castle, live in grand style, and people will become proud of us and accept us and our hospitality. A castle in the desert, Hans!'

And there, in a remote corner of the world, stands the grey sandstone Schloss Duwisib – forever a reminder of the love, devotion and understanding of a great woman, Jayta Humphreys.

Schloss Duwisib

THE FLIGHT OF THE HERERO

Everywhere in the gleaming sands lie the rusted parts of abandoned wagons, trek chains, thongs and canvas tarpaulins, along with the bones of men and cattle, and the graves of those fallen in the most grievous of deaths – thirst. For a trekker, there was no word that could instil greater fear than *dors* (thirst) – the stories of the Dorsland Treks live to this very day. Those who experienced a 'small thirst' on one of those treks never forgot the experience. The continual groaning of the oxen is the most heartrending sound that could ever come from an animal. Added to this was the blazing heat of the sun, the endless sand and the choking cloud of dust as they trekked onwards, becoming thirstier and thirstier.

One such Dorsland Trek has attracted very little attention in our country, probably because it was a black trek. The old newspaper *Die Brandwag* published the story in 1921.

It was the trek of the Herero out of South West Africa which went eastwards through the Kalahari and into the country of the Bamangwato, eventually coming to an end in Palala, in the Waterberg region of what is now the North West Province of South Africa. The size of this disastrous trek was unbelievable. More than 700 wagons were left behind in the desert, and more than 13 000 people died of thirst, the most terrible of all deaths.

The ovaHerero tribe originated in Central Africa and its people are exceptionally tall – an adult under 1,8 m is very unusual. At the time of this little-known trek, the majority of the tribe was educated and could read and write. High Dutch was their daily language. They built houses, wore European clothing and farmed, and were generally known to be a friendly people. It was said that their attitudes changed with the colonisation by the Germans, that they were influenced by the yellow people, and turned to murdering whites. I have heard this all too often in the stories of the Gqunukhwebe, the Xhosa and the Koranna at Mamusa, the list is endless. Behind the myth lies the greed to occupy land, and it was no different in the case of the Germans in South West Africa.

The Bondelswart Hottentots put up a fight on the plains surrounding the Karas Mountains and, when the Herero saw what happened to them, they were so shattered that the only option they could think of was flight. 'Rather face the Kalahari,' said the elders of the tribe, 'than face the Germans.'

So they prepared themselves for the long trek, before the German forces even reached their boundaries. They sent intelligence parties out to gather information about grazing, waterholes, Tsamma melons and general conditions, but nothing could have prepared them for the ordeal that they were about to face. The trek started and the Germans, following them to the last waterhole, reported that, even at this stage, they were following a path of dead and dying people and animals. Every waterhole was filled with dead cattle and the water trampled to mud. It is estimated that 4 000 Herero died, even before the big thirst began. The head of the trek was under Captain Samuel and the rearguard under one Julius, a preacher and schoolteacher.

When they left their homes there were more than 700 wagons, 14 000 people and cattle uncountable, but upon arrival in the Waterberg there were but 400 people and no animals except for a horse belonging to Samuel and the cattle given to them by the kindly people of Khama, the Bamangwato. It is estimated that in the desert 3 600 people died of thirst alone. There were very few old people or children that came through that crossing, and seldom has nature imposed her harsh code of 'survival of the fittest' more cruelly upon a people. Contrary to the hopelessly optimistic reports of the scouts, there was very little grazing to be had, the pan water was scarce and the Tsamma melons were green and bitter to the taste. Three days after entering the desert, the cattle began to die, and what made matters worse was the panicky knowledge that the Germans were after them. All the known water-holes were rushed by thousands of thirsty cattle and immediately churned into mud, so the cattle were unable to relieve their thirst.

Inevitably, within fourteen days the last of the 700 wagons had to be abandoned. Everything transportable was made into bundles and everyone, young and old, had to help carry. In the forefront was Samuel, trying desperately to keep order. At the back was Julius, making sure that the weak and frail were not left behind. On the flanks, daily, were patrols to collect Tsamma melons, which would be distributed among all the people. It took a lot of melons to keep the people going, of course, so as much meat as could be carried was made into biltong. But it soon became apparent that strict order could not be maintained and, within a week or two, the trek was so long and extended that the stragglers took fully three days to arrive at the place where the forward group had camped. Under these circumstances, of course, no fair sharing of meat and melons was possible. Contrary to what one would expect, there was very little selfishness, and heroic acts abounded.

The first to fall were the elderly and, almost every day, the rear section of the trek would pass small groups of them, usually lying under the shade of a thorn tree, having made their peace with God, and simply waiting to die. Usually the goodbyes and a little prayer had been said, and those who were strong enough moved on with the trek. Where a person had died in the company of another family member, he or she would be buried up to his or her neck in the sand. Mothers with suckling babies bore the brunt of the pain and very few made it through. 'You could count them on your fingers,' Julius said.

The unfortunate mothers with more than one child had an even worse time of it, and often you would see a mother walk the path three times, as she carried her children forward one by one, along the trek and, sooner or later, these poor mothers came to realise that one, or even two would have to be sacrificed, to save the last one. Many mothers actually had the courage to kill their children, instead of leaving them to a lingering death in the blazing sun. Samuel and Julius agreed – there was no option – though usually this decision was taken far too late and most of the mothers died shortly thereafter. One young woman, Maria, who gave birth to her first child at the beginning of the trek, used a galvanized iron bathtub as a sled and pulled her baby through the desert – and made it. Unfortunately, when a suckling mother becomes dehydrated, her milk dries up. Many babies died of hunger, usually shortly followed by the mother who would inflict knife wounds to her breasts in a vain attempt to give sustenance to the dying child. Julius recalled an elderly couple, long married – the woman was too weak and could go no further. The man was strong and would have pulled through, but decided to stay with his wife in the desert. They bade farewell to their children, their bundles were redistributed and the trek moved on, with the vultures always circling overhead.

The survivors went on, with feet and legs swollen, without skin, and bleeding. Their lips and tongues swelled up and cracked, so much so that it was almost impossible to eat the Tsamma melons. For two months they had not seen water.

Suddenly, these skeletons dressed in rags, heard voices calling them, but, with their burnt lips and burst tongues, all they could manage in answer was a hiss, as the Bamangwato tribe of Khama came into the desert to save them. Slowly, oh so slowly, the Bamangwato nursed the survivors back from the brink. Water was given in half measures to the weakest and the children first, then the others and, to those nearest to death, it was administered drop by drop, for drinking would have killed them.

After six months' recuperation, the remnants of the Herero tribe moved on to Palala in the Waterberg, where this terrible but largely forgotten epic was recorded, and is still spoken about very softly at night, around the fires.

JOB MASEGO

ob Masego was employed as a delivery worker in Springs in present day Gauteng when World War 2 broke out. He read about the war in the newspapers, but felt that it did not concern him until a visit one day by a close friend, Frans Makhanyua.

When Job opened the door that evening Frans stood there looking magnificent! He had joined the Native Military Corps and was in uniform. Job knew that the war was perceived by some as a white man's war. But he put aside the question of injustice at home and made the decision to fight for his country and freedom, like many thousands of black South Africans.

Job Masego joined the same unit as his friend and was posted to East Africa and then to Egypt with the 2nd South African Division. Here he was captured and placed in a prisoner of war camp. One day, sitting on the sand inside the barbed-wire camp in Tobruk, Job was thinking rather angrily about an event that had taken place the previous night. He had asked the Italian guards for washing water and they had arrogantly laughed in his face, remarking that he was already black and that washing would make no difference. When Job reacted indignantly, they had held him down and beaten him severely.

He was still furious as he absent-mindedly ran his hand through the desert sand. He felt something hard and smooth. It was a cartridge. It was not much use without a rifle, he thought to himself. As the area had not been cleared of debris before the camp was set up and having not much else to do, Job decided to continue to sift through the sand. He collected some 40 cartridges in all. Then it suddenly struck him that with the cordite contained in the cartridges, he could make a bomb and blow up something. Job systematically sifted and searched through the battle debris in the sand. He found pieces of fuse, which he was able to join into a four-metre length. He poured the cordite he had collected into a discarded milk tin. All of this he stuffed into his rucksack underneath his jersey and decided to bide his time.

Sometime later the prisoners were sent to the docks to carry cases ashore and it was there that the idea of blowing up a ship was born. Job's chance came on the third morning when, together with a number of prisoners, he was taken to a single-funnelled ship anchored in the bay.

Throughout the morning they were engaged in offloading supplies, mostly consisting of food. Having completed the job, the men were told that after lunch they would load cases of ammunition and drums and jerry cans containing petrol. Job knew this was his opportunity. He confided his plan to Koos Williams. 'This is our chance to get back at the Italians and also strike a blow for our people,' he said. 'But I will need everyone's help! When I am ready to place the bomb I want you and all the others to go over and distract the guards so that they'll not notice what I'm doing.'

The sun was setting as the end of the shift came and with it the opportunity to act. The men went over to the guards and Job slipped into the hold. He heaped straw over the milk can and soaked it in petrol. Leading a fuse, he scrambled up the ladder. He bent close to the hatch and touched the fuse with a lit cigarette. Luckily, his movements had not been spotted as the men had 'accidentally' dropped a case of ammunition overboard. The action had diverted the attention of the guards and only resulted in the culprit getting hit on the ear with the butt of a rifle. The ruse had worked. The prisoners were taken back to camp.

They sat in Job's tent waiting. Nothing was heard. Had the fuse gone out? Job went outside. 'Come!' he called to his comrades. 'Black smoke is coming from the ship!' At that very moment a sheet of flame appeared, followed by a massive explosion and then two more in quick succession. The guards appeared and hurriedly pushed the men inside.

The following morning the prisoners were marched down to the dock to carry on their work. The ship had all but disappeared and a number of drums were floating around in the sea. German officers lined up the prisoners and interrogated them in turn. Had anyone been smoking on board? Had they spotted any 'red balls' or mines in the water? The officers were forced to depart, none the wiser. The enemy was blissfully ignorant of the cleverly conceived plot!

Several nights later Lance-Corporal Masego and Private Masiya crept under the wire fence of their camp and escaped from Tobruk. They walked across the desert for 23 days sustained by a few meagre scraps of food saved from their daily rations. Just south of El Alamein, the South African Armoured Car Division picked them up and it was here on 16 November 1942 that Job's story was related to intelligence officers.

When the Eighth Army reoccupied Tobruk, navy divers were able to confirm the incident. Lance-Corporal Job Masego was awarded the Military Medal and the citation read as follows:

> For meritorious and courageous action in that on or about July 21st 1942, whilst a prisoner of war, he sank a fully laden steamer – an F boat – while moored in Tobruk harbour. This he did by placing a small tin filled with gunpowder in amongst drums of petrol in the hold, leading a fuse from there to the hatch, lighting the fuse and closing the hatch. In carrying out this deliberately planned action Job Masego displayed ingenuity, determination, and complete disregard of personal safety, of punishment by the enemy or from the ensuing explosion, which destroyed the vessel.

Job Masego is a true South African hero and one whose brave deeds should never be forgotten.

THE FIRST MISSIONARIES
IN THE TRANSVAAL

I n the year 1822, two wagons brought the first two missionaries to the Transvaal. They were Thomas Laidman Hodgson, accompanied by his wife Anne and their little daughter Mary-Anne, and Samuel Broadbent, his wife, their son and a second English nursemaid. These families, along with their friends, the Archbells, were to be the first missionaries in the Transvaal.

On 1 November 1822, just eleven months after the Andersons had returned from Klaarwater and taken charge of Pacaltsdorp, the missionary families were given instructions to go and spread the word of Christianity in the land of the Bechuana.

They started trekking from Graaff-Reinet, and passed what was to be the first town in the Orange Free State, namely Philippolis. Then, keeping close to the Modder River for water, they headed westwards, eventually crossing the lower part of the Vaal (Lekoa) River, near to where the town of Douglas stands today.

On 6 December 1822, they reached the small town of Campbell, and proceeded to Griquatown to the west. At both these mission stations the local Hottentots and Griquas pleaded with them not to go east to the land of the

Bechuana, as the country was being ravished by the Mantatees, who were attacking every tribe they came into contact with. However, nothing could dissuade the missionaries from their divine instruction, and they headed off northeast into the Transvaal, crossing the Harts River near the present Vaal-Harts irrigation scheme. They paid no heed to the constant warnings regarding the madness of their mission. Broadbent's simple response was, 'We are messengers of Christ. He is present with us and we will set up his banner in this land of darkness and war.' The coloured servants accompanying them thought differently. They fled.

At last they found a Koranna kraal, and it was here that the first brewing of afternoon tea was ever recorded in the Transvaal. Chudeep, the Koranna chief, begged the men to stay with him, as the earlier missionaries had done in Griquatown. Anderson's fame had penetrated even this far. The Koranna took all their trek oxen away, so they could not leave, and the tribe's talk of the Mantatees resulted in two more servants running away, one of whom was a Bechuana interpreter. They had just regained their oxen and were preparing to trek when a Koranna hurriedly entered the kraal on the back of an ox, warning them that the Mantatees were on their way. In no time at all, the Korannas had packed their belongings on oxen, and fled westwards.

The missionaries stayed put, knowing full well that if these were the hordes of Queen Mantatisi, they were as dead as dodos. They knew that talking would be utterly useless, but still, they stepped forward. There before them were not the Mantatees, but the very Bechuana that they had come so far to find. They were the Baralong Bechuana, falling back before the Mantatees. For over a week, the missionaries remained hidden in the dense bush, in order to avoid involvement in the battle between the Baralong and the Mantatees. They then trekked eastwards again, knowing full well that they were cutting off their only means of escape.

It was only the fact that the Mantatees had never seen a 'walking house' (ox-wagon) or white face before, let alone one saying 'come here, come here' in Tswana, that saved the families from being massacred.

Along the way, they saved a little boy who had survived the massacre of his entire family. His name was Liratsagae, and in later life, he became the first black printer in the Transvaal. They also saved a destitute little girl named Orphena, who grew to be a devoted family servant.

Sifonello, the Baralong chief, allowed them to build their little mission station just a few miles away from the spot where Wolmaransstad would eventually arise, and here Mrs Broadbent gave birth to the first white child ever born in the Transvaal. The young boy was only a few weeks old when the Hodgsons took both wagons away to fetch supplies from Griquatown. A horde of over 50 000 Mantatees swept down upon the Batlapin tribe near Kuruman and were going to attack Lattakoo, who was a Dithakong. These people lived under the chieftainship of Mothibi.

They were saved by Robert Moffat, who sent an urgent appeal to Griquatown for assistance. A commando of over 150 mounted Griquas with firearms let rip into the Mantatees. So deadly was the firepower that, after an hour, the Mantatees turned and ran and the might of Queen Mantatisi and the dreaded Ba-Klokwe was broken forever. The broken Mantatees retreated in the direction of Makwassie, where an ailing Broadbent was with his recovering wife. Mercifully, the hordes passed close to the little mission station, but did not discover it.

On his return, Hodgson was delighted to find his friends safe. They set about planting wheat, maize, beans, pumpkins, onions, carrots, beet and melons and were the first to prove that maize could grow in the Western Transvaal, without irrigation. Maize is the staple diet for many in that region to this day.

Edward Edwards then visited them, bringing them bad news. The missionary committee had sent instructions for the Hodgsons to return to Cape Town. They were devastated. After winning the respect of the Baralong, they were to leave their lifelong friends. The Broadbents wrote how they could not bear to go to the wagons to say goodbye, they just sat inside and cried. Broadbent's health deteriorated, and he had recurring premonitions that they should leave the mission.

They set out for Griquatown. No sooner had they left, than a fierce neighbouring tribe set upon the Baralong, inflicting heavy losses on men, women and cattle. The attackers razed the two mission station cottages to the ground. The Broadbents reached Griquatown, unaware of what had befallen the station. This was the layer of ash that my wife and I discovered some years ago.

Samuel Broadbent reached Grahamstown in November 1824. A year later, he left South Africa as an invalid and subsequently died. Such were the lives of the first missionaries in the Transvaal.

THE FIRST MISSIONARIES
TO GO NORTH

I t was some years ago, on a hot highveld summer's day, that my wife and I set off to try and locate the ruins of the mission station of Thomas Hodgson and Samuel Broadbent, the first mission station north of the Orange (Senque) River.

We found it just outside the town of Makwassie, which is a Bushman word for the indigenous wild spearmint bush they used in their natural medicines. It was in ruins. The grave on the outskirts had been dug up in a search for gold tooth fillings, the roof had been carried off and the place was in a shambles. Thank goodness the local farmer had the foresight to take the grave's headstone away and keep it in his shed, otherwise nothing of value or historical significance would have remained.

Next to the ruins, just under the ground's surface, was a layer of ash bearing testament to the fate of the first building that was razed to the ground by the marauding Queen Mantatisi of the Ba-Klokwe tribe. Slowly, my vision blurred as I gazed at the surrounding veld and recalled the events that had led up to the birth of the first white child in the Transvaal on 21 July 1823.

It all started with the remarkable trek of William Anderson, who, early in 1800, gave up his comfortable home in London, to sow the seeds of

Christianity. He was to go far beyond the boundaries of the then white south, as he trekked north of the Orange.

He was the son of a London merchant from Aberdeen, and for five weeks he trekked northwards with his London Missionary Society colleague, Kitchener. The northern boundary of the Cape was the Sak River. He crossed it and came upon Barend Barends, Chief of the Griqua tribe.

An old, dying Griqua of the Kok family told the missionary Dr John Philip many years later, that the reason they had allowed William Anderson to settle amongst them was because he had a wagon, and many other things that they coveted. When the time was right, their plan was to kill him and plunder his goods! But this reserved Scot went about his business, gaining the respect of all he came into contact with, and converting them to Christianity.

They gave him a site at a place called Aat Kaap, meaning 'Reed Fountain', which grew into the town known as Klaarwater, later to become Griquatown. No sooner had he settled, than an official British party called at Aat Kaap, a grim reminder that, if murder was being contemplated, the dreaded Cape Government would eventually get to know about it.

Attached to this party was another young British missionary named Edwards, who was on his way to attempt to found a mission station at Kuruman, which lay 100 miles to the north. These so called safeguards were short-lived. The Sak River mission was closed, and the Kuruman mission failed. Anderson and Cornelius Kramer, who had joined him, were on their own.

As the encroaching white communities slowly took up more and more of the indigenous people's land, the bastardised tribes were forced to move ever northwards. They comprised runaway slaves, people on the wrong side of the Colony's harsh laws, half-castes, interbred stragglers, naked Bushmen and Namaquas – a rabble of a people that were held together by one common thread – a bitter hatred for the British.

For four years, Anderson and Kramer shed their civilisation and lived with these people in their small portable huts made out of reed-mats hung over bent sticks similar to fishing rods. For years, they begged the leaders to settle in one place, establish a modicum of civilisation and attend the small reed church they had constructed, but to no avail.

In 1803, there came a great drought. The grazing turned to dust, the game moved northwards, and the now famished tribe followed suit, into the land of the Bechuana. They trekked through a starving land, the dryness taking its toll, even on the Korannas and Bushmen. When at last the rains came and the drought broke, this shattered tribe turned around and started its long trek back southwards to its waterholes once more.

It was then that Anderson made up his mind. He sent his ox-wagon south, over the Orange and into the Roggeveld, to fetch a load of seed-wheat. He and Kramer were able to fashion some farm implements and cleared a fair piece of land where they planted the first crop, praying daily to the Almighty that it would not fail. They dug a furrow all the way from the fountain to irrigate the crop. Slowly, from miles away, one could see the lush carpet of green begin to grow.

This opened up a brand new world for the nomads, and when the crop changed to white, the harvest began. It was a rich harvest indeed. The miracle of the loaves of baked bread convinced these nomads completely. They abandoned their nomadic existence and by the following season, all six of the fountain areas were under crops. The endless trekking was over, and the tenuous roots of western civilisation had begun.

One disaster struck the clan. It was the smallpox epidemic of 1805, and Anderson himself was struck down with the fever. However, as fate would have it, when the end of a long and hard road was approaching, none other than the well- known explorer, Dr Henry Lichenstein, poked his head through the door, and Anderson was nursed back to health in Cape Town.

He and his wife Johanna returned to Klaarwater, but in March 1820, with aching hearts and a big escort of sorrowful Griquas, they left Griquatown, never to return. Their names were passed down to future generations by the people that loved them so dearly.

RENSBERG'S KOP

ust off the N3 highway at Van Reenen's Pass in KwaZulu-Natal, is a little hotel called The Green Lantern, which services many of the 'Gauties' on their way to Durban. It is owned and managed by a friendly couple named Lew and Maria, who are well-versed in the history of the surrounding area, including the well-known story of Rachel de Beer. On one of my many visits there, Lew filled me in on another, less well-known story.

At the turn of the last century, the Rensberg family owned a farm in the beautiful foothills of the Drakensberg, called Rensberg's Kop. On one corner of the farm was a gentle hill leading up to a sheer cliff, which dropped into a cleft gorge halfway down. It was a lovely look-out site, as you could see the distant plains leading all the way to the mighty Drakensberg in the far distance.

One afternoon, the two Rensberg children, a boy of thirteen, and a girl not much younger, had run up that slope and were enjoying the magnificent view in the late afternoon sun. As the shadows began to lengthen, the girl got up and said, 'Let's head back home.' Her brother turned towards her, gave one last fleeting glance across the valley, then rose. It was then that his foot slipped, and, finding nothing to grasp, he plummeted over the side of the cliff into the gorge below.

His sister was dumbstruck, and stood frozen, staring at the empty space where her brother had just been. She tried to look over the edge, but she could see nothing. She ran to another prominent part and looked down. There she could see her brother – he was wedged down deep in the gorge.

She turned, and fled for home, where in a state of near-collapse, she bleated out her awful story. Her father ran for the horse, the farmhands for the saddles, and bearing water and rope, they set out for the krans.

On reaching the cliff, they called out to the boy, who by that stage had come around. He told them that he could not feel or use his limbs at all. 'He must have damaged his back,' his father thought. He went back to fetch hammers, more rope, steel spikes to attach the rope to, and a stretcher. By now it was dark, so they lit a fire. His mother stayed there all night, keeping vigil over her only son. The dawn must have seemed a lifetime away, but at first light, and with the assistance of other farmers in the area, they started to descend. The boy was still alive, but obviously racked with pain and very thirsty.

All day they toiled to get into that narrow gorge, but they could not reach him. They managed to get the rope to him, but he could not move his arms. No matter how his family pleaded, he could not move. The lengthening shadows heralded the onset of the second night. Again, his mother stayed up, blank-eyed from crying to her God for assistance.

It was the following morning at about 10 o'clock, while his father was still desperately trying to save him, that the boy called out to him, 'Ek ly vreeslik, Pa. Asseblief, skiet my.' ('I am in terrible pain, Father. Please, shoot me.') His father collapsed on his knees, and cried to the Almighty for help and guidance. He sobbed, his hands covering his face. Eventually, he rose slowly, and climbed the rope back to the top, where he went to fetch the rifle from his saddlebag.

'NEE, Pa!' screamed his now almost deranged wife.

'What must I do?' he asked. 'Must I leave my son for another bitterly cold night, and then allow him to die an agonising death?'

She walked to the edge and said goodbye to her son. Then a friend, with a gentle arm around her shoulder, led her and his sister away, and the father descended to the gorge. A single rifle shot reverberated around those mountains, and the very essence of life seemed to freeze in time and space. Friends said afterwards that although the bullet may have gone through the heart of the lad, it had definitely gone through the soul of his father.

The lad's father was never brought before any court of justice; the Law realised that the burden the father would have to carry for the rest of his days was heavy enough.

I took my drink and walked away. Lew's stories always do that to me.

So, if you are ever travelling through KwaZulu-Natal, and you happen to pass Rensberg's Kop, spare a thought for the family that sold up, and moved away.

Private Robert Hart

One of the first English-speaking South Africans to contribute to the making of our wonderful country, was Private Robert Hart. He was just eighteen years old when, having been confined aboard a British East Indiaman for four months, the young Scot caught his first glimpse of the Cape mountains in the spring of 1795.

Little did he realise that this fair country was to become his home, and that he was to be the first of the British Settlers, and a pillar of civilisation in the Eastern district. The town and the church that he founded still thrive to this very day.

As a penniless lad, he had run away from his Glasgow home and enlisted in the British Army, where he took part in the build-up of the war against the French. Now, he served as a member of the Argyllshire Highlanders, who had been cooped up in four vessels under the command of General Clarke, and were heading for Muizenberg to relieve General Craig's tiny force, clinging to a toehold in Simon's Town.

At that time, the French had overrun Holland, and the Cape therefore became their possession. Indeed, the French were overrunning most of Europe at that time, and Britain was not about to let the seaport to the

Eastern trade routes fall to the French.

When they anchored in False Bay, it was the very morning that the Dutch were advancing on Muizenberg to deliver a knockout blow to what they believed would be Craig's half-starved, dwindled force. Instead, they encountered four British man-of-wars, with their flags flying high. They fell back, and the issue was settled – the gate to the East Indies was slammed shut on France, and a second European nation was about to change the face of the landscape forever.

At dawn, on 14 September 1795, after a final skirmish where Wynberg stands today, the Dutch Commissioner, General Sluyken, surrendered. Eight hundred green-and-black kilted men proudly marched into the Castle at Cape Town, which was to be their home, and the headquarters of the 98th regiment, led by Private Robert Hart.

What a contrast it was to foggy Glasgow, or tough Stirling. 'Here is a divine climate, no fog, no damp, only clean, pure but sharp air,' wrote Lady Anne Barnard, whom Hart often saw from a respectable distance. She had arrived to play the part of the First Lady of the Colony to the current Governor, who had no wife.

Within a year, they received news that a great Dutch fleet was approaching, with the aim of recapturing the Cape. Hart's company, along with 2 000 infantrymen, marched northwards, through the tollgate that levied company taxes on the trickle of incoming trade from the farmers in the interior. They sweated and swore through the deep sands of the Cape Flats, for there were still no roads after 140 years of occupation. For nine days the men trudged northwards and arrived exhausted at Saldanha Bay, just in time to exact the surrender of Admiral Lucas and his trapped fleet.

Subsequently, Hart and his regiments came to visit all the smaller outlying towns in and around the Cape, where they sniffed out 'Jacobins and French principals'. Among the towns they visited were Stellenbosch, Paarl, Tulbagh, and the fledgeling Graaff-Reinet, which they visited in 1799 under Brigadier-General Vandeleur. They boarded the *Star*, and sailed into Algoa Bay. There they built Fort Fredrick, around which, much later, grew the town of Port Elizabeth.

Robert Hart loved the pioneer lifestyle, with all its dangers and hardships. He grew accustomed to the Frontier Boer, of whom John Barrow ungraciously wrote, 'Having nothing in particular to engage his attention, he is glad of an excuse to ride for some days, to go to church or hunt elephants, or to plunder the local blacks.' Exposed to dangers from his own slaves, wild Bushmen, local tribe raiders, lions, elephants, storms and floods, the Boer and his family were sustained by an immovable faith in God, with whom a Covenant was still to be made.

❖ ❖ ❖

After the Graaff-Reinet uprising, Hart and his companions pursued the last of the Rebels into the Bruintjieshoogte area of the Eastern Cape, where the Prinsloos and Van Jaarsveldts were arrested. This relatively minor incident became a veritable thorn in the Frontier Boer's side – it would fester slowly and eventually erupt in 1815, with the hanging of Hendrik Prinsloo, Stephanus Bothma, Abraham Bothma, Cornelius Faber and Theunis de Klerk. This event came to be known as 'the Slagtersnek Rebellion', and was never to be forgotten in the annals of Afrikaner history. It was used extensively to whip up patriotism in the 1880–1899 wars against the British.

It was in this beautiful area of Bruintjieshoogte, in the Eastern Cape, that Robert Hart and his wife Hannah decided to make their home. They called the government-granted farm Glen Lynden, and it was from here that the formidable Henry Francis Flynn set out on his epic journey to Natal. It was on this farmhouse stoep that the likes of Thomas Pringle, John Centlivres Chase and Robert Godlonton, the pioneer journalist, would sit and discuss the Frontier Wars at length.

In time to come, Glen Lynden was to be surveyed and laid out as the fledgling town of Somerset East, with Robert and Hannah Hart as the founder parents of the community. They were responsible for the building of the local church and appointing a Scottish Dominie, as well as the construction of the first school in the area, also staffed by Scottish teachers. Even today, the Harts' legacy lives on in the Eastern Cape.

THE STORY OF
ERNST LUCHTENSTEIN

Many men – soldiers, voortrekkers, trekboers, outlaws, etc. – for diverse reasons have chosen to disappear into the solitude of isolated places. One of the most interesting such stories that I have come across is that of Ernst Luchtenstein and the Karas Mountains of Namibia.

Ernst Luchtenstein's father was a transport rider, carrying supplies to the German army in the field during the war against the Hottentots. He later sent for his family. Frau Luchtenstein, along with Ernst, his two brothers and a sister, landed at Lüderitz bay in 1906. They travelled along the dusty road to Keetmanshoop in a convoy of seven ox-wagons, loaded with army provisions and the family's scant belongings.

Between the German outposts of Aus and Konkiep the train was intercepted by Cornelius, the feared leader of the Bethanie Nama. Ernst's mother, knowing that the country and its people were wild and wishing to preserve her family from certain death, ran up to Cornelius and knelt before him, begging him to spare them, but he told her to stand up. 'Kneel before God, but not before any man!' he said in perfect German.

The wagons were looted and all the military supplies taken, but not one thing was taken from the Luchtenstein wagon. There are so many tales of chivalry, of black men not harming women and children, particularly during the Frontier wars in the Eastern Cape – our history is full of them.

The family pressed onwards and met up with Ernst's father in Keetmanshoop. Ernst stayed in school only a few months and then decided to go and work for his father as a 'touleier' (the leader of the team of oxen). He and his father soon fell out, however, and Ernst went to live with the Mackay family.

The Mackays were a different sort of family. Mackay had married a local Nama woman, and Ernst had the privilege of growing up with the Nama, learning to speak their language fluently and finding out about game tracking and all the lore of the veld, including how to gather veldkos and medicinal herbs and their uses. The Mackay farm was called Paradise and was situated 22 km north of Keetmanshoop.

In 1914 at the outbreak of the First World War Ernst was, of course, conscripted into the German army. Both his brothers were captured by the South African forces, but Ernst remained free until German South West Africa was surrendered to General Louis Botha in July 1915. Having lived as he pleased for so long, Ernst did not take to the idea of becoming a prisoner of war. He had heard that all the German soldiers were to be interned. As a matter of fact, he ranked as a reservist and would have been allowed to return to the farm, but he knew nothing of this.

A train loaded with South African troops was going south and as they wore only the semblance of a uniform, he tore off his German badges and shoulder-straps and, dressed in war-stained khaki, he passed as a member of the Commando. Just before Keetmanshoop he jumped train and vanished into the vast veld of South West Africa.

If you have ever seen the Karas Mountains, you would be able to imagine the wilderness Ernst sought refuge in, convinced that, if caught, he would lose his freedom and be interned as a prisoner of war. The summer rains of 1915 had been far more abundant than usual. The natural springs and fountains had revived and veldkos was everywhere. Owing to his upbringing in the Nama family, Mackay, Ernst was able to live off the land. At the outbreak of the war he had buried his rifle along with fifty rounds of ammunition, and this he took with him into the mountains. His worldly goods consisted of a field-grey army greatcoat, a spear, a few mess-tins, his rifle and ammunition, and a mongrel dog that had followed him into the mountains.

Ernst trained the dog to catch dassies and each day when the dassies came down to graze, the dog would pounce, so providing a regular meal for both of them. Often Ernst would make Nama-type snares for guinea fowl and partridge and when this failed, he would resort to the age-old Bushman trap, consisting of a flat stone supported by a stick and baited with seeds. That stone fell upon many a guinea fowl! Ernst had so much meat that he seldom used his rifle, but when he did, he made sure that he brought down a kudu or a gemsbok. He cured the skins and used the leather to make shoes and clothing.

After six months of avoiding all humans, he felt it was safe to make contact with the Nama in the area, who gave him milk and later a goat. For the meat-satiated Luchtenstein this was an absolute luxury!

Beginning to feel secure, he visited local farmers near the mountains, but after almost eighteen months he learned from the local Nama that the police were looking for him. He became more careful and decided to wander off across the great plains to the Karas Mountains, where the last of the Bondelswart clan had made their stand against the Germans, prolonging the war for a further two years. From these peaks Ernst could scan an enormous area – westwards was the old dry bed of the Fish River and in the north-west he could see the cone of the extinct volcano, Brukkaros. This vista covered hundreds of square kilometres, but never did he see any signs of pursuit. It lulled him into a false sense of security and one afternoon, while resting in his little hut, he heard the sound of horses' hooves. He knew the game was up.

Two police troopers entered the hut. They said they had been searching for him for a very long time and that an army Captain in Keetmanshoop wanted to see him urgently! Despondently, he accompanied them to Keetmanshoop, but when he was taken to see Captain Tilley, the officer said: 'I want to go hunting and everybody around here says that not only are you the best shot, but you also know where all the kudu are! Will you take me hunting please?' All the way to Keetmanshoop Ernst had been thinking miserably about being put behind bars, so he was staggered by this outcome. Naturally he accepted gratefully! After the shooting trip Tilley gave him a contract to supply grass for army horse fodder and he made £2 000 in four months.

Finally, he was able to go farming, and the time he had spent in those mountains proved to be invaluable. He had come to know every hectare of ground there and, as land was cheap in those days, he purchased land where he knew it would rain. Later on, when the karakul sheep industry boomed, Ernst made a fortune. At one time he owned more than 400 000 ha – nearly 1 000 000 acres of land. However, a change in the land tax system forced him to reduce it to a mere 60 000 ha.

Later, he opened a general dealer's store in Keetmanshoop and used to fly to New York to buy goods. Often he would fly over the mountains and look down, reminiscing on how he had managed to survive and to succeed in becoming so wealthy.

Luchenstein's family and children have left Namibia now and are living in the Cape and the Northern Province. They contacted me after the story of their father was broadcast.

The strange
Ohrigstad phenomena

It is not very often that I record non-human stories, but the one I am
going to describe is, I feel, well worth a mention. Quite some time ago,
whilst visiting the Lydenburg district of Mpumalanga, ferreting out
aspects of our country's magnificent peoples and their histories, I came upon
the story of the strange phenomena.

My friends, Alistair and Marion Moirs, and I were travelling from
Burgersfort towards Ohrigstad when suddenly Alistair pointed to a mountain
range up ahead. It was a short range, but quite high. 'Have I ever told you the
story of the farm up there?' he asked. When I said no, he stopped the car and
proceeded to tell the most incredible story.

This saga started about thirty-five years ago when a local farmer in the
area, Duppie Papenfus, bought the farm Nooitgedacht 487 KT. Straddling the
top of the highest part of the mountain, it had never been farmed before. It
was virgin bush. Duppie acquired a bulldozer at a local auction and
proceeded to carve a road up the side of the mountain. At night he used to
camp out in a small tent next to the Vyfenhoekspruit, originally called the
Mamatali, which has its source at the top of the range. Some years later, when
the farm was running and the homestead completed, the Moirs often were

invited over for a Sunday braai. The scene was a very familiar one in our country, with the children playing and the adults chatting over a few cold beers. The children would always come to Duppie and ask for some bread. 'What for?' he asked one day. 'To feed the hungry snake in the river', was the reply. The adults just laughed and carried on their conversations and off the children would go, to return some time later.

One day Duppie's curiosity got the better of him and, after giving them the requested bread, he followed them at a distance. Down to the stream they went and then, keeping dead quiet, the eldest of the children put her index finger into the water and moved it up and down and side to side. Suddenly a head appeared out of the water, and Duppie stood dumbfounded as the children proceeded to feed an extremely large freshwater eel!

The Papenfus family was so amazed that they called in freshwater zoologists from a university and the following amazing facts emerged. These freshwater eels, upon reaching maturity, leave the peaceful ponds of that far-away mountain and travel down the Vyfenhoekspruit. They journey with the stream that flows down through Casper's Nek (named after Paul Kruger's father) into the Blyde River, and then into the Olifants. This eventually links up with the Limpopo and goes down all the way through Mozambique to reach the sea at Xai-Xai! The eels then swim away from the Mozambique coastline, travelling eastwards until they finally reach Morondava Bay on the west coast of Madagascar. Here they mate and spawn. The total distance travelled is 1 870 kilometres.

The second half of the story is even more incredible. The young eels or elvers start the journey back to Mozambique and, by some still unexplained DNA memory bank cell, these elvers reach Xai-Xai. Up the Limpopo they go, against the current all the time, up into the Olifants, then left into the Blyde and eventually the Vyfenhoekspruit and up the mountain – back to those self-same ponds from where their parents started the long journey many months before. This means that these eels, in their lifetime, complete a total of over 3 700 km, travelling half of that entire distance against the current.

I was ignorant enough to doubt the story until, some months later, I watched a BBC TV programme on the Scottish freshwater eels. These eels come down the Firth of Forth, go south around Britain and then head westwards – to spawn in Massachusetts Bay, off the east coast of the United States, over 6 000 km away! And then the young start on the return journey.

That excellent reference book *Smith's Sea Fishes of Southern Africa* tells us that these eels in the Ohrigstad mountains could be any one of four varieties of South African freshwater eels and can attain 1,5 m in length and weigh up to 20 kg. They have been observed wriggling up wet vertical cliffs and scaling dam walls. On the Vyfenhoekspruit there is a 10 m waterfall. No wonder they make the uphill journey and climb whilst still young and very small.

What an astounding country we live in!

THE ADELAIDE DUTCH
REFORMED CHURCH

Adelaide, a small, restful village in the Eastern Cape, not far from
Somerset East, came into existence as a military outpost during the
Frontier Wars against the Xhosa and Pondo during the middle of the
19th century. It remained a sleepy, delightful little sheep-farming hamlet and
was eventually occupied by the British forces during the Anglo-Boer War of
1899–1902.

During their occupation of Adelaide, the British commandeered the local
Dutch Reformed Church and converted it into barracks for their men. The
Rectory they converted into stables. This did not go down too well with the
local Afrikaans townsfolk, but there was nothing much they could do for, as
is customary in such times, the occupying forces had scant regard for the
property and possessions of the Adelaide townsfolk.

After the war and the withdrawal of the troops, the local community
wished to restore their place of worship. Throughout South Africa, however,
there was a dire shortage of money. Everyone in Adelaide was willing to lend
a hand and donate their labour, but there were no funds to buy the materials
essential for the restoration.

Then a strange thing happened. Three months after the failed restoration

The Adelaide Dutch Reformed Church

donation drive, into the town came two long-wheelbase transport or commissariat wagons. They were piled high with fine cut timber, along with a beautifully hand-carved pulpit and matching chair. The congregation were astounded! They immediately withdrew some of the nastier names that they had found for the British officers and troops during the occupation of their beloved town. They now realised that the British people had a conscience and had sent the timber all the way from England as an apology.

The delighted members of the congregation immediately set to work and within a few months, the restored church and rectory was proudly standing. It looked spectacular and the people settled down to their normal Sunday routine.

A few years later, a letter addressed to the Mayor of Adelaide arrived. It said:

To: The Honourable Mayor, Adelaide, South Africa
From: The Mayor of Adelaide, Australia

Dear Sir,
It is with some trepidation that we enquire as to whether a consignment of oak wood, which we ordered from England about two years ago for our new church,

has not, perhaps, by mistake been delivered to your town in South Africa instead of ours.

Well, there was not much that the town council could do, the restoration was complete. Instead they had photographs taken of the beautiful new interior of their church and sent them off to the Mayor of Adelaide, Australia, together with an explanatory letter telling of how the British had commandeered their church during the war.

And that is how the interior of the church was restored and still stands today, a monument to a lovely mistake.

THE MYTHOLOGY
OF THE ELAND

I f you travel around this wonderful country of ours, and you are not in any particular hurry, take time to view the beautiful rock art, left to us by the ancient San people who populated the entire area. You will have no choice but to be left in complete awe. The designs, colours, structures and intricate variety of these three-dimensional drawings, captured in numerous caves and shelters all across our land, will make you marvel.

It is an undisputed fact that the Drakensberg World Heritage Site has the greatest collection of rock art anywhere in the entire world. Some of these sites have never been opened to the public and probably won't be if vandalism persists.

I remember reading a Lourens van der Post book, many years ago, which described the hunt of what was probably the last Bushman on the plains of the old Orange Free State. Small horn tips were found tied to his belt and feathers and quills in his pouch. This was probably the murder of the last of these gifted painters, killed because they were considered to be vermin. Right into the beginning of the twentieth century, it was legal to purchase a licence to hunt these gentle folk.

I have had the privilege of staying with these people in the Kalahari

Desert, some twenty years ago, and all I can say is that it changed my view and approach to life forever.

If you take the time to go and see some of this magnificent art, one thing will strike you: the preponderance of paintings that depict the Eland. These paintings are scattered all over our country, and here's one of the reasons why.

The Eland is considered to be one of the most revered of all animals, amongst the indigenous people of the southern part of Africa. It played the most important part in days of old. It saved the Earth Mother. Here's the story.

Ninawatu, the great Earth Mother, looked down from her mountain and saw the fighting, the killings and the bad things that humans were getting up to. She was devastated, and pondered upon the reasons for it. Then it dawned upon her. It was her fault. She had created the people the way they were. She was solely to blame. The complete responsibility lay upon her shoulders. Weighed down by this terrible realisation, she went to Ranadu, the pitiless judge, who, along with his six assistants, had no emotions. The sentence was harsh; she was to spend three months in the underworld. Ninawatu disappeared from the Earth, and, overnight, the Earth froze. The grasses died, the trees died, and even the rocks lost their spirits. The cold iciness of despair descended upon the Earth. Ninawatu was placed in the grips of the cruel hag Nomhoyi, and was repeatedly raped and beaten by the hag's son Sondakati, the monster. She knew that she could not flee; she had to pay her penance.

The animals of the Earth could stand it no more, and Imbube, the lion, called a meeting of all the animals. 'Ninawatu must be rescued,' he said. 'We must choose the one to do the deed.' Impofu, the Eland was chosen above all others to rescue the Earth Mother from the underworld because of the strength of his back, the gentleness of his nature, and the size of his heart. The giant boulders at the back of the cave were parted, and Impofu descended the darkening tunnel to the underworld. He came upon the Insenika River, the river that flows with the blood that has been shed by all the unnecessary wars and killing in the world above. He found her in a deserted hut in the village. Her hands and feet were bound. He chewed through the ropes, lay down for her to climb onto his back, and galloped away as fast as his legs could carry him. Sondakati the monster was in hot pursuit, shouting and screaming for his claimed wife to be returned. Impofu paid no heed. Sondakati fired his deadly arrows at Impofu. On he ran for the entrance, over the Insenika River, to the tunnel leading back to the Earth. He was struck in the neck and began to falter. 'Please pour your strength into me, so that I may complete my given task', he pleaded with the Earth Mother. As they came through the rocks at the entrance, Impofu fell. The Earth Mother dismounted and cradled Impofu's head in her lap. As his spirit departed, she gathered it up, and threw it into the skies, where she turned it into stars. The indigenous peoples know it today as the constellation of the Eland.

THE NURSEMAID OF
MRS LINDSAY

T he now very famous diary of Private Buck Adams detailing life on the Eastern Frontier of South Africa during the early 1900s, contains a story that shows to what lengths love can drive people. The same story was recorded in the Fort Beaufort Museum and has subsequently been proved to be factual.

A young woman grew up together with her childhood sweetheart in a tiny English village. Ann was expected to marry John Marvell as the two were inseparable – or so it appeared. On no particular day or occasion, John Marvell just simply upped and disappeared, leaving neither a note nor any explanation as to why or where he was going. Ann was totally mortified!

Being a young woman of strong will, she decided on her own course of action. John had always said that he would like to be a sailor and she was convinced that he had run away to sea. She was determined to find her lover and one day, just like him, Ann quietly slipped away from her village. She had borrowed her brothers' clothes and dressed as a man in order not to attract attention along the way – in those days women did not travel unaccompanied.

Soon afterwards she signed on as an assistant steward and so she began her first trip aboard a sailing vessel. Even if it meant sailing right around the world, she was determined to find John. She enquired at every port of call, but alas, in vain, for John had 'taken the shilling'. He had joined the army, under an assumed name!

Undaunted, Ann continued her searching and in 1842 she obtained a post aboard the SS *Abercrombie Robinson*. A sailor's lot in those days was not a comfortable one, the hours were long, the work hard and the accommodation was uncomfortable and cramped. Not to mention the sadistic punishments and the miserable food. A typical daily ration consisted of a pound of mouldy ship-biscuits, three quarters of a pound of salted beef or pork and three quarts of water. Twice a week they received one pound of bully beef and half a pound of bread. The biscuits were usually Liverpool 'pantiles' and harder than the hobs of hell. They had to be banged on the side of the hold before being edible, not so much to soften them as to bang out all the weevils and maggots. The salted meat was generally horsemeat and one could not tell what was more rancid, the salted pork or the butter!

Amidst these primitive conditions, Ann was accepted by her fellow sailors and her gender was never questioned, until, one day, whilst working on the rigging, she slipped and fell onto the deck. It was when she was taken to the doctor that they discovered that she was, in fact, a woman.

Again we see how fate can play such an enormous role in one's life, and in this case it led to the end of Ann's quest. Aboard the *Abercrombie Robinson* was the 91st Regiment, headed for the Cape of Good Hope. After Ann's real identity was discovered, the wife of Lieutenant-General Lindsay, the Commanding Officer of the regiment, took Ann under her wing and employed her as a nursemaid for her children. The *Abercrombie Robinson* docked in Cape Town and the troops and everyone else disembarked. The following evening a gale force wind and storm hit the Cape and the *Abercrombie Robinson* was driven ashore and totally wrecked, leaving the unfortunate Ann with no other choice but to accompany Mrs Lindsay, with the regiment, to the Eastern Frontier outpost, Fort Beaufort. During this time Ann became very close to the Lindsays and eventually confided the story of her love quest to them.

One afternoon, she returned from a walk with the children, clearly in a state of shock, but she refused to divulge what had happened. Eventually, it came out. She had noticed that the sentry on duty outside was none other than John Marvell!

Lieutenant-General Lindsay's assistance was called on and the guard rosters checked but there was nobody by the name John Marvell. The soldier was paraded and, under close questioning, the man known as Mullins broke down and confessed that he was John Marvell. The use of another identity was not an unusual occurrence in those days. Many men, for varying reasons, enlisted under false names. The Colonel then contrived a meeting between Ann and John. It is difficult to imagine how John felt faced with his childhood sweetheart after all that time and thousands of miles away from his home. A very touching reconciliation, however, took place between the two and once more they plighted their troth, and decided to marry as soon as John had become a sergeant. The Colonel then saw to it that John was promoted and their wedding day was fixed.

On the eve of the wedding, John was returning from Grahamstown. Before him lay the Koonap River, in full spate. He could not bear the thought of any delay and plunged in. He managed fine until halfway across, but then he tired and as he did so he was swept downstream by the relentless flood-waters. His struggles were in vain and he drowned.

Ann was inconsolable. It is said that she nearly died of grief. 'So long in searching and waiting,' she later said, 'so close in presence and time, but, alas, never ever to be.'

It was some years later that she eventually recovered sufficiently to marry Troop Sergeant-Major Samuel Moffat of the Seventh Dragoon Guards. She bore him two sons and a daughter and lived a hard but happy life.

Ann Moffat died in the autumn of 1851 and is buried in an unmarked grave at Peddie, between King William's Town and Grahamstown. Where precisely is not known and I would certainly love one day to pinpoint its exact location.

THE TOTEM OF THE BAMANGWATO

Throughout the world, different groups of people, clans or tribes, have special symbols in the form of animals or natural objects, otherwise known as totems. African tribes are no exception. This is the story of how the Bamangwato people of Botswana derived their special totem.

Mythology tells us that many, many years ago, the totem of the Bamangwato tribe was the kwena, or crocodile, and that the great-grand-father of the late Sir Seretse Khama later changed it to the puku. A puku is a little, very shy, grey and brown duiker, with a white underbelly, and a small set of straightish horns.

At the time of this change, the whole of southern Africa trembled under the wrath of that mighty Matabele warrior, Mzilikazi, who along with his followers had fled Shaka's Zululand. By attacking numerous tribes in various northern parts of the country, the Matabele were partly to blame for the Mfecane, the desolation of huge tracts of land in and around the central parts of South Africa.

The Bamangwato, living in the northeastern part of Botswana on the eastern fringe of the Kgalagadi, were no exception. The Matabele were pillaging and laying waste to vast sections of their land. As they passed through Chief Khama's homeland, they encircled the Bamangwato army, trapping the Chief. When his army scattered, he had to flee for his very life.

The capture of a leader of Khama's stature would ensure being fêted by Mzilikazi, and all the Matabele warriors strained every nerve to overtake the fleeing leader. Each tried to outrun the other, and gradually, the blood-hounds were reeling him in. Exhausted, he stumbled, but the shouts of joy from his pursuers gave new strength to the man's aching legs. He had to get away and rally his tribesmen, and drive off the scourge of this Matabele warfare. Up ahead lay scattered trees and bushveld, and if he could just reach it, he may be able to elude his hunters. He forced his muscles into one last burst, and, for a moment, the hunters lost sight of the fleeing chief.

To his right was a type of bramblebush. He dived for cover and scrambled into it. Ignoring the thorns, he crept under a fallen tree trunk. His heart was pounding like a hammer as he lay there. He was too scared to even realise that he was not alone in the thicket, for alongside him, not even flinching, lay a little puku. The creature seemed to sense his distress and lay absolutely still, just watching him.

The warriors were now upon the thicket. 'He may have tried to hide in there,' he heard somebody say. 'He may have skirted it and used it to hide his fleeing,' said another. Two warriors approached the thicket and, using their spears, started prodding the thick bush. One of the assegais struck the log, and the puku bolted. He rushed out into the open and sped away into the distance.

'He's not in there,' someone said. 'If he had gone in, the mpuzi (which is the Matabele name for a duiker), would have already bolted upon his arrival. Come on, we have no time to lose, we must capture and kill the Chief,' and away his hunters ran into the distance.

The chief of the Bamangwato lost no time at all making good his getaway and, upon reflection, became convinced that the puku was sent to him from the Great One. Why, otherwise, did it not flee when he arrived? Pukus always flee when they come into contact with human beings. But this one didn't, not this time. The puku had consciously decided to stay, in Khama's time of greatest need. The Great Chief never forgot this incident.

Thankfully, the Bamangwato tribe survived the Matabele, who eventually went northeast into the area that was occupied by the Mashona people, whom they invaded and conquered. They founded what was to be called Matabeleland, now a part of Zimbabwe.

Chief Khama called a kgotla (a meeting of all the heads and sub-heads of the different sub-tribes) of the Bamangwato people, and, when he had completed the story of how the puku had actively saved the royal line of the Bamangwato tribe, the elders reached a unanimous decision that the tribal totem be changed to the puku, which it still is to this day. It also meant that as a sign of thanks and veneration, from that day forward, nobody was ever allowed to hunt the puku.

THE OPENING UP OF
SOUTH AFRICA

For the first 190 years of settlement in the southern part of Africa, there were no roads leading into the interior of the country at all, making bartering and trade on the other side of what van Riebeeck called 'the mountains of Africa', nigh impossible.

In 1830, the Governor of the Cape, Sir Lowry Cole, an Irish General who had served under Wellington, was in a rage. Viscount Goderich, the British Secretary of State for the Colonies, had rebuked him for building a road without prior consent, and was now threatening to charge the entire cost to Sir Lowry Cole's personal account!

Sir Lowry was incensed. How was it possible that someone with such responsibility could be so lacking in vision? The opening up of that first man-made road, the now famous Sir Lowry's Pass, through the Hottentots Holland mountains, would facilitate trade from the eastern part of the Cape, and go a long way towards alleviating the poverty and the lack of goods and services in that area. At that stage, the only link to that area was an often-impassable wagon track through Tulbagh's Kloof.

However, the first man to attempt to end the isolation of the Western Province was, in fact, Lord Charles Somerset. Not wanting his Royal Africa

Corps to be distracted by Cape Town's 'Taverns of the Seas', Somerset occupied their time on the construction of the Fransch Hoek pass. This first mountain road gave access to the Swellendam and Mossel Bay area, but, of course, the Outeniqua Mountains were still an obstacle to the North and East.

Little did anybody realise that within 200 years of occupation of the Cape, there would be names on roads that would live forever: There was Montagu's Pass, built by Colonel Montagu using convict labourers from the Cape gaols; Bains Kloof, built by the eminent Scottish Engineer, Sir Andrew Geddes Bain, and Michell's Pass in Ceres, named after Lieutenant-Colonel Charles Michell who was also Sir Lowry Cole's road builder. Dr William Stanger, after whom the KwaZulu-Natal town Stanger was named, was to build what became known as 'the road of South Africa'.

Sir Lowry Cole

The second chain of mountains that blocked the Cape from the northwest was pierced by the so called Mostert's Hoek Pass, giving access to the Warm Bokkeveld and Koue Bokkeveld areas, along with the Roggevelt and Neuweveld, which became rich fruit-, wheat- and sheep-farming areas.

Sir Andrew Geddes Bain

Before the roads were constructed, these areas were all desperately poor and uncultivated. A certain Jan Mostert, who lived at the foot of the Mostert's Pass, had built a rough wagon-track up that pass, and all wagons had to be taken to pieces to get up and down that mountain.

The next chain of mountains that had to be conquered was the Hex River range, and even the indomitable Bain himself, who had traded well into the interior, is on record as having complained about the area's unforgiving rock and sand drifts, as well as the extortionate farmers who charged a fortune for passage.

Another of these natural barriers to trade was what is now known as 'Cradock Kloof'. An army officer in the 1840s reported that this was the most impossible place for horses, much less wagons, that he had ever encountered. It was almost as perpendicular as the face of Table Mountain in places, and the pass, which was only 9 km long, would normally take a wagon three full days to clear, allowing for accidents and delays.

Within twenty years of Sir Lowry's departure from this country, all those routes had been opened up, and the interior began to flourish. In the Diary of Hendrik Hamelberg, we read that in 1855 he took a horse-drawn vehicle on a jaunt to places like Paarl and Stellenbosch, not realising that a mere ten years prior to this, a horse- drawn vehicle would never had made it, and an ox-drawn vehicle would have taken weeks to cross those flats. These days we time it in minutes!

By then, John Montagu, who had fathered the imaginative road-building schemes in the Cape, lay dead in an exile's grave in England. Andrew Geddes Bain, who had constructed the Queen Victoria's Road from Grahamstown to Fort Beaufort, was killing himself inch by inch as he laboured with his road up the Katberg Mountains. Colonel Michell, the Surveyor-General of the Cape who built Sir Lowry's Pass, died in England only three years after leaving the country that he had served so well.

The debt that South Africa owes to these pioneer road-building men is too huge to contemplate.

THE LEGENDARY
IVORY

Among the many ancient tales and myths that I have come across in Africa, from the Lost City of the Kalahari to the Kruger Millions, nothing has intrigued me more than this story of a mysterious elephant burial place.

When the hunters of old used to gather around the campfires of Africa at night, the talk was sure to turn, sooner or later, to a place that was known as Ivory Valley. This was a great cemetery to which dying elephants, guided by instinct, were said to make their way.

Frederick Selous, Trader Horn, Henry Hartley, Oswold Cotton and many other famous adventurers believed the legend implicitly. The reasons were numerous and the stories enchanting, but the legend of the elephant cemetery in the Kaokoveld has persisted, based mainly upon two facts.

The first is that the Herero people would appear from time to time, carrying heavy loads of valuable ivory tusks – tusks which had obviously not been cut off newly killed elephants. 'We found them in the bush' would be their standard reply. That was their story and they stuck to it. No hunter could ever persuade a Herero to lead him to this apparently endless supply.

The second supposedly indisputable reason that the hunters gave was that apart from the elephants they shot or trapped, they never found elephant remains. Elephants are certainly the easiest animals to spot and the Kaokoveld was teeming with them. Their giant spoor could be seen for miles around the waterholes. Herds, stampeding along the horizon, were regularly seen, but never any dead elephants. It is true that some elephants in the wild live to be a century old, but even then, amongst those enormous herds, there were surely deaths each month? The question the hunters of old asked was where did the dying elephants go?

The solution to the puzzle lay, it was said, in a mysterious valley. When the elephants knew death was upon them, trumpeting the shrill call of finality, they would vanish into the secret valley, where the huge skeletons of their ancestors lay bleached by the blazing African sun.

As far as I know, there has never been a thorough search for the Ivory Valley of the Kaokoveld. In other parts of Africa people have combed tropical forests and bush, quiet lakes and mountain craters to find the elephant sanctuaries. But what lies hidden under the ever-shifting sands in the barren stretch of land in the Kaokoveld, has never really been explored.

Few records were kept about the early exploits of ivory poachers in that then uncharted land. Yet, in times gone by, many bold Boers crossed the Kunene River, returning from the former Portuguese Angola with great loots of ivory.

One Boer recorded how a chief named Oorlog, described as a potentate of mixed ancestry, had captured him. He told how Oorlog (meaning 'war' in Afrikaans) believed that all the elephants in the Kaokoveld belonged to him. The man was taken captive and then a runner sent to the police post on the very edge of the Kaokoveld with the news. He was tried for ivory poaching, declared not guilty, but fined £50 for entering a forbidden territory without a permit. This man swore until the day that he died that Oorlog had told him of the valley of ivory and that no white man would ever learn the secret whereabouts of this most holy place.

Donald Bain, a well-known South African hunter, once camped near a waterhole on the elephant trail in the Kaokoveld. They pitched camp in darkness and did not notice that the tent stood between two elephant paths.

'Just after midnight,' Bain recalled, 'I was raised by the barking of my dogs, and the trumpeting of an elephant. I sat up and saw a mountain on legs coming towards me. Instinctively, I rolled over, expecting to be crushed. For a few seconds, there was pandemonium, the dogs barking, the native bearers shouting and the elephant trumpeting. It had caught its legs in the guy ropes. Mercifully the elephant passed on, crashing through the undergrowth.' Bain then described what he felt was a very eerie experience. 'After all was over, I saw my dog Fritz, standing there shivering from head to foot and yelping for all the world as though someone was beating him.'

The elephants of the Kaokoveld have been protected for many years now and one does not know what changes have been wrought in their ancient patterns of behaviour. Perhaps the cemetery is still in usage? Who can really tell?

Let us conclude with a poem by Cullen Gouldsbury – it may help to convey some sense of that secret place.

> Pile upon pile of bleaching bone, and a foul miasmic breath,
> With now and again a mighty moan, to break the hush of death –
> Sluggish streams, and silver beams, of a silent moon on high –
> God forefend, I should meet my end, in the place where elephants die.

The demise of the Bushmen or San

I t was not long after Van Riebeeck landed at the Cape in 1652 that he heard tales of a people called the Sonqua, but several years passed before the first recorded contact was made. We are told of a Dutch official named Wintervogel who came upon a party of Bushmen on the Berg River; and this place of encounter is still known as Sonqua's Drift.

The Bushman or San lived in the interior and were described by the settlers as 'an entirely wild nation, without cattle or houses, but well armed with hunting bows and spears'. The Europeans did not initially perceive them as a serious threat, although at this time three Dutch burghers, engaged in shooting hippo in the Berg River, were murdered by Bushmen. Such remained the status quo for nearly a hundred years.

According to their mythology, the Bushmen had originally come from the north. They entered the area of the Great Karoo, where they found vast herds of game. Let me add that this migration took place thousands of years before the arrival of the Dutch. George William Stow, a pioneer in Bushman research, spent many years patiently copying rock paintings and gathering artefacts and stone implements which, as he stated, were 'unquestionably the title deeds of the Bushmen'.

The caves of the Bushmen and their ancestors are richly adorned with painted scenes of trance dancing and their intimate relationships to nature. It was here too that they roasted their 'uintjies' or bulbs, pummelled their grass seeds and stored dried locusts for the coming winter. They also roasted termites, still today called 'Bushmen rice'. And with the arrival of the full moon they danced the 'mo-koma', or dance of blood, in which both men and women would leap about, around and around in a circle, until the trance state was reached, and the blood gushed from their nostrils.

The Bushmen did not cultivate plants but their knowledge of bulbs, herbs, trees and scrub was intimate and deep. It represented the accumulation of centuries of information passed down from the beginnings of time.

The secrets and stories of these people are absolutely fascinating and should you be interested in finding out more, I would recommend that you read books such as *Miscast* by Pippa Skotnes and *Stories that float from afar* by Professor Lewis-Williams. The astronomical knowledge of the Bushmen never ceases to amaze me. After Dr W.H. Bleek had mastered the Bushman language and written down the legends, 'The dawn's heart' and 'The dawn's heart child', it became apparent that the Bushmen had been observing with the naked eye movements of the planet Jupiter, and its satellites, long, long before European astronomers.

Incidentally, lions never bothered the Bushmen. If lions were encountered during the day, the Bushmen would run directly at the animal, shouting at the top of their voices and waving their arms. Seeing such unnatural behaviour, the lions would simply turn tail and flee! At night they sprinkled on the fire a special ground powder made from a fungus, which grows only on anthills. Lions found the smell so repugnant that they kept a wary distance.

The Bushmen watched, year after year, as the white man entered their traditional hunting grounds. At first they did not protest. In the course of centuries the pace of settlement picked up. The farmers trekked to the land where the present town of Ceres is to be found and named the area the Warm Bokkeveld because of its vast herds of springbok. Then they entered the area higher up and named it the Koue Bokkeveld.

From the Bokkeveld, the settlers went to the Roggeveld, where wild rye used to grow and before the 1750s they had settled in the Calvinia district, which the Khoekhoe knew as Hantam. Ten years later the valleys between the Langeberg and the Swartberg had been settled and the more adventurous farmers had begun entering the Nuweveld area around present Beaufort

West. In time the area of the Camdeboo (meaning 'Green Heights' in the Khoekhoe language), lying between the towns of Graaff-Reinet and Aberdeen, was occupied. On the west, the settlers made their way up into Namaqualand, as far as the Kamiesberg and by 1760 there were white farmers in the Sneeuberg range.

Year after year, decade after decade and century after century, the Bushmen watched in growing horror the unstoppable creep of European farmers over more and more of their land, a process which forced them to withdraw progressively further from their home grounds.

A fundamental difference between the Bushmen and the Europeans was that the Bushmen hunted primarily for food and then only on a small scale, while the settlers hunted to eat, but also to sell meat, skins and ivory. They even hunted 'for fun'. When a Bushman hunted, he did so with a simple bow and arrow that had a limited range, so the game usually had a fair chance. The hunt was long and difficult. The white man hunted with a musket! This was like murder in comparison.

However, the stage was set, the cauldron of conflict was starting to boil and during the 1770s it boiled over. A farmer named Coetzee van Reenen sent a white overseer to look after his flocks along the banks of the Zak River. It was known that he was a brutal man who shot Bushmen people for no reason. There were many farmers like the overseer who considered the Bushmen not to be human beings. The Bushmen eventually retaliated, and slew the overseer with an assegai.

It was revenge for all the horrors suffered under this man. On the farmers' side, however, it was considered murder with no extenuating circumstances. A strong commando was sent up to the frontier and many hundreds of Bushmen were massacred. As soon as the commando had departed, the Bushmen rose up as one. From the Kamiesberg in the west to the Stormberg in the east, they went on the rampage. Farms were ravaged and farmers and their families brutally murdered. As a result, more commandos were raised and the wholesale slaughter of the Bushmen began. It was the start of a guerrilla war.

Prisoners were sometimes taken all the way down to Cape Town. In 1772 a band of 58 men and women, of all ages, was tried for the murder of Rogge-veld burgher Hendrick Teutman, his wife and daughter. The most gruesome punishments were handed down. All the children were flogged, the women were hanged and the men were killed by means of 'breaking' on the wheel.

Some years later when the famous botanist, Thunberg, was travelling in the Roggeveld, he came across a commando that had killed over 100 Bushmen. The commando told him of another detachment that had wiped out over 400 in the Sneeuberge alone. It became the policy of the Dutch East India Company to exterminate the Bushmen and in the nine-year period between 1786 and 1795 at least 2 500 were killed and more than 600 captured. Not many men were taken alive for they usually fought to the last arrow.

Shot, powder and handcuffs were readily supplied by the government for such expeditions. A surgeon's report on one particular conflict contains a significant statement concerning the attitude of the people. He stated quite simply: 'The Bushmen have no fear of death.'

The last stand of the Bushmen in the Sneeuberg area has been recorded and makes for poignant reading. The Bushmen had retreated into the mountains and were surrounded by a commando. Cut off among the rocks at the edge of a precipice, they fought for the last time. One after another, they fell as the sharpshooters fired, until only one man remained alive. As the man put his last arrow to the bow, the commando leader touched by the man's bravery, called out and told him that if he surrendered, his life would be spared. The Bushman looked at him and shouted, 'A chief knows how to die,' and, releasing his last arrow, he jumped off the precipice. For many years sun-bleached bones could be seen on the ledge far below.

During the nineteenth century Dr Bleek, his daughter and Lucy Lloyd befriended Bushman convicts working on Cape Town's breakwater. They learnt the Bushman language and worked hard at preserving some of their beliefs. In 1875 Dia! Kwain told the following story to Lucy Lloyd. It concerns a dream about the death of Dia! Kwain's father. She recounted his story as follows:

When I was with a Boer, I dreamed that we were cutting up a sheep. The Boer came to us as we were cutting it up and said that he would beat us to death. The dream spoke to me thus, and I told the Boer not to kill us … for I did not want him to kill my father … I would work out both what I owed and what my father owed. And the dream said to me that I saw my father lying dead in the Sun's heat. AND I WEPT.

And I asked the Boer, did he think it was such a big thing that we had killed, that he acted like this? I dreamed that the Boer drove us before him …

And when day broke, I arose and told my wife that a dream had told me that we were cutting up a Boer's sheep. I saw my father standing there dead. And the wind was in the north, and I asked her, did she not see that the sky looked like it was going to rain, just as the dream had told me, that the dust was covering the sky. Therefore I should go and talk to the Boer about the ox, I should see what was happening that had made me dream of father, that the Boer had killed us. The dream had told it to me, just as if a person had spoken. Therefore we will go home, we will go and listen at the huts, and see whether we do not hear news …

And my father's eye was blinking before I was gone …. Rainwater, which was not little, was falling. I said to my wife … you seem to think that my dream was not clear. I shall see things that my dream told me about. I SHALL SEE IT. THEN YOU WILL SEE.

We returned home to where we lived with the Boer and we stayed two nights … the wind blew, as if it was begging from me, just as the wind had done in my dream when I dreamed about father that … the Boer had killed us … when the sheep bleated. The dream had told me this.

And my mother said to me that I seemed to have disbelieved the dream and to have thought I should see father again, though the dream had told me I should not see him again. Yet, now I saw her, and she had come to tell us that father had died leaving us … and mother asked me, did I not see that the dream had spoken the truth … So the dream I had told her about had not deceived me …

The springbok had afterwards passed the hut, as if they were not afraid, mother did not know where the springbok came from. They were not few and they came and played as they approached the hut were my father lay dead. The springbok appeared to be moving away. And the wind really blew following them. THEY WERE RUNNING BEFORE THAT WIND.

It was really father's wind, and you yourself feel how it is blowing. You know it used to always blow like that whenever my father was shooting game.

I spoke to my wife and told her about it. I asked her whether she did not realise that I was feeling my inside that was biting.

As the wind blew past I felt my insides biting …

I felt that when one of my people was dying.

MY INSIDE ALWAYS ACHED WHEN IT WAS ONE OF MY PEOPLE.

This complex description is not the product of a savage mind but represents a poetic vision of a people with a unique understanding of family and nature. Today, tragically, only small groups of the Bushmen people survive and I can say with pride that I have had the privilege of spending time with them in the Magalagadi Desert in Botswana. It was an experience I shall never forget.

The history of Curry's Post

I n the late 1800s, George Curry, a retired Sergeant Major, established a staging post alongside the wagon road between Durban and the Transvaal goldfields at Houtboschrand. His enterprise became known as Curry's Post, and it grew to be the first centre of the district. It comprised two hotels, a blacksmith shop and a couple of stores. In its day, Curry's Post was a very busy little spot, until the railway line and the relocation of the road left it isolated in the countryside.

Back in those days, the land in this vicinity was very uninviting. Huge stones covered the sides of the hills, making cultivation nigh impossible. Added to this, visibility was very poor, as the high-lying area from Curry's Post to the Karkloof attracted heavy fog and mist.

The first known owner of Houtboschrand, now Curry's Post, was a Mr Dobson, who was a survivor of the ill-fated *Birkenhead*, shipwrecked off the Cape coast. His is a story that needs to be told.

In the early 1860s, Captain Lucas, who was also a survivor of the *Birkenhead*, and a good friend of Dobson's, left Pietermaritzburg in a light trap with two chestnut horses to travel to Ladysmith, a journey of 110 miles. There he was to collect £10 000 in gold. The horses were changed several times along the way, as it was a long haul.

On his return to Houtboschrand, he noticed six men of dubious character lurking nearby. When Dobson took his friend's horses from the trap into the stables, he signalled for Lucas to follow him, and the six men disappeared. Dobson told Lucas that these men, thinking that Dobson was an ally, had told him that they were planning to hold him up, and steal his gold. He advised Lucas not to rest, but to carry on immediately. Dobson gave the horses water and oats and Lucas a cup of coffee.

Re-loading his gun, Lucas promised not to divulge the identity of the person who had told him about the six men, and rode off. Soon he spied two of the men halfway along the cutting. The other four, however, were nowhere to be seen. Lucas's horses were travelling at a dangerous speed of 12 miles per hour down a steep incline, but not wanting to be robbed, Lucas considered this the best plan of action.

As it turns out, he was right. One of the men ran at the horses' heads and fell amongst the hooves of the nearest horse. A second man made a jump at the rear of the trap and fell backwards over the wheel. Two of the outlaws were killed that day at Curry's Post. Captain Lucas, however, did not wait around, as the other four would-be thieves were as yet unaccounted for. There was great rejoicing when Captain Lucas finally reached Pietermaritzburg, with all of his gold intact.

Henry Curry, George Curry's brother, was the innkeeper at Curry's Post. He married Mary Ann Stead in December 1852, when she was 20 years old. When Henry died in March 1919, he left his entire estate to charity, and for the next two years until her death, his wife had to trek to the Master of the Supreme Court in Pietermaritzburg each month to get an allowance, for she had no other form of income after he died.

Today, Curry's Post lies off the N3 highway between Durban and Pietermaritzburg, but still boasts a wonderful little restaurant, where the owners were more than willing to share this story with me. Go and visit, it's well worth the stop.

George Rex
of Knysna

The life story of George Rex, the founder of the beautiful coastal town of Knysna in the Southwestern Cape, is well documented by his great-granddaughter Sanni Metlerkamp, in a book called *George Rex of Knysna – the Authentic Story* (Howard Timmins, 1955).

The exact details of how George Rex arrived in the Cape remain a well-kept secret, making it difficult to separate fact from fiction. Nevertheless, the story began when Rex left England aboard a British East Indiaman, under sealed orders of the Admiralty, in 1797.

But what had induced his father to send him into lifelong exile? It appeared that he had fallen in love with one of the King's daughters from a subsequent marriage, effectively his half-sister. The daughters of George III and Queen Charlotte led very cloistered lives, and their suppressed passions had resulted in them indulging in several 'liaisons' with equerries at Court.

The story of Rex's parentage makes for fascinating reading. He was said to be the offspring of King George III and a Quaker woman, known as Hannah Lightfoot.

The story goes that, when the Prince first saw Hannah sitting in the window of her uncle's drapery shop in St James Market, London, he was struck by the fair maiden's beauty, and demanded to meet her. A discreet meeting was arranged, and the romance grew over time.

One must remember that this was a blatantly immoral age; lovers for the women and mistresses for the men were considered to be common practice. Royalty had mistresses as well as wives, and to be 'under the protection' of some great person was a position to be greatly sought after.

But demure young Hannah was not prepared to become anyone's lover, not even the Prince Regent, although she loved him deeply. Over time, Prince George realised that marriage was the only way he could gain her affections.

Now begins a web of intrigue and deception. Upon hearing of the Prince's affections, the Royals were enraged, and gave Hannah's uncle a bribe of £500 to have her hastily married off to a young grocer named Isaac Axford of Ludgate.

On 11 December 1753, Hannah was taken to a clandestine marriage chapel in Mayfair, where a bizarre marriage ceremony was conducted, despite Hannah's refusal to say 'I do' and not allowing the groom to place the marriage ring on her finger.

On emerging from the chapel, she was seized and carried into a waiting carriage. With shouts of 'Royalty!' from the driver, the carriage sped off and disappeared, never to be seen again. Isaac Axford's attempts to establish the whereabouts of his so-called bride were in vain.

The woman who helped Hannah to escape from the chapel, and the one sitting inside that carriage as it sped away, was none other than Elizabeth Chudleigh, lady-in-waiting to Prince George's mother, and later to become the notorious Duchess of Kingston. It was said that she herself had succeeded in committing a bigamous marriage. She had achieved this very cleverly.

To annul her first marriage, she had to prove that she was, de facto, a virgin. She consented to the examination, but requested that, as it was such a private examination, she be allowed to cover her entire body in an extra large blanket. This wish was understandably granted. Of course, what the examiners didn't realise, was that a suitable young chambermaid was ushered in under the drape, and the hymen was declared intacto. The Duchess was nobody to be fooled with!

But back to the story of the son of King George and Hannah Lightfoot, and his arrival on South African soil. Before leaving England, the young George Rex had an audience with his father, King George III, who made him a notary and gave him a warrant proclaiming him Marshal of the Vice-Admiralty of the Settlement of the Cape of Good Hope, which was then a British possession. The King also told him that he could choose himself any tract of land 'as far as the eye could see', on condition that he never returned to Britain.

In October 1797, Lord McCartney of the Cape appointed him Registrar of the Courts Martial at the Castle, for the purpose of trying 'piracy, felony and general disobedience', as well as 'treason, desertion and espionage'. George Rex therefore came to play an important role in public life at the Cape. He occupied an office at Admiralty House, situated in the naval yard on the shores of Table Bay. In 1812, Admiral Stopford bought a house for the Admiralty in the Gardens and named it Mount Nelson, the very site of the Mount Nelson Hotel in present-day Cape Town.

George Rex purchased his first house in Table Valley, called *Schoonder Zigt*. The house sported lavish reception rooms and a ballroom, and had magnificent views over Table Bay and Bloubergstrand.

It was around this time that Rex took a common-law wife, Cape Malay slave Johanna Rosina van der Caab (of the Cape). 'Van der Caab' was a surname for slaves born in the Cape. They had four children together. In 1808 George Rex and Johanna Rosina parted, and in 1809 Rex married Carolina Margaretha Ungerer, who, in a strange twist of fate, was Johanna's second daughter from a previous union. Carolina bore Rex an additional nine children.

As is the case so often in history, fate plays a large part in determining people's outcomes, and for Rex it was no different. The Cape reverted to the Dutch in 1803, resulting in George Rex's post becoming vacant.

Then a terrible thing happened. The *Mary*, an English whaling vessel, put in at Table Bay. Oblivious to the fact that her country was at war with the Dutch, her officers and crew were taken prisoner and transferred to another vessel. They were to be dispatched to England in exchange for prisoners of war. Miraculously, the crew escaped, managed to board their vessel and made a clean getaway out of Table Bay. The Dutch Governor, Janssens, was furious, and ordered that all British subjects were to leave the country within 60 days. Non-British subjects were forbidden from having any dealing, or to associate in any way with those under the ban. Numerous properties were sold under duress, including Rex's *Schoonder Zigt*. Many treasures, valuables and antique pieces of furniture were sold for virtually nothing, as supply outstripped demand. The British subjects were totally ruined.

Commissioner-General de Mist, who was superior to Janssens, was travelling while this proclamation was issued. When he returned to the Cape, he repealed Janssens' proclamation, and ordered that all British subjects were to be interned in Stellenbosch. But, alas, the damage had already been done.

By this stage, George Rex had ventured many times inland towards the east, where he had discovered a delightful lagoon with its two, now well-known, heads. He had climbed up the inland mountain and surveyed the land 'as far as the eye could see'. The entire area that was granted to him by King George III, was from Belvedere to the west, and eastwards towards what was originally called *Bahia Formosa* by the Portuguese discoverer Masquita Pasterella, in 1575. It was later renamed Plettenberg Bay by Governor van Plettenberg, in 1778.

Because the land he had chosen had been granted by the King, and because of his ancestry, the Dutch Governor granted George Rex the required permission to remain in the country and to return to his farm in Knysna. George Rex wasted no time in leaving the Cape, and journeyed eastwards to begin a brand new existence in one of the most beautiful stretches of coastline this country has to offer.

There are quite a few interpretations of the origin of the name Knysna, but the one I favour is that in the old language of the Outeniqua Khoekhoe there were two words *!Nys*, and *!Na*, which, when put together, literally mean 'the place of wood'. To me, this seems most appropriate, as beautiful yellowwood and stinkwood trees proliferated in that area in those days.

Along with his family and all their worldly possessions, George Rex undertook the arduous and perilous journey to Knysna by wagon, pulled by enormous spans of oxen. He finally reached Knysna in the summer of 1805. Rex's original grant of land between Knysna and Plettenberg Bay was a 3 954-acre stretch of grasslands, hills and valleys undulating down to the sea – he named it Springfield. From Dutch loan farmers, he obtained the further farms Melkhout Kraal, Welbedacht, Sandkraal and De Poort. He retained the name Melkhout Kraal, and promptly changed the others to Eastford, Westford and Portland respectively. The combined area of the five farms was 21 423 acres, of what is now prime real-estate today. He later acquired all the land on the western side of the Knysna basin, which brought the total land holdings to almost 25 000 acres.

Melkhout Kraal

The land immediately opposite Melkhout Kraal on the western side, he called Belvedere, and the land that continued towards the sea he called Brenton, in honour of Sir Jaheel Brenton.

For any ship, crossing the bar through the beautiful Knysna Heads was rough and treacherous, but once in the lagoon, the waters were so calm and placid that the sailors had named it Featherbed Bay. Today, it is owned by the illustrious Smith family. J.L.B. 'Fishy' Smith was responsible for discovering the coelacanth, the prehistoric fish once believed to be extinct. His enigmatic son William is known to South African children as the face and voice of the TV Education channel.

George Rex's relations with Johanna Rosina, and Carolina (mentioned earlier), bore him a total of thirteen children, six sons and seven daughters. The first child, Edward, was born in 1801, and the last, Thomas Henry, was born in 1834. His sixth child, Fredrick, fought in the Fourth Frontier War, and, together with his brother-in-law Thomas Bain, the son of the famous Andrew Geddes Bain, they wrote the well-known Afrikaans poem *Kaatje Kekkelbek*.

Child number seven, Caroline, married Scotsman Thomas Henry Duthie, who came out to the Cape with the 72nd Highlanders, and they became the official residents of Belvedere. To this day, the Duthies of Belvedere are a veritable institution in Knysna.

There were countless comings and goings of distinguished guests to Melkhout Kraal and Belvedere. Everybody who was anybody experienced the congenial hospitality of that wonderful family. Queen Victoria's second son,

His Royal Highness Prince Alfred, Duke of Edinburgh, went elephant hunting there in 1867, and the Earl of Caledon visited in 1811.

The spring in the garden was called 'Lord Charles's Spring' after numerous visits by Lord Charles Somerset, who presented Betsy Rex with a hand-cut ivory chess set from Persia. With Lord Charles Somerset's party in 1817, were, amongst others, Colonel Bird, Cape Colonial Secretary, and the famous Dr James Barry, who masqueraded for over 70 years as a man. It was only after her death that her Cape Malay manservant, whom she had retained all her working life, discovered that she was in fact, a female.

❖ ❖ ❖

No attempt at telling the story of Knysna would be complete without the epic of the opening of the Heads as a harbour for timber and other trade. George Rex was convinced that the passage through the Heads was navigable, others thought very differently after Sir Jaheel Brenton sent the brig *Emu* to try crossing the bar, enter the lagoon and load a cargo of timber bound for Cape Town.

Alas, the *Emu* hit a headwind crossing the bar, and was badly damaged on the rocks. She barely made it into the lagoon and was beached at Leisure Island, where her remains lay for many years. The rock bears its name to this day, Emu Rock. The Captain, one Lieutenant Forster, his wife and child, were to board the *Podargus*, which was sent from Simon's Town to fetch them. Captain Wallis was in charge of the *Podargus*, and had been instructed to anchor off the Heads, and to send a small boat to load up the crew and return to *Simon's Town*. He had other ideas. He saw that the wind was favourable, decided on a bearing, and headed straight for the opening between the Heads.

The *Podargus* was the first brig ever to cross the bar successfully without inflicting any damage. Wallis collected his passengers and the stores rescued from the *Emu*, and promptly sailed out again. George Rex and the Cape Admiralty were delighted, as this was an absolute milestone for trade in the area. Until that time, timber had had to be hauled all the way to Plettenberg Bay to be loaded, and this had been extremely costly.

The next ship to navigate the Heads successfully in October of 1817 was the *Dispatch*, and from this time onwards vessels regularly called in to load timber, mainly for the dockyards of the Admiralty at Simon's Town, but also to take the excellent timber to the dockyards of England. The coastal trade started to increase, and Lord Charles Somerset found it so important that he decided to place a pilot, with a boat and crew, at the Heads, for the protection and reassurance of trading ships.

The Dispatch *successfully navigated the Knysna Heads in 1817*

Captains Walker, Skead and May were all responsible for the erection of two beacons. The first beacon, a white one, was placed on Barrel Point, on the eastern side of the Heads. A second red beacon was placed on Leisure Isle. By aligning these two beacons and having a favourable wind, any medium-draft ship could successfully navigate the entrance to the lagoon.

A suitable piece of land was found, and the first signal station was erected on the eastern head, and named Melville, in honour of Viscount Melville. A suitable site for shipbuilding was located, just west of Melville, and a slipway was laid down. The building of a brig commenced in August 1820, but due to rising costs and an accidental fire, the project was halted and moved to Simon's Town. Thus ended the Admiralty's shipbuilding scheme at Knysna.

The first pilot to be sent to Knysna in 1818 was John Gough. Despite his sterling credentials, the leisurely lifestyle of the area seemed to distract him, slowly eroding his sense of duty at the signal station. He was often away, either in the Lange Kloof or at Plettenberg Bay, instead of being at his post. In February 1830, George Rex reported to the Admiralty that vessels destined for the port were being put at great risk, for in favourable weather conditions, the incorrect flag was flown, and there was no pilot to go out to the vessel. Also, on 12 December 1829, the brig *Adolphus* was lost because the incorrect flag was flown, and she had tried to come through the Heads in adverse weather.

John Gough was replaced by a man name Flinn, and thus began a spate of pilot tragedies, starting with the drowning of Flinn and, uncannily, within a short space of time, the drowning of his replacement. Then came the wrecking of the brig *Harmony*. One of the last pilots was John Benn, after which the leisure cruiser currently owned by William Smith is named.

Insurance underwriters had by now pushed their premiums up to a level at which it was no longer profitable to do business, and with this came George Rex's chance.

He decided to build his own brig, and become his own underwriter.

On the Westford bank of the river, at the slipway which still stands there to this very day, George Rex laid the keel of his 140 ton brig the *Knysna*. On 26 July 1831, she sailed out through the Heads with her first cargo of timber, destined for Cape Town. She was constructed of seasoned stinkwood, and she plied her trade not only to the Cape, but as far as Mauritius in the east, and Saint Helena Island in the west. Because of the insurance underwriters' perceived risk, and the *Knysna* captain's excellent knowledge of the local conditions, the *Knysna* made the region in general, and George Rex in particular, extremely wealthy.

In November 1836, the *Knysna* made her historic voyage to the Buffalo River mouth, notorious for its shifting sands, in present-day East London. She was laden with stores badly needed by the troops on the Eastern Frontier, not to mention the 1820 British Settlers, who were isolated on distant farms.

George Rex's old and trusted skipper, Captain John Findlay, was excited at the prospect of being the first to sail up the Buffalo River. So, late in October 1836, the *Knysna*, with three 'men of the name of John', set sail for East London. The men were John Findlay, the skipper, John Rex, the son of the owner, and John Bailie, a retired British Navy lieutenant.

The *Knysna* reached the mouth of the Buffalo on 11 November 1836.

Upon their arrival, Rex and Bailie went ashore, and on top of a hillock, later to be named Signal Hill, they promptly raised the Union Jack in the area that was to become the prosperous harbour and town of East London.

Captain Stockenstroom, who had replaced Colonel Smith as Commandant of the Eastern Frontier, was so pleased at the sight of the *Knysna*, that he named the place Port Rex. Yet, as no ships other than the

Knysna called there for the next ten years, the name fell into disuse and, in 1847, Governor Harry Smith changed the name to East London.

A memorial tablet in honour of the founding father of East London, John Bailie, was erected. It is a great pity indeed that no mention was made of the important part played by the Rex family of Knysna, in the founding of that city.

❖　❖　❖

Before we come to the end of this brief account of the life of George Rex, let's have a look at some of his family. It is known that he had a brother named John, and that John died at a young age. However, the facts surrounding his death are uncertain, and there are three different versions. Firstly, that he became demented and committed suicide. Secondly, that he went to America, fell overboard and drowned, and thirdly, that he went to India, became a judge, and was drowned on the passage back to England. Which one of the three is correct, I do not know, but there is one incident, which relates to option number three, that I feel throws some light on the subject.

A British East Indiaman, returning to England on a voyage from India, sent a message to Rex that it was to disembark at Plettenberg Bay before visiting Melkhout Kraal. George Rex was normally a calm man, but when the time came he was very excited by this forthcoming event, and personally oversaw the preparation of the wagons and equipment needed on the trek down to Plettenberg Bay.

He travelled down in his wagon, accompanied by horses and many slaves, who set up camp. The ship duly arrived, dropped anchor in the Bay of Formosa, and a longboat was lowered over the side. The entire party, including, I believe, his returning brother, disembarked, and the oarsmen struck out for shore. Rex was standing on the beach, eagerly awaiting the party.

Then suddenly, there was a sudden squall, unusual for that part of the coast. It swamped the boat, sinking it with all on board. Standing helpless on the shore, and watching the death struggles of those so near and dear to him, was seared into Rex's memory forever. It was a tragedy he would never forget. He took the canvas covering off the wagons, and, as the dead were washed up onto the shore, he gently wrapped them and buried them.

It is said that there was one man that he would not allow the slaves to touch. He personally wrapped him, dug his grave, and buried the man all by himself.

He returned to his home, a very sad and quiet man, and it took quite some time for him to recover from that specific tragedy. Not one word would he say about it to his wife and family, and the names of those people, and their relationship to him, would go with him to his grave.

It is said that many years later, these graves were pointed out as a group of grass-covered mounds, a little way up the path leading from the original parsonage to the church, and one was quite small in size. I presume they have disappeared now, as there were no headstones to mark the spot.

George Rex died on 3 April 1839, and his mortal remains were buried on the farm Melkhout Kraal. Anne, one of his daughters, died in December of the same year, and lies next to him, under the trees. While the descendants of the original Rex family have dispersed to all corners of the globe, one gets the feeling that they retain a very strong sense of where their roots are.

George Rex's grave at Melkhout Kraal

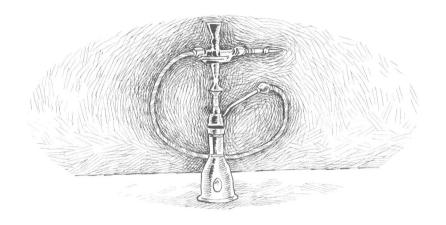

Of doctors and discoveries –
Dr Atherstone

I t is rare indeed that fate allows a person more than once to occupy
centre stage in the theatre of fame and fortune. But this did happen to
Dr William Guybon Atherstone, celebrated surgeon, botanist, geologist,
musician, artist and statesman. The first event made him a household name
in his own country and the second, twenty years later, made him world-
famous.

He was two years old when he arrived with his father, Dr John Atherstone,
in South Africa in 1820. Later in life, he took up residence in Grahamstown
where he attended Stephenson's Grammar School, at the famous Yellow
House. After a spell at Uitenhage, he returned to Grahamstown in 1831
where he was apprenticed to his father, in order to qualify for the medical
profession.

A few years later, at the age of sixteen, he was appointed Staff Medical
Officer to the Governor, Sir Benjamin D'Urban, during the Sixth Frontier
War. By the age of eighteen he was a fully qualified medical practitioner!

One incident that left a deep impression upon the young man was his
interview with the famous Voortrekker leader, Piet Retief. News reached Dr
John Atherstone that his friend Retief was going to lead one of the Treks.

Much perturbed, he and William rode over to Mooimeisiesfontein, to persuade Retief to abandon his plan and stay. However, Retief was adamant and, bidding his friends a sorrowful farewell, he chose his path of destiny – one that ended on a lonely hill at Umgungundlovu in February 1838. One cannot help but wonder what the course of South African history would have been, had the persuasion of Atherstone senior been successful.

The day, Wednesday, 16 June 1847, was a memorable one in the annals of South African surgery, for it was on this day that Dr William Guybon Atherstone performed the first operation in this country using anaesthetics. Before the advent of anaesthetics, an operation was a nightmarish horror of incredible shock and excruciating agony for the patient concerned, so it is fitting that both Dr Atherstone and his patient, one Frederick Carlisle, should be remembered. *The Grahamstown Journal* published an article about the operation ten days later.

Mr Carlisle, Deputy-Sheriff of the Albany district, had all but lost the use of his leg and gangrene was starting to set in. He said the pain was so unbearable that he would gladly have his leg amputated if the pain would stop. After several experiments using different kinds of apparatus, with and without valves, Dr Atherstone succeeded in producing the required degree of insensibility, by means of a simple hubble-bubble container from a hookah pipe.

The patient, convinced of the powerful effects of ether, consented to have the leg removed, but stipulated that the operation could not start until he gave the word. After ten to twelve inhalations of the ether, he reached down and pinched himself, then continued to inhale a short while longer, pinched himself again and said 'I'm drunk enough now – you may begin!' The tourniquet was immediately tightened and at the same moment the first incision was made. The patient did not feel or show any signs of discomfort, still mechanically opening and closing his nostrils with his own hand. So perfect was the insensibility that the assistants let go of the patient altogether. For the rest of the operation, Carlisle lay motionless on the bed. Once the leg was removed and the nerves and blood-vessels taken care of, the bottle was removed and the patient, still holding his nose, became talkative and even humorous as he gradually recovered from the stupefying effects.

He had inhaled ether for about four minutes. He then asked, 'Why have you removed the bottle of vapour?'

Atherstone replied, 'Because the operation is over, your leg has been off for some time now.'

'Don't talk nonsense to me Doctor', said Carlisle, 'I'm a reasonable man, just tell me why you have removed the bottle.'

'You don't require it any longer, your leg is off!'

'Impossible, I don't believe it, let me see for myself.' Upon seeing the stump, he said, 'God be praised, this is the greatest discovery ever made. I have been totally unconscious of everything – the sound of the saw still rings in my ears, as if in a dream from which you awoke me, but I never felt any pain ever!'

So the first trauma-free operation was recorded in *The Grahamstown Journal*, and preserved for posterity. But as far as Dr William Atherstone was concerned, fate had a much more far-reaching event in store, one that would make him renowned in the world.

❖   ❖   ❖

Some twenty years later Dr Atherstone, who in the meantime had become quite well known as a geologist, received a strange parcel in the post. He carelessly tore it open and read the covering letter.

Colesberg
March 12 1867

My dear Sir,

I enclose a stone which has been handed to me by one John O'Reilly, as having been picked up on a farm in the Hope Town district, and as he thinks it is of some value, I send the same to you to examine, after which you must please return it to me.

Yours very sincerely,
Mr Lorenzo Boyes
Acting Civil Commissioner
Colesberg.

Atherstone was greatly excited and rushed off to the local jeweller, Mr Galpin. Galpin tested the stone for hardness and agreed that it was a diamond. On the way home, the excited Atherstone saw Professor Peter MacOwen and showed him the stone. MacOwen suggested that in order to make absolutely certain, they should test the stone's specific gravity. Off they went to the house of the Catholic Bishop, the Right Reverend James Richards, and there in the Bishop's study, with a hair pulled from Atherstone's head and fastened with a small bit of wax on the stone, they completed the specific gravity test. The results were positive. The Bishop grabbed the diamond, strode over to the window pane and scratched his initials on the glass. This pane is still in the Roman Catholic Presbytery in Grahamstown, with the inscription 'Initials of the Rt Rev James David Richards – cut with the first diamond discovered in South Africa, 1867'.

Sir Percy Douglas, the Lieutenant Governor of the Eastern Cape, had just returned to Grahamstown and a state dinner had been organized for that night. Atherstone thought this a fine opportunity to make his discovery known, and he whispered to a friend, Advocate Henry Blaine, that during the toasts he was going to stand up and make his announcement. Blaine was horrified. 'For heaven's sake, Doctor, don't do it – remember the Sand River Gold.' He was referring to a previous statement Atherstone had made at a similar dinner, claiming that gold had been discovered in the Orange Free State. The 'discovery' had proved to be fraudulent and Henry Blaine, knowing the doctor's optimistic nature, wished to save him from further embarrassment, but to no avail. Amid a great hush, the doctor rose to his feet and made the announcement that was to have such far-reaching effects on the economy of our country, and continues to do so to this very day.

Dr Atherstone wrote to Boyes congratulating him and informing that the stone was a 21,25 carat diamond worth £500. The stone was sent to Cape Town, acquired by the Governor, Sir Philip Wodehouse and sent to the Crown jewellers Hurst & Boskell in London, who confirmed the analysis. It was then proudly sent on to the Paris Exhibition for display.

Not much happened after that, as people were very sceptical. One said that the place in which it was discovered was salted with diamonds from Brazil. Another put forward the interesting theory that ostriches must have deposited the diamonds there. But the optimistic Atherstone would not be discouraged.

Fortunately, an even more bizarre event then took place. We have learnt how Honest John O'Reilly handed the first diamond to Mr Boyes of Colesberg. Boyes gave Van Niekerk, the farmer, on whose land he had picked it up, his half-share, £250, and this then got the old farmer thinking. If just one of these 'worthless' stones was worth £500, he must try to find more of them.

He remembered that a Bushman whom he knew had a similar, but larger stone, which he carried in a dirty old skin bag around his neck. Van Niekerk set off to find the Bushman, but failed, as he had wandered off into the wilds. Van Niekerk left a message for the man to contact him when he returned.

One morning Van Niekerk awoke to find the Bushman patiently waiting for him on his veranda. He had the bag around his neck. To the Bushman's absolute amazement, the farmer gave him 500 sheep, 10 oxen and a horse for the stone. Van Niekerk then set out for Hopetown, where the stone was examined and declared to be an 83,5 carat white diamond. Van Niekerk sold it to Lilienfeld Brothers for £11 200 and returned home a rich man.

The stone was sent to England and was subsequently purchased by Lady Dudley for £25 500. This is how the famous 'Star of South Africa' came into existence.

In this way the South African diamond rush began, with incalculable results for our country and, although many far bigger stones were subsequently found, such as the Cullinan Diamond weighing 3 025 carats, not one has ever had such far-reaching effects as that small 21,25 carat stone which so excited Dr William Atherstone on that day in 1867.

THE STORY OF
SARAH HECKFORD

O n 30 June 1839, in Dublin, Ireland, was born Sarah Maud Goff. From a landed gentry background, she inherited, on both sides of her family, a tradition of service. The army, the church and laws she learnt about from her father, and good works and community service from her mother. Along with a dose of puritanical intolerance and an independent turn of mind, this background in Victorian England assured her a position in society.

Her mother died when she was six years old and having contracted tuberculosis, she was doomed to be partially lame, with a slight hump on her right shoulder. She remained self-conscious about this and would never allow a photograph be taken from the left-hand side.

Sarah studied, becoming competent in music and painting and, at the age of twenty-two years found herself financially independent. At that time there were no women doctors in England and she began caring for the sick and poor. Sarah took her inspiration from Elizabeth Blackwell. Elizabeth was born in Bristol in 1821, emigrated to America in 1832, then studied medicine and was awarded a PhD in 1849. She obtained permission to study at St Bartholomew's Hospital in London. Both women met Florence Nightingale, who was at this time still living at home. What a tragedy it was that facilities in England for higher education were denied to women at that time!

In 1866 the great cholera epidemic, which had arrived from Egypt by ship, struck London. Extra nurses were desperately needed and Sarah volunteered. She met a doctor, Nathaniel Heckford from Calcutta, who was a mere twenty-two years of age, but had already won gold medals for medicine and surgery. On 28 January 1867, the twenty-six-year old Sarah married the twenty-three-year old Dr Heckford, much to the displeasure of her relations.

At this time there were no hospitals that would admit children under the age of two years, so Sarah took £4 000 of her debentures. In January 1868 they started the East London Hospital for children, in Butcher's Row. During this period Charles Dickens used to visit the hospital and they remained good friends until his death in 1870. Nathaniel, the love of Sarah's life, died in 1871 at the tender age of twenty-nine, and was buried in the Goff's cemetery plot in Woking, Surrey.

The British, represented by Sir Theophilus Shepstone, had annexed the Transvaal Republic in 1877, and the broken-hearted Sarah decided to make a new life for herself. She purchased 100 shares in the Transvaal Mining and Trading Association. Lame, widowed and in poor health, she set sail for South Africa. She arrived in December 1878 in Durban. Having bought a horse and, in the company of a transport rider, she rode into the Transvaal, westward to Rustenburg, where the business venture she had bought into was supposed to have been situated. She stayed at the local inn, only to discover that the whole thing was a hoax. The scheme did not exist. Her money was now running low and she realized that if she did not get a job with lodgings, she would be in desperate trouble.

The local clergyman arranged a post for her as a private tutor to the two Jennings daughters on the farm Nooitgedacht, in the Hekpoort valley. The Jennings' were quite a family themselves, being second-generation 1820 settlers who had trekked up to the Magaliesburg and started farming. This was a pleasant period for Sarah. In the winter months the family would trek up to the Northam region for the cattle to enjoy the winter grazing, returning to the farm with the onset of spring.

Sarah, however, was becoming restless and, having learned quite a lot about farming, she persuaded William Jennings to sell her a portion of the farm Groenfontein. It was during this period that she employed an Englishman named Edgerton, who was 'down on his uppers'. She then acquired a wagon and twelve 'salted' oxen, and decided to become an itinerant trader, a 'smous'. Male smouses were common then, but a woman smous – unheard of! She left Nooitgedacht and trekked to the markets of Pretoria, where she bought supplies of all sorts of commodities the farmers required. On the way home, she sold her goods along the valley. The northern part of the country was now being opened up, and she decided to ply her trade on the Great North Road. Northwards she travelled with Edgerton as her 'voorlooper', leading the oxen. She would trade her goods at settlements such as Marulaskop and the Nylstroom district, and then head back to Pretoria. On one of these expeditions she entered an agreement with Makopane (Makapan), trading very successfully in grain with the Chief until the outbreak of the so-called 'Gun War' in Basotuland caused a shortage of grain. She fell out with George Edgerton, her presumed lover, and he went off to the Basotu War never to be heard of again.

She soon realised that war between the Boers and their British rulers was imminent and moved onto the farm she had bought. The First Anglo-Boer War broke out in 1880. Anstruther was defeated at Bronkhorstspruit, Colley was defeated at Majuba, the British sued for peace and the Transvaal was returned to the Boers. This heralded the end for those farmers who had supported the British. Business in the Transvaal had collapsed. Banks were calling in their loans and many people were going bankrupt. She decided to head for Natal. On the way her oxen sickened and died, a Boer shot her beloved dog 'Prince' and at Harrismith, she gave up. She eventually made it to Durban where she sailed for England.

We know very little about Sarah's life between 1881 and 1887, other than the fact that she helped out in the East End Hospital. However, as happens with so many people who leave this country, the memory haunted her. She longed for the African sun and the bush and, in May 1888 she arrived in the boom-town of Johannesburg, where gold had been discovered only two years before. The bondholders had foreclosed on her farm and she set herself up as a sharebroker in Booysens. Her timing could not have been worse! March 1899 saw the mines hit pyrites and yields plummeted. The boom collapsed almost overnight and the biggest slump in the history of Johannesburg began.

Sarah weathered the storm, found a buyer for her farm, settled the bond and, with the little that was left, she decided to go transport-riding and farming. She bought a 'Burgher's right' farm out near Middelburg on the road to Mozambique, invested in two wagons with oxen and set about remaking her fortune by transport-riding on the Great North Road. It was here that she found the ideal farm, 'Tobias zyn Loop', and, when the railway came, she was bought out at a handsome profit. The business grew, especially now that she had the capital for trading. She moved to the northern Transvaal, loaded her wagons and travelled the 110 kilometres down the Klein Letaba area, where she supplied the miners at the Birthday Mine with their requirements. She bought the farm Ravenshill and worked out the first farm-schooling scheme in the Transvaal, launching the Transvaal Women's Educational Union in 1898.

In 1902, after the Second Anglo-Boer, she sailed for England, where she was treated as a celebrity. She caused a sensation by attacking Emily Hobhouse, declaring how very little the latter actually knew about the entire situation! She soon returned to the Transvaal and took lodgings on the corner of Du Toit and Schoeman Street, Pretoria. In 1903 she took ill and on 17 April she died, at the age of sixty-three years. Her obituary which appeared in the *Pretoria News*, was written by Vere Stent, secretary to Cecil John Rhodes.

And so, a tremendously brave and indomitable woman of pioneering spirit lies resting peacefully in the Wesleyan section of the old cemetery in Pretoria. She is an example to us all.

Rachel de Beer

If on your way down the N3 towards Natal, you afford yourself the
pleasure of stopping off at Van Reenen Village and visiting its historic
Little Church and the lovely old wayside inn called the Green Lantern,
owned by Lew and Maria, you will become acquainted with the area in which
this story takes place.

Just to the north of the village runs the old road from the Transvaal to
Port Natal, and the pass is known as De Beer's Pass. It is named after an old
Freestater named Herman de Beer, who in the late 1870s owned a farm on
top of that part of the Drakensberg between the Transvaal Republic and the
Orange Free State.

One of the biggest dangers in the area is the cold. During the winter
months, snowfalls are often accompanied by winds that drop the temperature so swiftly that even during the day animals have been known to freeze
to death on those open plains.

One winter Herman de Beer was visited by a man of the same name, who
was looking to buy a farm in that area. He was accompanied by his wife and
two children, a boy of six or seven and a girl of twelve years named Rachel.
They had a small number of stud cattle, along with some sheep and goats

and, as there was an unoccupied hartbeeshuis on the farm, Herman offered to let them stay there, to afford the man a chance to look around for a farm.

Scarcely a week later, just after midday, a terrible storm came in from the south-east. Heavy dark clouds came rolling over the mountain peaks and the icy wind cut through the thickest clothing like a knife. The young animals from the summer lambing season had to be attended to immediately and everyone on the property, even old Herman, was busy carrying the young lambs into the barns, and herding the cattle into the kraals where they could huddle together to ward off the bitter cold. The younger De Beer was not rich and with his comparatively few cattle and sheep he could scarcely afford to lose any. When he had accounted for his herds, he noticed that a young cow, which had only just calved, was not accompanied by her new calf. As the herd had not been far from the house, it was easy to follow the spoor to locate the new calf. Night was falling fast, no time could be wasted and everyone had to help in the search. Rachel, or Raggie as she was called, was an energetic young girl who had grown up with cattle and already helped her father to take care of his herd. She often acted as herder and could milk cows, inspan a team of oxen and drive a wagon. So it was decided that the father, along with a Koranna assistant, would look further afield while Rachel searched the area nearest to the house.

Just before leaving, the young brother insisted on going with Rachel. It was bitterly cold, but these children were accustomed to a hard way of life and even their mother saw nothing wrong in the boy accompanying his elder sister. After all, it was close to the house and they wouldn't be away that long. So she wrapped him up warmly in a sheepskin kaross and the two of them went searching for the calf.

It is not necessary to drag out this tragic story. It was long after dark that the father and his Koranna servant returned, but Raggie and Boetie were still not back. The storm was vicious. The wind was so strong that it was difficult to keep one's direction, and the falling snow was turning to ice. The alarm was raised. The mother lit a big dung fire next to the house. The father, along with the Koranna and another two servants with lanterns, all heavily wrapped up in blankets, started the search for the children.

Throughout the night they searched, shouting, calling and shooting continually, but to no avail. At dawn the storm began to abate. The wind died down and the snow ceased to fall. At this stage the mother joined the search, but there was scant hope in anyone's heart. What shelter was there on those cold plains? The only possible hope was that they had found refuge in a deserted antbear hole.

Just after sunrise, one of the labourers picked up the spoor. The children had walked through the first and then the second dale and had evidently become completely lost in the storm and the darkness and, when the labourer signalled and the rest of the search party joined him, this is what they found.

A relatively big termite mound had been hollowed out with a sharp stone, to resemble the oven used by the trekkers. The mound might have been partly hollow when Raggie found it. She had made many such ovens for her own mother. Chipping away with a stone, in the bitter cold, with her little brother lying next to her almost unable to move, and slowly freezing to death, she had managed to make the excavation big enough for him to squeeze into.

It had long been dark when she had carried him over fifty metres to the termite mound. Her arms must have been almost paralysed when she started digging, but she worked without stopping, though slower and slower in the cold, until the hole was finished – and then she had made her final decision.

She was found naked, with only her small velskoens on her feet, curled around the entrance to the little cave she had dug, completely blocking it. She was dead, her body almost as white as the surrounding snow. Inside the ant heap was Boetie, curled up tight and close to death, and over his clothes were those of Raggie – her dress, her petticoat and her thick sheepskin jersey wrapped around his little legs and her kappie on his head.

The bitter cold wind blew a little softer that day, over the frozen fields of the eastern Free State.

EVENTS IN THE LIFE OF AN ENGLISH OFFICER AND GENTLEMAN

There were many interesting characters sent out to South Africa from foreign shores and some have played an important part in the formation of our country. Others have left lasting impressions, both good and bad. One man, I feel, has been wronged by history and on a certain level used as a scapegoat for the wrongs committed by others. The man in question is Colonel Anthony William Durnford.

We pick up his story in Pietermaritzburg where he was a Major in the Royal Engineers, placed in charge of a group of Natal Carbineers. He was given the task of pursuing Chief Langalibalele, the head of the Hlubi tribe, in the vicinity of the Natal Midlands.

Langalibalele had been instructed by the government of Natal to register his tribe's rifles with the authorities. He had ignored the order three times and Durnford and his men were sent to bring in the recalcitrant chief.

Langalibalele's spies had told him of this decision and, along with his cattle and his men, he hotfooted it to the safety of Basutoland. Major Durnford and his men headed up the Bushmen's River Pass in the Giant's Castle area of the Drakensberg. After a bit of a mix-up, they eventually linked up with another section, only to find Langalibalele and his men already at the pass. In the ensuing fight, Durnford's horse, his treasured Chieftain, lost its footing and both horse and rider tumbled down the side of the pass. Miraculously, both survived the fall, but Durnford's left shoulder and arm were severely broken, as a consequence of which his arm was rendered useless and he had to carry it in a sling for the rest of his years. In that fight five men were killed. All were buried in the pass where they fell, and today there stands a monument to the men in Pietermaritzburg Market Square.

A strong party under Captain Allison, another famous name in the history of Natal, was sent to Basutoland, where they managed to capture Langalibalele. The Chief was to be banished to Robben Island but instead was kept at De Oude Molen, outside Cape Town. The township, Langa, formed later in the vicinity, was named after him. As a result of this rebellion the Hlubi tribe was broken up, their lands were confiscated by the State and the people who survived were captured and parcelled out as itinerant labourers to the various frontier farmers in the Midlands district.

Durnford did not agree with the handling of the Hlubi and took exception specifically to the policies and procedures of Sir Theophilus Shepstone, the head of Native Affairs in the Colonial Government. It is at this juncture in his life that he became estranged from colonial society in Pietermaritzburg. He became a virtual social outcast, to the extent that somebody even went as far as poisoning his beloved dog, Prince.

Durnford and his wife were separated. He said it was because she spent money too freely, but it was rumoured that she had taken a lover in town. His very liberal attitude toward the black people of Natal distanced him from colonial society and drew him closer to that other well-known champion of the downtrodden, the Rev. John William Colenso, or Somtsue, as the locals called him. Colenso also disagreed fundamentally with what was happening and he was not shy in making his opinion well-known. As a result of the handling of the Langalibalele affair, Durnford broke off his lifelong friendship with Shepstone and never spoke to him again. He found the actions of the government, in general, and those of Shepstone, in particular, utterly despicable.

Durnford found solace in the arms of the Bishop of Natal's youngest daughter, Francis Sarah Colenso. The 50-year old Durnford became the lover of the eighteen- or nineteen-year old Francis. Francis saw Durnford as her knight in shining armour and loved and idolised the man until her dying day.

Later, in 1879, we find Durnford commanding the reserves at Middledrift, while Lord Chelmsford's centre column crossed the Buffalo River to begin the invasion and destruction of the Zulu empire. Durnford sent a message to Chelmsford stating that an attack by the Zulus on Natal was imminent and that he wished to move his men to a new and better position of defence. Here is the reply he received from the bungling Lord Chelmsford:

> Dear Durnford, unless you carry out the instructions I give you, it will be my unpleasant duty to remove you from your command and to substitute another officer … You have simply received incorrect information and your change will make it impossible for me to carry out my plan of campaign. I trust you will understand this plain speaking and not give me further occasion to write in a style that is distasteful to me.

I do not wish to delve into the details of the battle of Isandlwana, but Durnford arrived with his trusted Natal Native Contingent and they participated in that terrible battle begun by the British to destroy the might of the Zulu Kingdom forever. However, Durnford acted like the true man and soldier that he was and died at the head of his men.

Francis was utterly devastated by the death of the man she loved. Some years later she wrote a book about their life together called *My Chief and I*, under the pseudonym of Atherstone Wilder. It is a book well worth reading. And near to where this brave man fell, there is a monument to all the men who perished on that fateful day. It reads as follows:

Not theirs to take the day,
But falling where they stood,
To stain the Earth with brave men's blood.
For England's sake and duty
Let neither praise nor blame be placed upon their epitaph,
But let it be simple like that, which marks Thermopylae
Go! Tell it in England, you that pass us by
That here, faithful to their charge
Her soldiers lie.

THE PEDI AND
MAFOLOFOLO

As you drive towards the scenic Mpumalanga Lowveld, with its majestic beauty and abundant game reserves, you may not realise that you are travelling through an absolute treasure trove of history. In the eighteenth century, the Pedi tribe had become a great and powerful people, and by 1800, King Thulane, with his capital in the beautiful Steelpoort River Valley, raided as far south as the Vaal (Lekoa) River, west as far as the Magaliesberg and north as far as the Soutpansberg. In those days, there was a thriving trade in ivory, horns, skins and metal goods, and people spanning the Northeastern Transvaal linked the traders from Inhambane and Delagoa Bay with the people deep in the interior.

In the nineteenth century, the Pedi vied for control of the land against the powerful Swazi Kingdom to the east. This tension was exacerbated in 1845 with the arrival of a group of Trekkers, who immediately laid claim to the land and started subjugating their neighbours. The local youngsters had to go to the Cape and find employment to enable them to buy guns and keep the threat at bay. By 1860, an uneasy stalemate existed between King Sekhukhune and the Trekker community at Lydenburg.

At a place called Botshabelo, 'The Place of Refuge', a band of Pedi

Christian converts, under the leadership of Reverend Alexander Merensky, had built a mission station. By late 1870, Botshabelo boasted 1 600 inhabitants, a mill, a store, a wagon-building shop and the largest school in the Transvaal at that time. At the heart of this settlement was the church – built by the converts from stone, bricks and thatch. At the height of apartheid in the 1960s, Botshabelo was still a thriving educational and religious centre. However, it was soon declared a 'black spot', all its tenants and peoples were removed and their homes destroyed.

Today, a number of these structures still stand – the church, the mission and Fort Merensky. Fort Merensky was originally built to repulse a revenge attack by the Pedi or an attack from the Ndzundza Ndebele, whose Chief Mabhogo had his capital Erholweni near where Roos Senekal stands today – but that is a story for another time.

In 1864, a group of Pedi, who had converted to Christianity, left the heartland of King Sekhukhune and followed the missionaries to set up Botshabelo. This group was led by Johannes Dinkwanyane. Despite the educational facilities and all the industrious work done there, there were mounting internal conflicts at the mission. The elders questioned the missionary's intolerance of age-old practices and beliefs such as initiation, lobola, rainmaking and the fertility festival. Many were also angered by Merensky's refusal to allow them to acquire land of their own and were rightly embittered by missionary insistence that they meet and respect Boer demands for payment of tax and supply of labour.

These grievances led Dinkwanyane and 300 of his followers to leave the mission in 1873, and saw them faced with a difficult choice. If they stayed in the Transvaal, the Boers would not allow them to acquire land. If they went back to the Pedi Kingdom, they would have to abandon their Christian faith.

They settled in an area which fell on the margin of both Boer and Pedi control and, alongside the Spekboom River, they built Mafolofolo, 'The Place of Gladness'.

The entire village was surrounded by a high stone wall with shooting holes, and inside lay further fortifications along with caves and a necessary supply of water. At the heart of the settlement, they built a church, large enough to accommodate the entire community on Sundays. During the week, it doubled up as a school.

Dinkwanyane attempted to create a Christian community independent of direct control by the Pedi or the South African Republic, but in the

Transvaal of the 1870s, there was no room for Mafolofolo. Local farmers and officials saw it as a profound threat to authority and security and demanded its destruction. Local missionaries, fearing that it would become a magnet for their own converts, refused to provide religious assistance for the village and some even agitated for its destruction.

It was this absolute determination to bring Dinkwanyane to heel, which caused the outbreak of war between the Pedi and the Zuid-Afrikaansche Republiek in 1876. During the first battle of that war, the Boers, who had linked up with the Swazis, marched on Mafolofolo, and after failing to breach the outer wall with their four-pound canon, hung back, leaving the Swazis to do the fighting. After a desperate battle, the Swazis managed to breach the town's defences, killing Dinkwanyane along with most of his followers.

But the destruction of Mafolofolo proved to be the turning point in the First Sekhukhune War. As the Swazis were outraged by the Boer cowardice and duplicity, the Boer commando had to continue into the next battle without the Swazi shock troops. This led to the defeat of the Boers by Sekhukhune, leaving the way open for the annexation of the Transvaal by the British through Natal.

It is a pity that we have forgotten Dinkwanyane and Mafolofolo – in their attempts to blend a Christian value structure into an African Culture, they were responsive to a rapidly changing world. The solutions they adopted speak so powerfully to our present-day South African realities.

SCOTTY SMITH

If ever there was a character in our history who, along with Dick Turpin, Ned Kelly and Jesse James, deserves a place in the rogue's gallery of the world's 'Gentlemen of the Road', it is our very own Scotty Smith. He is notorious as a cattle rustler, horse thief, highwayman and outlaw, secret service agent, IDB trafficker, confidence trickster, soldier of fortune and half a dozen other things besides. He was loved, feared and hated throughout the northern borders of South Africa for almost three decades and, as a young boy, I knew of the Welcome Beer Hall in Potchefstroom, where the bullet holes in the counter were a reminder of one of his escapades.

Born George St Leger Gordon Lennox in 1845, the eldest son of a Perthshire landowner, he received a good education, which included subjects such as land surveying and veterinary science. He landed in Cape Town in 1877 and for the next forty years this country was his home and was where he earned his dubious fame.

At the end of 1877 Scotty was in Kokstad, working as a military farrier, when he received a message that his bank in Glasgow required his presence. He calmly deserted his regiment, went to Scotland, sorted things out and returned, only to be punished for dereliction of duty. He was sent to King

William's Town, where he decided that army life was not for him, and so began his long career in brigandage. His desertion set the pattern for the future. He commandeered two of the best police horses, and scarpered!

It is totally impossible to recount the events of this man's doings in any coherent order, so I am going to set down some of the better known escapades of this fascinating man.

This story is probably the first of his escapades as it took place shortly after his desertion from the army. In his old age, he was extremely proud of this particular event and understandably so, because in subsequent exploits he never quite reached the same heights of ingenuity.

He rode from King William's Town to Fort Beaufort, where he sold the two stolen horses and, with his real identity undetected, he took on a job as an assistant foreman with a road construction gang. He and the foreman soon became good friends and, as the road under construction passed through many farms, they were entertained hospitably by many farmers, including one particular elderly couple, at whose home there was always a bed and a hot meal awaiting them.

Unfortunately, the old man died and, at the reading of the will, an amazing disclosure was made. Practically all he possessed had been bequeathed to the lawyer, while his wife was left penniless. Hurriedly, the lawyer wound up the estate and placed the assets up for auction. Almost £10 000 was realised and deposited in the lawyer's bank account. The widow, meanwhile, was too frail and heartbroken to challenge the will.

Scotty was not prepared to let this matter rest and, on obtaining a copy of the will, concluded that it was a forgery. He sent it with a covering letter to the bank manager, suggesting that the signature be verified by a handwriting expert. He also decided to take independent action to assist the widow, just in case nothing came of his letter.

On the night on which the money was deposited in the Bank, Scotty was in town and the following morning Fort Beaufort awoke to the electrifying news that the Bank had been robbed of £10 000, with no clues left as to the identity of the thief. A reward of £1 000 was offered for the capture of the thief.

Some time later, Scotty and his foreman were sitting in their camp. The latter looked very worried. 'What's the matter?' asked Scotty.

'It's my wife, she is seriously ill and requires specialist treatment and I haven't the money. But if only I could capture that Bank robber …'

'I think we can rectify that situation', said Scotty. 'First let's get the reward money straightened out.' They set off to the bank.

'I have certain information that could lead to the successful capture of the thief and the return of the money', said Scotty, 'but first we want a written undertaking that the £1 000 reward money will be paid.'

The delighted bank manager drew up the document and signed it. Back at camp, Scotty gave his friend the copy of agreement saying that the money was as good as in his pocket, and informed his friend that he had robbed the bank, and that he should call the police and have him arrested.

'Rubbish', said his friend, 'and even if you had, I would never turn you in.'

Scotty, assured him that no gaol could hold him and promised him that he would remain behind bars only until the reward was paid out. In this way he persuaded his friend to turn him in. Scotty was sent to prison for robbery. The manager, however, would not hand over the reward because after searching Scotty's lodgings, no money could be found. He visited Scotty in gaol and broached the subject of the missing money.

'What have you done about the will?' asked Scotty.

'You were right', was the reply. 'The will was forged and the matter is now in the hands of the police. You did a good thing there, Scotty, the money really does belong to her, which makes it more incomprehensible as to why you stole it.'

'It should be obvious', said Scotty. 'I have no faith in the law, and I was making sure that she received her just due, whatever happened.'

Thereupon, they came to an agreement. Scotty, handcuffed, would show the bank manager where the money was hidden and the widow in turn would receive the money. Scotty led the manager to a mound of earth some distance out of town, slipped his handcuffs, overpowered the manager and tied him up seated on top of the mound. Climbing on to the manager's horse, he said, 'I have never broken my word, and I don't intend to start now. You are sitting on top of the money and I will tell the first person I see in town of your whereabouts and you will be rescued.' He was true to his word, the bank manager was found and the money recovered. As Scotty had been arrested, the bank paid the reward money to the foreman whose wife could then have the treatment needed, and the widow received her inheritance.

There was a countrywide hue and cry about the audacious gaol breaker, but Scotty was already riding hard for the north-west.

In order to appreciate fully the antics of George St Leger Lennox, it is necessary to have a broad understanding of not only the territory but also the people, places, politics and events of the last quarter of the 19th century. The area we are talking about stretches from Kimberley, westward towards Klaar-water (now Griquatown), then north to Postmasburg and Kuruman, turning east to Mmabatho and Zeerust, south to Mamusa (the present-day Schweizer-Reneke), down to Bloemhof and then back to Kimberley. This is the area that later briefly would be known as the Republics of Goshen and Stellaland.

Various tribes, all engaged in internecine warfare – wonderful pickings for freebooters and filibusters – occupied this area. In the northern part were the two Baralong rivals for power, the pro-British Montsioa at Sehuba and the pro-Boer Moshette at Kunana. In the south were their counterparts, the Batlaping Chief Mankaroane at Taung and the Koranna Chief Massouw at Mamusa. It was a troublemaker's paradise. These various chiefs would hire the freebooters on the usual conditions – retention of half of the booty and half of the farmland taken from the chief's rivals.

But these mercenaries had drawn up a gentleman's agreement amongst themselves, that if they faced each other in battle, they would deliberately aim high. This was so strictly observed, apparently, that only two white men were actually killed in these skirmishes.

The Transvaal freebooters in the north were having a good time. The pro-Boer Chief Moshette had appointed Nicklaas Gey van Pittius as his agent and with his help, had inflicted a crushing defeat on Montsioa and burnt his capital, Sehuba. The land seized from Montsioa was used for setting up the Boer puppet-republic of Goshen.

In the south, things had gone badly for the pro-British section. Massouw, the leader of the Koranna, was causing a great deal of trouble. The ancestors of these Koranna had originally lived near Table Bay, but European expansion had forced them ever further to the north-east. Their wanderings had resulted in an almost continuous battle for existence, with all the peoples of the interior viewing them as enemies. They eventually established themselves at Mamusa on the west bank of the Harts River, where they converted a natural hill into a stronghold with a stone fortification on the summit.

In October 1881, Mankaroane and his white mercenaries attacked Mamusa but were defeated by Massouw, who then offered a farm and half the loot captured to every white man who would fight for him. The generous terms attracted a mercenary army of 400 desperadoes under one Sarel Petrus Celliers, who then kept up constant raids on Mankaroane's cattle herds. Poor

Mankaroane had fallen out with the English and was also under threat from Gasibone, chief of another rival Batlaping tribe.

To recoup his losses, Mankaroane attacked Massouw at Fourie's Graf, but he suffered a crushing defeat and the very symbol of his power, a ship's cannon, was captured, causing many of his tribesmen to desert him.

This was how matters stood on the wild frontier when Scotty rode into the town of Taung. He was then about thirty-seven, sported a big red beard and had a striking personality. He summed up the situation pretty quickly and offered his assistance to Mankaroane. 'We are too weak to drive the Boers out of our country', Mankaroane told Scotty, 'so we must stop them from settling down, we must raid their camps, we must steal their horses, and keep them shut up in their laager. We must steal their cattle, so that they will be so busy protecting their herds that they won't attack us. When they find that they cannot remain peacefully on the farms, they will get tired and return to their own country.' This I find a very interesting strategy, one not dissimilar from that employed by the Xhosa in the Eastern Cape frontier wars.

Before long Scotty had recruited, organised and armed his own private army consisting of about thirty tough whites and sixty local tribesmen. Scotty and his band threw themselves wholeheartedly into the fray and on more than one occasion, made a clean sweep of the cattle in Boer encampments. He acquired arms and ammunition, clothing and provisions for his men. He had no scruples in breaking into some convenient store. It is known, for example, that he broke into Charles Daly's store in Bloemhof. Daly, incidentally, was himself another interesting character. He had survived the wreck of the *Birkenhead*, was a good friend of Paul Kruger, and was the only man given a magazine licence by the Transvaal Government to supply its forces. However, he arrived one morning to find that the shop had been raided. Pinned to the door was a list of all the stores taken, with a note from Scotty saying that he would pay in due course. The strange thing about this man is that he always kept his word, and there are numerous incidents which proved this.

Scotty's lively band had their own war song, which went like this:

> Come saddle up my horse
> And strap my billy on
> To hell with the Lime Juice Parliament [referring to the Cape]
> We'll fight for Mankaroane

Now cheer boys cheer and never be afraid
We're marching in the ranks of the Stellaland Brigade
As we march along, we'll sing this little song
And fight for good old Mankaroane!

There were a few incidents that took place before Scotty formed his little army, and I feel that the following two, in particular, need retelling.

On one occasion, Scotty was in a very tight corner, so hard-pressed by the police in fact that he actually abandoned his horse. By means of some ruse, however, he managed to escape and trekked across the veld on foot. After some time he came across wagon tracks and overtook a few transport riders in charge of three wagons. Scotty asked whose outfit it was. They replied that it was Jan Coetzee's and that he had ridden on ahead as they were so near to home. 'I am Piet Coetzee, Jan Coetzee's nephew', said Scotty. 'You must give me a lift.' He climbed into the wagon, lay down under the tent and went to sleep, to be awoken later by the sound of horses approaching. Somebody asked the transport riders whether they had seen him. When they said they had not, the men turned their horses and rode away in a different direction. On reaching the farm, Scotty brazenly introduced himself to Jan Coetzee as his nephew. In those days most Boer families had so many nephews and nieces that Oom Jan did not doubt Scotty's story at all.

He was immediately invited in, given food and drink and generally made comfortable. All went well until, as was customary, Coetzee and his wife tried to establish to which branch of the family he belonged. Scotty became more and more embarrassed until, cornered, he decided to put his cards on the table. He told them who he was and what had happened and ended up by asking Oom Jan for a horse. 'I haven't any money at the moment, but I promise you faithfully that I will pay you when I can', he said. Oom Jan agreed without question. 'I have heard a great deal about you, Scotty, and how you have helped many people.' True to his word Oom Jan saddled up a good riding chestnut, his wife gave Scotty a satchel of provisions and he rode away. Many months had passed and Oom Jan had forgotten the incident, when Scotty came up to him in Johannesburg Market Square one day and told him he wanted to pay for the horse. Jan Coetzee named a fair price and Scotty promptly paid him double!

Scotty was a master of disguise and this got him out of many tight corners, for example when he was declared the South African Republic's most wanted man, with a price of £500 on his head. Some of the leading Transvaal freebooters, such as Groot Adriaan de la Rey, Nicklaas Gey van Pittius and Gert van Niekerk were eager to claim the money and they all did their best, but to no avail. On one occasion Groot Adriaan, brother of the famous Boer War General, Koos de la Rey, in a determined effort to capture Scotty, assembled a commando of western Transvaal farmers and set out on his trail. Scotty soon heard about their plan and, instead of doing the sensible thing and going to ground until the danger was over, he decided to play a prank on the posse. After changing the colour of his hair and beard, he set out with a friend and came upon the posse near the village of Amalia. Riding up to the leader he enquired where they were going. 'We are searching for Scotty Smith', came the reply. 'Oh!' Scotty exclaimed, 'my friend and I are also looking for the damned scoundrel! Do you mind if we join you?'

Groot Adriaan agreed to this and so Scotty had the peculiar delight of taking part in a fruitless hunt for himself! This went on for two days. Then Scotty told the Boers that, as he and his friend were now a long way from home, they would have to start back in the morning. He thanked the commando for allowing him to take part in the search and said, 'Every night you have taken it in turn to stand watch, and we've done nothing. As it is our last night, we would like to do our share of guard duty so that you can all have a good night's rest.' The men were only too glad to accept this considerate offer and, needless to say, when they awoke at dawn the next day, not only had Scotty and his friend disappeared, but all the horses had vanished as well.

Though our hero seems to have borne a charmed life, not all freebooters were so lucky. Close to the western border of the Transvaal, not far from Massouw's camp at Manthe, is a deep ravine known as Honey's Kloof. It was here that James Honey, one of the toughest and most reckless of the filibusters, met a sudden and violent death. Honey, a mercenary fighting for the Koranna chief, Massouw, had a bitter quarrel with his fellow adventurers over the distribution of the land and booty. Honey apparently tried to incite the Koranna against them and they decided to have their revenge. They captured him after a struggle and set off back home. It was an extremely hot day when they came upon the spring in the kloof and they went to rest the horses and quench their thirst.

Honey also begged for water. They loosened the riem around his wrists and, as he knelt to drink, one of his captors shot him in the back of the head.

Honey toppled slowly over into the stream, staining it red with his blood. The commando then threw his saddle down beside his body and rode away.

African herd boys who found the body reported their find to the authorities and the matter was referred to Sir Charles Warren. As a result Sarel Petrus Celliers, the former commander of Massouw's mercenaries, was arrested along with Gert van Niekerk and others, but owing to lack of evidence, all were later released. However, the story does not end there. According to local legend, shortly after the tragedy, a strange thing happened. To the amazement of the Africans living around Manthe, the eye of the spring began to recede gradually down the kloof until, a year later, it was fully sixty metres away.

The locals swore that Honey's ghost haunted the place and that every year, on the anniversary of the murder, a shot could be plainly heard in the area. 'The spirit that inhabited the spring', they told their children, 'was very angry because the blood of the white man had defiled his waters. So he went to live in another place.'

❖ ❖ ❖

We leave Scotty himself now and take a brief look at what was happening in that area and how it was affected by larger political events. In July 1882 a peace treaty was drawn up between the Transvaal Government and chief Mankaroane, in terms of which a large portion of Batlaping land was taken away and used to establish the Republic of Stellaland, with Vryburg as its capital. In July 1883, amid great jubilation, the Republic was formally proclaimed by freebooter Gert van Niekerk and its flag – a white star on a green background – was ceremoniously hoisted. Stellaland and Goshen were now nominally independent states, with the Transvaal exercising a vague and ill-defined suzerainty over them.

This was Rhodes' worst nightmare, as the famous Missionary Road seemed likely to be incorporated into the Transvaal and his 'Cape to Cairo' dream was fading fast. So imminent was the danger that Rhodes urged Her Majesty's Government to annex Bechuanaland to forestall the designs of the Germans in South West Africa and the Transvaalers to the east.

The man selected to help maintain peace and order in this unruly area was the Reverend John MacKenzie. MacKenzie was a zealous political missionary and took very little trouble in hiding his virulently anti-Boer sentiments. The new Commissioner arrived in July 1884 and took strong action immediately. He accepted Montsioa as a British subject, declared the area a British Protectorate, then promptly lowered the one-star flag and raised the Union Jack – all on his own authority. The freebooters went wild. They wanted to lynch him, and there was also huge resentment in the Transvaal Republic. Their Commissioner's action took the British Government completely by surprise and they decided on a complete reversal of policy. They rapped him over the knuckles, ordered the lowering of the British Flag, the raising of the one-star and had him recalled, replacing him with none other than Cecil John Rhodes himself.

Rhodes arrived in Vryheid and, early one morning, went to Niekerksrest on the banks of the Harts River, where he met Van Niekerk, De la Rey and other Stellaland leaders. The Boer mood was very ugly. De la Rey particularly was spoiling for trouble, saying, 'Blood must flow, blood must flow'. But Rhodes knew exactly how to handle this kind of situation. 'Nonsense', he replied. 'I'm hungry. Give me breakfast first, and then we will talk about blood.'

His appeal to traditional Boer hospitality did the trick. Over breakfast the aggression and suspicion gradually subsided and soon they were on friendly terms. Rhodes actually stayed in the Boer camp for a week and became godfather to De la Rey's grandchild. Soon a deal was struck. Rhodes guaranteed the Boers' possession of their farms and cattle and they in turn agreed to accept British rule. Once again the tribes, in this case the Batlaping, lost out on a deal struck between the British and the Boers.

Further north in Goshen, Montsioa was also getting the dirty end of the stick, eventually being forced to surrender practically all of his lands to the freebooters. Gey van Pittius took charge and declared the country Transvaal territory, whilst S. J. du Toit hoisted the Vierkleur in triumph. On the very same day, Paul Kruger boldly annexed Goshen to the South African Republic. This really put the cat among the pigeons. There was a tremendous outcry at the Cape and Rhodes asked for British military intervention.

Sir Charles Warren set out from the Cape with a large force and arrived in Vryburg early in 1885. Those in favour of British rule were jubilant, but the Transvaal Government's reaction was immediate and dramatic. President Kruger withdrew the annexation proclamation and Du Toit hauled down the Transvaal flag. The southern part of Bechuanaland, incorporating both Goshen and Stellaland, became a Crown Colony while the northern part became a British Protectorate. The short-lived, inglorious era of the freebooters came to a sudden end.

Meanwhile, Massouw was still causing trouble to the north with his persistent cattle raiding, and the Transvaal government decided to take action. A force of nearly 1 000 men was raised, with the Commandant-General himself, Piet Joubert, in command. Joubert, always a cautious man, upon reaching Mamusa attempted to negotiate a peaceful settlement with the Chief, but the younger members were itching for a fight and, led by one of the more impetuous young Commandants, Piet Cronje, they climbed the hill up to Massouw's fort and demanded the Chief's immediate surrender. A heated argument ensued – a shot was fired and bloody battle was joined. So fierce was the fray that within minutes ten Boers lay dead.

However, by the end of the Battle of Mamusa, Massouw had suffered a terrible defeat. The Chief himself and all of his counsellors were killed. An extremely unfortunate aspect of the battle was that a large number of women and children were caught up in the crossfire and also perished. The Koranna tribe which, for more than a century, had trekked all the way up from Table Bay, was finally completely destroyed. Fewer than 100 people escaped with their lives that fateful day. They were dispersed among the surrounding tribes and soon lost their identity.

Today the sole reminder of this bloody massacre is the town of Schweizer-Reneke. The name commemorates two of the Transvaal Boers who lost their lives in that battle, Captain C. A. Schweizer and Veldkornet G. N. Reneke. Maybe it is time we looked at this place name again and, in the interests of reconciliation, take the other side into consideration.

❖ ❖ ❖

As for Scotty, the fall of Goshen and Stellaland made very little difference to his life. He remained a law unto himself – nobody could prevent him from going where he wanted to and doing exactly as he pleased.

During Sir Charles Warren's expedition to annex southern Bechuanaland, Scotty was hired as a guide. Shortly after this Scotty purchased a farm and a store in the Kheis area on the Orange, now Senqui, River. But he did no actual farming there. This was merely a cover and a convenient hiding place for stolen stock, before they were re-branded and prepared for market. He acquired a second farm just outside of Amalia village, not very far from Schweizer-Reneke, which he also used for grazing and fattening his purloined cattle. This area is still known as Diewedraai.

A gunrunning exploit of his, into Basutoland, is well worth the telling. In 1871 this country, at the request of King Moshweshwe, had been taken under the protection of the British Crown. But the proud Basuto people had in no sense been conquered. They were still ruled by their King and almost every man possessed a rifle. In 1880, after the Zulu War, the Cape Government, fearing this large force of armed tribesmen, tried to disarm them and many rose in rebellion. The so-called Gun War ensued and, after three years and an expenditure of £4 500 000, it reached an inconclusive end. The rebels were 'defeated', but allowed to retain their weapons, with a strict embargo on new importations. Inevitably, it became the ambition of every Basuto to possess an illicit firearm. They were all prepared to pay a premium and this set of circumstances was just right for our man.

Having secured a large number of Snider rifles, muzzle-loaders and soft-nosed bullets, along with a quantity of powder, Scotty trekked across the Free State, to Ficksburg, near the Basutoland border. He hid his wagons in the bushes close to the road and boldly rode up to the frontier alone. The Veldkornet guarding the border with a handful of men hospitably offered him a cup of coffee. After gaining the man's confidence, Scotty said, 'Look, Meneer. I have some very important information for you. I know that there is a lot of gunrunning taking place, and I have found out that Scotty Smith is the main culprit. What's more, I will show you how he does it! As a matter of fact, I have had a tip that he has just run a cargo into Basutoland, and they have not yet been collected. He's hiding them in a drift on the Caledon River and they are to be collected tonight.'

The officer became very excited. 'Can you show me the place?'

'Yes', Scotty replied. 'It's about twenty kilometres south of here. I don't know if Scotty will still be there, but you had better take all the men you can, as he's a pretty desperate fellow.'

The officer was greatly impressed with the charm of the genial stranger and decided to take no chances. He ordered all his men to mount their horses and, leaving the post to its own devices, they rode hard for a couple of hours to the south. When they came to a drift Scotty and the Veldkornet dismounted and reconnoitred the area. They found no one and the officer ordered the men to picket their horses. They followed Scotty on foot to a bend.

'There!' cried Scotty. 'That's where they are hidden.'

'But surely the powder will spoil in the water?' said the officer.

'Scotty's a sly one', came the reply. 'The boxes will be watertight.'

The men began probing the water and, sure enough, they found one box, then another, then another, but they were too heavy to lift and the entire patrol came to assist. Scotty wandered casually away until he was around the bend, and then ran swiftly to the picketed horses. After setting them loose and stampeding them, he mounted his own steed and galloped back to the border post where he had left his wagons. He quickly inspanned and drove the wagons safely past the deserted border post to the rendezvous deep inside Basutoland.

Meanwhile, the Veldkornet and his men had managed to get some of the enormously heavy boxes to the bank and had prised the lids open, only to find them filled with river boulders. When they looked around for the stranger he had disappeared and so had their horses. They had a long and weary walk back to their post.

Another of his favourite stories concerned an encounter with the Jewish diamond thief. Scotty was transport riding at the time when he happened upon a pedlar walking along the road and offered him a lift. He noticed that the man appeared to be highly agitated and kept glancing over his shoulder.

'What's the matter?' asked Scotty. 'Is something troubling you?'

'It's nothing, it's nothing', the pedlar muttered. They were nearing the border when the man let out a yell.

'The police, the police! They are after me!' Scotty turned his head and saw a small posse in the distance.

'Hide me, hide me!' cried the stricken passenger. He flung himself flat on the bed of the wagon and Scotty quickly threw a sail over him and piled some boxes and packages on top.

The police rode up and immediately asked Scotty if he had passed anybody on the road.

'Yes,' replied Scotty, 'I saw a pedlar some way back, if that's the fellow you are after. He's a small man dressed in a dirty corduroy suit and wearing a slouch hat.'

'That's him', cried the Sergeant, 'that's our man alright'.

'What's he done?' asked Scotty.

'Stealing diamonds', came the reply. 'He's got quite a packet on him.'

'Well, if you want to capture him you'll have to retrace your steps. As soon as he saw me coming, he branched off into the veld.'

"Where was that?' the sergeant enquired.

'About four kilometres back there is an ironstone koppie with a small dried-up vlei next to it. That was where I saw him turn off.'

'Thanks!' shouted the Sergeant. 'We'll get him alright. Goodbye!' And he and his men thundered back the way they had come.

At that moment Scotty stuck his hand in his pocket and felt a hard package. A slow grin spread over his face and, stooping down, he whispered to the pedlar, 'I've put the police off the scent, but you had better stay hidden for a while longer.' He opened the parcel and, seeing a number of fairly large diamonds inside, he placed it in one of the wagon boxes. 'It's alright, you can come out now', he called.

The man got out and said, 'Please give me the packet I slipped into your pocket when I thought the police might find me.'

'What packet?' asked Scotty. 'I don't know anything about a packet. You must be making a mistake – look for yourself.' The pedlar ran his hands over Scotty's person but found nothing and, in spite of the man's protestations, he denied all knowledge of the stones. The pedlar kept on wailing, moaning and threatening, until at last Scotty could take no more. He grabbed the man by the shoulders and shouted, 'I've had enough of this nonsense, I hid you from the police and that's all the thanks I get. You accuse me of being a thief! Clear out of here or I'll put a bullet through you, as sure as my name is Scotty Smith!'

A look of horror and fear appeared on the man's face when he realised to whom he had entrusted his precious diamonds and, jumping off the wagon, he ran off across the veld.

Many are the recorded stories of our hero and villain, but there was a side to this cattle thief that touched many hearts, especially women's, in those very harsh times.

During a certain Bloemfontein court case, which Scotty attended – not so much for the court proceedings as for the general information he could pick up from the farmers – he noticed that the Landdrost possessed a particularly fine horse. That evening he slipped into the Landdrost's stables and led the horse out without anybody noticing a thing. He hadn't gone far out of town when it started raining and, soaked to the bone, he knocked on the door of a rather run-down homestead. A woman opened it rather hesitantly.

'Can you put me up for the night?' Scotty enquired.

'I would like to, but my husband isn't here and he made me promise not to admit any strangers while he is away and now I hear that Scotty Smith is in the neighbourhood.'

The older generation, from whom these stories were learnt, told me that when they were children, their parents always used Scotty's name to make them behave. 'If you don't stop that I'll tell Scotty Smith to put you on his saddle and ride away, and you'll never see your poor mommy again!', or words to that effect.

However, on this occasion, Scotty just laughed. 'You have nothing to be afraid of', he said, 'That scoundrel won't show his face while I am here. As a matter of fact, I am after Scotty myself, and the local Landdrost has lent me his personal horse. Don't you recognise it?'

'Yes,' said the woman, 'I know this animal well! I'll give you a room for the night. Take the horse around to the stables whilst I make some supper.'

After they had finished eating they sat and talked for a while and Scotty noticed that his hostess was somewhat sad and distracted.

'What's wrong?' he asked. At first she would not say, but later the story came out.

'I don't know what's going to happen. I told my husband not to do it, but he wouldn't listen to me. He backed a bond for a friend for £200, and now the man has cleared out, and we can't find him anywhere.'

'Don't worry', Scotty comforted her, 'and don't sit up for me either. As soon as the weather clears I'll be off on Scotty's trail.'

He thanked her for her hospitality, paid her, and she retired. Sometime later the storm passed and Scotty got up and rode off into the night. In the morning his hostess rose and went through to the kitchen and there, under a plate on the table, was £200 in bills with a note: 'Best wishes from Scotty Smith.'

Of course the old freebooter did not usually have so much money at his disposal, but he always kept his promises. If he promised a certain farm in the area that their stock would be safe, it was never touched and if he said he would pay for what he called 'borrowed' horses, he always did so, without fail.

Mr David Cowan, a well-known citizen of Victoria West in days gone by, was away on a visit to Beaufort West. A stranger turned up at his house asking for accommodation for the night. His wife was dubious about taking him in, for the usual reasons. But when she confided her fears to the stranger, he laughed. 'You needn't be afraid of Scotty Smith', he said. 'He has never been known to harm a woman.' Mrs Cowan was still rather doubtful but eventually took him in, gave him an outside room and took him his supper. The next morning she sent him some coffee. The maid brought it back. 'The man has gone,' she said, 'but he left a letter on the bed.'

'Thank you for the room and food', it read. 'I am sorry I have had to borrow two of your horses. When your husband returns, tell him to go to the Beaufort West Hotel in ten days time, and he will find them there.'

Mr Cowan did this and found the horses waiting for him at the Hotel.

But it was when it came to befriending the poor and lonely widows in distress that Scotty was in his element. There seems to have been a plentiful supply of poor, lonely and distressed widows in the Orange Free State and western Transvaal at that time. As always, Scotty arrived, looking for a place to sleep and, with his usual tact, had very little difficulty in discovering what the widow's problems were. The farm was bonded and the bondholder was foreclosing the following day. 'How much is the bond?' Scotty asked. '£400' was the reply. Without any hesitation, he dug his hand into his pocket, extracted a thick wad of notes and counted off £400. 'Now, when the man comes tomorrow, you must pay him in full and demand a receipt – that is very important.'

At first the widow demurred and would not accept the money. 'It is quite all right,' said Scotty, 'I will not lose on the deal. You can be sure of that.' She did not understand, but eventually gave way and agreed to do as he said.

The following morning, the bondholder arrived and found, to his great annoyance, that the widow had the money. However, there was nothing he could do about it but give her a receipt and ride away. He had not gone far when, from out of the bushes, appeared a man holding a pistol, who robbed him of all the money he had just received, took his horse from him and galloped away. The following day Scotty visited the farm. The widow was very grateful and asked for his address so that she could eventually repay him. 'Don't worry, the debt has already been settled in full', said the stranger. 'You don't owe me a penny. Goodbye.' And he rode away.

When the First World War broke out in 1914, Scotty Smith was one of the first to offer his services to the Union authorities and was attached to Military Intelligence with the rank of Warrant Officer. Dressed in khaki slacks and shirt, he wandered about, spying on the rebels and reporting their movements and activities to Headquarters.

Soon after war was declared, some of the men who had been Boer leaders during the Anglo-Boer War thought that they now had an opportunity to overthrow British rule in South Africa, and went into open rebellion. Among them were Commandant General C. F. Beyers, one of the renowned bittereinders, along with General Christiaan de Wet, whose original farm Roodepoort is now a suburb on the West Rand of Gauteng. His farmhouse, by the way, was the first one burnt in the Transvaal by the British. I have no doubt that General Koos de la Rey would also have joined these rebels, but he had been tragically shot in a roadblock incident in the Johannesburg suburb of Booysens. But that's another story.

In South West Africa, the Germans had concentrated powerful units at Nakop and Raman's Drift, while across the border at Upington and Kakamas were large detachments of the Union Defence Force, under the command of General Manie Maritz, another Anglo-Boer War hero. In October 1914 there was a sensational development. General Maritz deserted to the enemy, taking a large number of men with him. This might have proved a very serious matter, but for some reason, the rebels received very little support from their countrymen. The rising had to be suppressed, however, before Louis Botha could invade South West Africa.

Scotty took part in the invasion of South West Africa, and this story was related by Mr Greeff, who at fifteen had joined the 20th Mounted Rifles (later known as Breytenbach's Light Horse). The campaign took place in the middle of summer, and the sun beat down mercilessly on them. It was not too long before the water carts were empty and, to make matters worse, the commissariat department had broken down and there was no immediate prospect of obtaining fresh supplies.

The position grew more and more critical. In order to spare the horses, the men dismounted and led them. Fortunately, they knew they were near Lutzputs where there were wells of drinking water, and this thought alone kept them going. However, they arrived only to find, to their horror, that one of the wells had dried up and the retiring enemy had polluted the other. A fight had taken place between the rebels and the 8th Mounted, in which the latter had been defeated. The enemy had collected some of the bodies and thrown them into the well before they withdrew. Many of the soldiers were in a state of collapse and the horses were in an even worse plight. The stench from the well was so terrible that the animals refused to drink. One of the men then had a brainwave. He smeared axle grease up some of the horses' nostrils and in this way gained some relief for the animals, but quite a few actually died of thirst. The officer in charge was desperate and began sending heliograph messages appealing urgently for help.

'Luckily for us', he reported, 'Scotty Smith was in the area and came to our assistance. He arrived at midnight, and we were told to fall in. With Scotty at our head, we set out, leading what remained of the horses, staggering and stumbling through the desert. Fortunately we did not have far to go. Scotty led us straight to the dry bed of the Molopo River. He quickly chose a spot and told us first to picket the horses, then to dig. We had no entrenching tools, so we began excavating a fairly large hole with our hands. The men formed a line and the sand was stuffed into nosebags, and passed along. The sand was soft and before long we were down about a dozen feet. Suddenly one of the men let out a hoarse yell. In a parched, croaking voice he shouted, "Water, boys! Water!" And there, seeping up between the smooth, round river stones, was a thin clear trickle of fresh water. Thank goodness Scotty had had the foresight to picket the horses, otherwise there would have been a stampede.'

True to the tradition of a crack Imperial Cavalry Regiment, these irregular volunteer Union troops looked after the needs of their horses first, before relieving their own thirst.

The year 1919 was a black one for Scotty's admirers all over South Africa. The old veteran contracted influenza and was confined to bed. He became weak but refused to give in. Every now and again a faint smile would cross his lips, as he remembered perhaps something of the full life he had led. Just before his death, he sent a Bushman to call his friend, the priest but, alas, by the time the priest had arrived, Scotty was no longer in need of human sympathy and comfort.

Scotty Smith was buried in the Upington cemetery and a simple metal plaque was erected over his grave. It reads:

> George St Leger Gordon Lennox.
> Gone but not forgotten. Never will his memory fade.
> Wife and Children.

And so South Africa lost one of its folk heroes. Scotty had said to a friend over a fire one night: 'I was born two hundred years too late. You see, my weakness is that, when I see a bunch of good cattle, I want to own them. In modern times this is looked upon as stealing. Two hundred years ago taking other people's cattle in Scotland was known as rieving, and a successful riever was a highly honoured member of his family group. And if the cattle had been rieved from south of the border, the riever was acclaimed a Scottish hero.'

Maybe he had a point.

THE MYSTERIES
OF THE SEA

The sea has its moods – sometimes calm and gentle, sometimes raging with unbelievable fury. It has always intrigued mankind, and from all over the globe there are both wonderful and frightening tales of these forces of watery fury. Our coastline has been no different, and is regarded as one of the fiercest on Earth.

I have stood at Splash Rock, at Port Edward, during a raging storm. I have watched the almighty force unleash, sounding like a huge canon shot, smashing upwards into the very heavens, a polite reminder to us of our proper place in the universe.

In the 1870s, Durban experienced a high tide that flowed over the Point wharf, and continued to the steps of the old Point Hotel. Four months later, in Table Bay, the tide rose four feet higher than expected, then receded, only to do it again fifteen minutes later.

In September of 1883, the entire coastline from Port St Johns to Port Alfred was pounded with the heaviest seas ever recorded. The reason? The volcanic eruption of Krakatoa, and for months the evening sunsets were blood red from the dust in the atmosphere.

Another interesting incident involved the Port Elizabeth Harbour Board nightwatchman – he recorded three high tides one night, and was promptly suspended for drinking whilst on duty. The following day, news came in from other centres, and the Board apologised accordingly. We are all aware of the pull of the moon, and of the spring tides when the sun, moon and the Earth align, but there are some phenomena that we still cannot explain.

Take the incident at Dwarskersbos, a little fishing hamlet up the West Coast with no more than a dozen houses at the time this incident was recorded. Although the settlement was usually protected by dunes and scrub, on that particular day the older and wiser fishermen had dragged all their equipment way past the normal high-water mark.

At about 3 o'clock the next morning, most of the seasoned fishermen were lying awake, listening to the unusual fury of the waters they so deeply understood. They knew their source of income well, but none of them had ever heard it so fierce before.

The rhythmic, pounding roar became louder and louder, and nearer and nearer. The first of a number of waves crashed through Dwarskersbos, then a second, breaking over the village, which was already two metres underwater. Dwarskersbos literally came apart at the seams.

The villagers came to their senses, and struggling to carry their furniture and belongings, they fled from the fury of the beast. More huge columns of water crashed down onto the drowning town. Great waves, more than ten metres high, crashed over the matchstick houses, the raging winds screaming through the village all the while.

Nobody slept that night, for you cannot sleep when you can hear the beating of your own heart. Some said that they were so scared, they could hear the beating of their spouse's heart!

Although various theories were put forward to explain the disaster away, personally, I can understand why most fisher folk remain so superstitious to this day.

A second incident worth mentioning occurred in the early 1930s, at a lovely spot just east of the Knysna Heads, called Noetzie. It was summer, and many people were in the water. Pretty soon, the tide started to come in, and people started to notice that huge shoals of fish were coming in with the waves. Those on the beach ran into the surf and collected numerous varied species of fish, and carried them ashore. It was not long before the entire beach was covered in tons of fish – providing a veritable feast for the seagulls.

In amongst the fish that were washed up, there were some species of fish never seen in those waters before. Sanni Meterlerkamp, a descendent of the Rex family of Knysna, documented some of these strange creatures. Some, she said, had snouts not dissimilar to those of pigs, others sported brown manes from nose to tail. There were red fish, purple fish, striped and rainbow-coloured fish. The local folk gathered as many as they could, cleaned them, and then began salting and smoking them.

Noetzie residents must have eaten salted fish for quite some time after that.

An academic later supplied a scientific reason for this strange phenomenon. He explained that there are intensely cold masses of water that normally lie deep beneath the Agulhas current. Nearer to the coast, these waters can come closer to the surface, and, when certain conditions prevail, these icy waters rise to the surface. The fish are stunned or killed, and the tide brings in the rich harvest.

I am not one to question the rhythms and moods of the sea, but wise enough to grant it the respect it justly deserves.

THE RESTING OF PROPHETESS NONTETHA BUNGU

ontetha Bungu was a Xhosa prophetess and religious leader in the East London, Middeldrift and Fort Beaufort districts of the Eastern Cape. She was born in the little settlement of Toyise, near King William's Town, in about 1875, and grew up there as a part of the Amaqaba community. Very much like the king of the Bapedi in Venda, the Amaqaba had little time for missionaries. They dressed in the way of the old, and rejected most of the western ways, preferring to follow their traditional manners and customs. They did not buy into the new way that was being thrust upon them.

Nontetha was very fortunate to have survived the Grim Reaper's visit that came with the influenza epidemic of 1918–19. She preached and prophesied to her faithful followers, very much like Makazana, Umlanjeni and Nonqase had done in times long gone. But, things and times had changed.

In 1921 there was an uprising, at a place called Bulhoek, where the police opened fire on the Israelite Church community. Two hundred people lay dead. The authorities, upon seeing Nontetha's growing following, did not want a repeat of this incident, so they arrested her for what they termed 'seditious behaviour'. With hindsight, this was an obvious move on the part of the authorities to silence her, and to stop the movement from gaining momentum. She was placed in the Fort Beaufort Asylum, which was some distance from her home.

The Amaqaba organised protest marches, demanding her release. This behaviour continued for three years, until the authorities eventually released her. She was told that her release was subject to the condition that she ceased preaching to her people. She did not. She was re-arrested and placed back in the Fort Beaufort Asylum.

The ensuing protests became so fiery, that in 1924, they removed Nontetha from Fort Beaufort to the Weskoppies Mental Hospital, just west of Pretoria. The community continued undeterred with protests and demonstrations, demanding her release. The authorities at Fort Beaufort responded lamely, saying that she was no longer there.

In 1927, the community, their appeals having fallen on deaf ears, took matters into their own hands. The congregation set out for Pretoria on foot, walking the entire distance of just over 1 000 km to lobby for her release. They were rebuffed, and many of them were arrested for the defiance of not carrying a pass. 'We do not carry them,' they said, 'because we shouldn't have to, in the country of our birth.'

Again, in 1930, they undertook the same journey, which received the same response. In the interim, eight Xhosa chiefs had journeyed to Pretoria, and prominent members of the Xhosa community had shuffled backwards and forwards, all to no avail. Nontetha's supporters' unwavering spirit in the belief that what they were asking for was both just and right, their interminable patience and reasoning, is nothing short of humbling. It is no wonder that Tata Madiba belongs to such a truly remarkable people.

There were absolutely no valid reasons to incarcerate Nontetha because of her mental state. The authorities simply used this as an excuse to prevent her from continuing with what they called 'seditious preachings'.

On 20 May 1935, Nontetha Bungu died of cancer of the liver and stomach at Weskoppies Mental Hosptial. She would never see her beloved home or people again. The hospital superintendent sent the usual regulatory telegram, informing the family of her death, and instructing them to come to Pretoria to claim the body. Unfortunately, telegram deliveries in that remote and isolated area were extremely slow, and by the time her family and the elders received it, she was already buried in a pauper's grave.

Nontetha's people requested that the body be returned to the family for reburial. The authorities refused on the grounds that, firstly, it would be prohibitively expensive, and secondly, regulations did not allow for the exhumation of a body within the first two years of burial. Her only son, Menzeleli, went to Pretoria to request permission to move her body. His request was declined, but he was showed the gravesite. The family eventually gave up the quest.

In 1997, an American scholar of African religious belief and custom, named Robert Edgar, visited the church that was founded by Nontetha. On being told her story, he was so moved that he inwardly resolved to take action. He traced all possible records, and discovered that she was buried in the New Cemetery in Pretoria. He found the original site of her grave, but the area was long since overgrown.

He found an old map, and had the site surveyed. Then, having obtained the necessary permission, and with the help of archaeologists and numerous supporters, the remains of Nontetha Bungu were exhumed.

On 25 October 1998, the reburial of Nontetha Bungu took place at Khulile, near the little church that she had founded. A grave travesty of justice had been partly rectified. You see, in our country, before we try to heal the wounds, we need to see and understand them. I hope that this incident takes us one small step further along that road of progress.

JOHN MONTAGU

One of the unsung heroes of the development of our country is the relatively unknown John Montagu. He was Colonial Secretary of the Cape under the despotic Lord Charles Somerset, as well as the ego-king Sir Harry Smith.

The towns Montagu, Somerset West, Somerset East and Harrismith, were named after these gentlemen. Sir Harry Smith went as far as naming the following towns after events that he was personally involved in: Aliwal South, since renamed Mossel Bay, was so named after his defeat of the Sikh Indians at a place called Aliwal in India, and Aliwal North was named after the same event. He renamed his family home in Britain Aliwal House. Ladysmith was named after his wife Juana, and so was the now-deserted town of Juanasburg.

But back to John Montagu, the only gentleman amongst the three. It was Montagu who fathered the great transformation of the road structures in the Cape. He began very imaginative schemes for the construction of the road network by utilising convict labour from the various gaols dotted around the Cape Colony.

This had two major effects. Firstly, it opened up transportation to and from the outlying areas, leading to massive growth outside the confines of

Cape Town, and secondly, it provided for the employment and rehabilitation of prisoners, by giving them a technical skill, which could lead to employment after they had served their sentences.

As Secretary to the Colonial Government, John Montagu controlled virtually all of South Africa's public service from 1843 to 1852. He had originally been stationed in Tasmania, where he was second in command to the Tasmanian Governor. However, he was abruptly suspended after successfully launching a far more humane system for the treatment of transported convicts, or 'remittance men', as they were then referred to. It seems that politics was indeed involved in this abrupt removal of Montagu.

Along with his entire family, he caught the first ship back to England, and pleaded his case to Lord Stanley, who was then Secretary of State for the Colonies. On reviewing the case, Lord Stanley exonerated Montagu completely and offered him the Colonial Secretaryship of the Cape Colony.

During those times, the successive Governors of the Cape use to spend a lot of time away in the war-torn Eastern Cape, so Montagu, de facto, would be in charge. What the people did not know was that this man, who would work a twelve-, and often fifteen-hour day to free the Cape Colony of its crippling debt, was a completely ruined man.

Here's what happened to him. Having been forcibly removed from Tasmania, Montagu decided to sell his Tasmanian estates by proxy. The mail, transported by sailing vessel in those days, took months each way, and hence the sale was transacted at the height of the Australian economic slump. When the news eventually reached Montagu, he found to his horror that he was now no longer a man of considerable independent means, but rather a debtor for many thousands of pounds.

The news completely shattered the man and his family, but they faced it together. He had to withdraw his eldest son from Cambridge University. He sold his country house in the Peninsula and moved into Cape Town so that he could walk to work, and, behind the scenes at home, the most stringent economic practices were put into place to cope with the financial disaster. Little did Montagu's fellow dignitaries know what a predicament the Montagus were in. Yet, even through all of this, he remained a man of honour and dependability.

It was towards the convicts of the Cape Colony that this remarkable man revealed a heart of mercy. In those days, the prison conditions were appalling. Many prisoners were kept in stocks overnight to prevent escape.

There was no reward for good conduct, no training for reformation, and certainly no after-care.

Montagu himself had fought at Waterloo, so he understood and believed in discipline, yet he also believed that prisoners should be properly fed and clothed, and, above all, trained for a better life afterwards. He therefore started the prison road gangs.

He concentrated these convicts into two major road camps, where days were set aside to teach illiterate convicts to read and write, and to learn the truths of religion. At the end of their sentence, they were granted a bible as a gift from the State.

These rehabilitated men were snapped up by farmers at superior rates of pay, for they were now trained, disciplined and excellent labourers. Such was the mind of that man.

John Montagu

In just two and a half years, John Montagu had fully settled the long outstanding paper debt of the Cape Colony, which the Colonial office had exploited year after year as an excuse for not constructing harbours, roads and bridges. Now, they had no more excuses.

To decide where his convict gangs would build roads, he inaugurated the first National Road Board of South Africa, and created the Local Road Boards of the Cape Colony. This man laboured ceaselessly, but it took him the rest of his strenuous life to repay the £21 000 he owed in Tasmania. It was two months after the final payment, whilst away on sick leave in England, that this courageous man died, haunted by the knowledge that he could bequeath his wife and family nothing.

Here was a man of such mercy, to whom the gods showed no mercy at all. A man who is owed a great debt by our country. Long may his name live on.

DR JAMES BARRY

Her true origins are vague, to say the least. Some say that Dr James Barry was the daughter of a Scottish Earl, yet others say that her father was the Duke of York, second son of King George III, and that her mother was the daughter of the famous General Barry. Irrespective of her background, the Cape Archives are full of anecdotes about what she was like, and the mark she made on society whilst at the Cape of Good Hope.

Born in 1795, she graduated as a medical doctor from Edinburgh University in 1812, at the age of 17. Throughout her training, she masqueraded as a man. They tried to teach her boxing, but she kept protecting her chest. She took up fencing, and became very proficient with the rapier. She joined the British Army and served in Spain and Belgium, later in India, and in 1817 she became the staff surgeon at Cape Town under Lord Charles Somerset, who was then Governor of the Cape. He seemed to dote on her, and with hindsight, I am convinced that he was aware of her gender.

She was only 1,7 m tall, and used to wear high-heeled boots, wrap towelling around her rather delicate waist and stuff cotton wool into the shoulders of her uniform to bolster her image. In this ridiculous garb, she would strut around Cape Town in full uniform, sporting long spurs and a huge dragoon's sword. Hardly anyone ever crossed the diminutive doctor, for her temper was as short as her sword was long. Her favourite threat was delivered in a high-pitched squeaky voice, 'I should much like to cut off yer ears!'

She was forever in trouble, and often guilty of breaches of discipline, yet always seemed to be let off the hook. One day, a clergyman sent a message to her requesting that she extract one of his teeth. 'Does this fool think I am but a vulgar tooth puller?' she yelled at the messenger. She went to her farrier, armed him with a hand-vice and pliers, and sent him off to the clergyman. Upon arrival, he informed the man that the doctor had sent him to pull the tooth of a donkey! When an official complaint was laid, Lord Charles told the man to let the matter rest.

What was the reason behind this absolute protection, even when she was so clearly flouting the rules? The answer is simple – she was brilliant at her job, and was often referred to as 'the most skillful physician, but the most wayward of men'.

She was the champion of the poor and wretched, exposing scandal after scandal of the terrible conditions in the prisons. When a malignant epidemic called 'rotkoors' broke out in the Swartland, she diagonosed it as European typhus, and set out the standard treatment.

She heard that the lepers at Hemel-en-Aarde, a leper colony just outside Caledon, were being starved and were running away. She personally went to investigate. 'Nothing could exceed the misery of the lepers,' she wrote. The hospital was filthy beyond description, and many of them chose to die rather than face the squalid conditions. She appealed to Lord Charles, who saw that the colony was reformed, and she prescribed a diet of milk, rice, coffee, vegetables, mutton and bread.

The people worshipped her. She found the Cape Town gaol in an appalling state, and promptly reformed it. The official guilty of this state of affairs decided to get his revenge, and she was summoned to appear in court. She tore the summons up and refused to answer any questions, saying that she was beholden to the Governor, and the Governor only. The court sentenced her to one month's imprisonment, but Lord Charles set this aside. Her comment on the matter? 'If I had had my sword on when Mr Fiscal proposed sending me to gaol, I would certainly have cut off both his ears to make him look smart.'

Dr Barry often accompanied Lord Charles Somerset on tours of the Colony, and on one occasion, they were the guests of George Rex of Knysna. What she and George Rex discussed about their possible royal past will never be known, but they did remain in contact for a long time.

It was in September 1828 that the Cape bade farewell to 'die kapokdokter', when she sailed to Kingston, Jamaica. After that she took postings in St Helena, Barbados, and then Trinidad in 1844, where she went down with fever and delirium. Surgeon-General Sir Thomas Longmore tended to her and thus found out that she was indeed a woman. When she came round, she begged him to keep it a secret as long as she lived. He did.

Her overseas service ended in 1864, when she returned to Britain. There she died, all alone on 26 July 1865. Her manservant asked the charwoman to lay out the body. On dressing what she had thought to be a man's body, the charwoman ran back to tell the manservant that their beloved doctor was a woman!

She was buried at Kensal Rise cemetery, where her simple headstone reads:

Dr James Barry,
Inspector-General,
H.M. Army Hospitals
Died July 26th 1865
Aged 71 years.

Although Inspector-General was the highest rank to which any army medical officer could rise, I feel that she deserved much more for all the work she did for people, not only in our country, but across the entire globe.

A MAN OF MERCY

Contrary to popular belief, there has been a wealth of goodwill shown by South Africa's English speaking community over the years. This is exemplified in the story of Peter Davidson, the Minister of the Scottish Settlers Church in Adelaide in the Eastern Cape.

His congregation comprised the settlers that Robert Hart had taken to Glen Lynden, on the wild frontier of the Baviaans River, in 1820. These people had fought war after war on that frontier, and they could scarcely rank as liberals on questions of race. His wife, Janet, was the daughter of Alexander Walsh, one of Glen Lynden's earliest pastors, and his community was at Koonappos, later to be named Adelaide.

One Sunday in 1879, the Davidsons and their children went up through the beautiful Makazana Valley to deliver holy communion at the church at Glen Thorn, situated at the foot of the Great Winterberg. The children all filed into the church with their mother, except for golden-haired Ebenezer. As he was not yet four, he was permitted to play outside during the service.

Once the devotion was over, it was discovered that young Ebenezer Davidson had disappeared. Members of the congregation, together with farmers from the surrounding areas, scoured the bush, riverside, hills and dales for days on end – all to no avail. Ebenezer Davidson was never seen alive again.

The family were overwrought with grief. The family tombstone in Adelaide bears testimony to their sorrow. It reads: 'Mysteriously taken on June 22nd 1879.'

Fourteen years had passed, when a local farmer called Jack Pringle came to bring Peter Davidson the first authentic news about his missing lad. A Xhosa informer had heard a woman blurt out the long-kept secret at a beer drink. It was said that two Xhosa men had seized the boy that Sunday morning so many years ago, and had killed him. They had mistaken him for the son of another farmer, who had beaten their brother until he had died. It was a mistaken revenge killing.

The little skeleton was eventually discovered on top of Governor's Kop, just above Glen Thorn. The culprits were soon hunted down and captured. As this was the time of the Frontier Wars, one could bet one's life on the eventual outcome of the sentence.

Then came the most unexpected turn in that era of violence. Peter Davidson came forward in the courthouse, to plead for the life of his son's murderers. What this took from the old minister, alone, in the long hours of the night with his God, we will never know. But his plea was successful, and thus he prevented a second family from being plunged into mourning, to avenge the death of his son.

Sometimes I think, in the times we now live, that we could all take a leaf out of old man Peter Davidson's book.

The Settlers' church at Glen Lynden

MODJADJI

S hould you stand on the top of Pypkop Ridge near Duiwelskloof and cast your eyes over the forest-clad folds of the Walowedu Mountains, you would be gazing at the ancient lands of Modjadji – 'The Transformer of the Clouds' – 'She who must be obeyed'. And as you stand and watch the mists and the greenery of those ancient mountains, you have to keep blinking, for you tend to slip away into an ancient time, a time in which Rider Haggard immortalised a Queen called 'She'.

It is told in the legends that there was a time long ago when there were no people in this part of the world, only the beasts of the forest. The hoarse bark of the baboons, the soft sighing of the winds, and the roar of tumbling waters, were the only sounds. All the people lived away to the north, in Monomotaba. Among those tribes there was one whose priests told of their origins near 'the great waters that had no end'. These priests and chieftains wore around their necks, blue beads, the sacred *uhulungu ha madi* or 'beads of the sea' – the emblem of royalty and relics of a culture possibly older than that of the Phoenicians.

And in the forest depths, parents told their children tales of fierce warriors and ancient cities, and a lost race who lived in the land of their forefathers –

a white race, whiter than the Arab slavers who pillaged their cities. But time and the bush had swallowed this race of white people, and the people of the blue beads were called the BaVenda – 'people of the world'.

One day there came from West Africa a warlike tribe, pillaging and looting, and the people were forced to flee southwards to the mountains now called the Walowedu. Amongst the tribes who fled were the Lobedu, led by a woman who, it was said, was a white woman. Her name was Modjadji.

Who was this woman? Was she the daughter of some captive white woman, or of one of the tribes from that far-off land near the waters that have no end? Was she the descendant of some noble house, with the blood of Semitic kings in her veins? Or was she a waif, thrown up on some remote slave market? Modjadji, on the rocky heights, her priests guarding her from prying eyes, and weaving an aura of mysticism and dread power of the spirit world around her, to such effect that, when the white people arrived, they called the area Duiwelskloof – 'The Valley of the Devils'.

It was said that Modjadji's lovers were either killed or became her slaves and that her male offspring were all put to death. Only a female child, who had to be conceived incestuously, could inherit the mantle of tribal rule. Whatever the land and people who bore her, Modjadji had the blood of conquerors in her veins and, as her tribesmen were not great warriors, it was by the fairness of her body, the cunning of her mind and the savagery of her heart, that she created and moulded a great kingdom out of the tribes who settled in that area.

So great was the fame of this sorceress that chiefs of the Basuto, the Shangaans and others came to pay her homage and brought gifts of young girls as handmaidens to the queen. Even Shaka, the great Zulu king, who feared no man, dreaded the magical powers of Modjadji and sent a deputation headed by Dumisa, his own personal sangoma, to propitiate the Rain Queen.

When Modjadji reached old age, she would announce her successor and retire into a cave, take a special type of poison made from the spine of the ngwenya ('crocodile') and then die alone. Her people believed that she was immortal and that her spirit entered into the younger female, thereby ensuring a continuous reign. What we do know is that the whiteness of her skin slowly, over generations, grew darker and darker. Then in 1894, came the white man, with guns.

Modjadji suffered her first major setback at the hands of Commandant-General Piet Joubert of the Zuid-Afrikaansche Republiek, and the reigning

Modjadji died by her own hand, after the Commandant had broken her power.

It is said that, until then, no white person had ever seen Modjadji and the old woman who shuffled out and spoke to Piet Joubert was a fake. The real Modjadji had been taken away to safety. The tribe was severely punished for deceiving General Joubert and later the real Modjadji was dragged into his presence. After this ignominy, she took poison, and died the ritual death of her ancestors.

The present Modjadji still resides in that area, but receives visitors and can be seen in her kraal by all and sundry. A strange and interesting rider to this story is that the latest DNA testing has proved that the Lemba – a subgroup of the baVenda, do actually spring from semitic stock – makes one wonder, doesn't it?

❖ ❖ ❖

As the sixth Queen Modjadji, Makobo Caroline Modjadji, has just been installed, let us have a closer look at how hugely significant she is to the Lobedu people.

To her tribe, Queen Modjadji represents the very essence of their history, culture and belief system. I am reminded of what the great Roman Statesman Cicero said, over 2 000 years ago.

> Cultures, without their history, doom themselves to remain trapped in the most illusionary tense of all – the present. For, when trapped in the present, you become akin to a child. You know not from whence you come, nor whither you go.

This statement, I feel, is immensely relevant to all of us in South Africa today. We need to re-establish our roots, or start growing new ones, so that we can understand our origins, otherwise, we will never know where we are going.

In the sixteenth century, an African princess named Dzugudini had an illegitimate child by her own brother. To escape the wrath of her father, she and her followers fled, eventually finding sanctuary in the fertile forest of Daja. They have been there ever since.

In the early 1800s, they had as their chief a mystical philosopher called Mugudo. He contemplated the fact that, in all royal families, the sons fight for the kingship. He solved the problem by killing all of his sons. He told his daughter that she was to be Queen upon his death, and said that the ancestors had ruled that, as the tribe had come about in an incestuous manner, she was to marry him. Should her offspring be male, they were to be killed. The first daughter born would be the next Modjadji.

The first Modjadji became renowned as a rainmaker, and her fame spread throughout the land. She was an elusive, secretive queen, hidden deep in her forest village. Nobody could ever gain an audience with her, as she worked through deputies. The African tribes were petrified of her, yet at the same time she was deeply revered. The Zulus, who held her in particular renown, called her Mabelemane – 'the four-breasted woman'.

Rumours about Modjadji abounded. Many thought her to be immortal, but this was not the case. In 1854, the mantle was passed on to her daughter. Her paternity, as well as the source of her rainmaking magic, remains a secret. All we know is that male offspring do not ascend to the throne – only females.

In 1881, a German missionary named Fritz Reuter, with money donated by Fraülein von Mending, supplicated Modjadji for the right to build a missionary church in the area. Modjadji pondered the meaning of this new arrival, who was telling her followers that her secret doings were not the work of God.

In 1884, Modjadji struck. The small community of Christian converts, under a preacher chief named Kashane Mamadeba, were killed and the church was burnt down. As the white settlers grew more numerous in the surrounding area, so the drought worsened. The Lovedu began burning the outlying farmsheds, and the settlers fled. The outlying local peoples were known as *batsanene* or *tzanene*, after whom the town Tzaneen was named.

There lived in the area a chief named Maguba, who was tired of being told that he had to pay taxes to the Transvaal Republic. He went to war in 1893, withholding taxes, raiding cattle and generally making it unpleasant for the returning settlers. This prompted General Piet Joubert to arrive with a commando from Pretoria, and he rallied the settlers near Haenertsburg.

Maguba and his warriors retreated deep into the bush, near the lovely Debogane Falls. The commando could not flush them out. Piet Joubert called for Swazi mercenaries, who went into the bush and, finding two women, killed one and tortured the other until she revealed Maguba's hiding place. Halfway up the kloof, which still bears Maguba's name, they found him. There they killed him, cut off his head and presented it to Piet Joubert. Joubert demanded reparation from Modjadji, as some of her men had been with Maguba. She was to pay 300 head of cattle, or come out and fight. Joubert had broken the might of Modjadji.

In 1896, at the sacred place of Naulini, she called for the traditional cup of poison. After her animal skin, which held the rainmaking magic, had been removed, she was buried in the traditional standing position, with a man beside her.

May the new Modjadji rule her people with a wise, just and firm hand, so that her people will always know where they came from.

The revered fifth Modjadji who died in 2001

SARAH BAARTMAN

I t is very heartening to see ordinary South Africans taking an interest in the history of our country. They are starting to question the old biased stories and examine the past with new perspectives. This and this alone will eventually break down the enormous barriers and fill those voids that the old kind of history-telling created.

The story of Sarah Baartman is a case in point. It is also a very topical one as her remains have only recently been returned to South Africa and buried in her country of birth.

We know quite a lot about Sarah's life but what we hardly have any record of, and what we can only imagine, is the immense personal pain and suffering that this young woman underwent during the years she was a virtual slave on foreign shores. Her fate was not dissimilar to the two Inuits, who, on being captured by Captain Frobischer off the coast of Baffin Land, were locked up in a cabin. On the journey to England the Inuits were monitored on a rotational basis by the crew, to confirm the gross speculation that they might 'mate' as animals!

'Saartjie' as she was known until recently, was Khoekhoe. It is believed that she was born near the Gamtoos River in the Eastern Cape. She left her home as a young teenager. In March 1810 she was living near Cape Town when a ship's surgeon, Alexander Dunlop, met her. She was enticed with promises of fame and fortune to board his ship and accompany him to London. He promised that within two years he would make them both rich, for one of Sarah's striking characteristics, at least as far as Europeans were concerned, were her large buttocks or steatopygia, which is the result of fatty tissue around the buttocks.

Written into Sarah's contract was a clause in which she agreed 'to be viewed by the public of England and Ireland just as she was'. Like so many girls who are attracted to the bright lights, she was lured into the life of what effectively was a stripper and later a prostitute.

She was displayed at the home of Dunlop's partner, Hendrick Caesar, in York Street, Picadilly, London, to anyone who would pay the entrance fee and, in time, became known as 'The Hottentot Venus'. Led onto the low stage like an animal by her keeper, Sarah was exhibited, wearing only the scantiest of clothing. Her keeper gave her orders in Dutch, instructing her to 'sit, stand and turn around' and generally walking her around for the audience's enter-tainment. It was noted that, on a number of occasions, she was reluctant to obey and that the keeper had to threaten her. At one performance, it is said, a Dutch-speaking man who was in the audience tried to ask her questions, but Sarah's keeper immediately drowned out her replies and then led her weeping off the stage.

This was the period of the growing anti-slavery movement in Britain and Dunlop therefore quickly drew up a new contract. It was dated 20 October 1810 and covered a period of five years retrospective from the date on which Sarah had been removed from the Cape Colony. The contract stated the following conditions. She was employed as a domestic servant and for this job she would be paid twelve guineas a year. She agreed to exhibit herself in public in the nude. And, finally, she would be free to return to the Cape after the five-year contract period. Dunlop's move was none to soon, for the Attorney-General intended taking action against him, based on affidavits supplied to the State.

The case was heard on 24 November but the new contract proved to be watertight. A year after this celebrated case, on 7 December 1811, Sarah was baptised by the Reverend Joshua Brookes at the Parish Church of Christ in Manchester, with permission of the Lord Bishop of Chester.

In September 1814 Sarah was taken to Paris and fell under the control of a keeper of wild animals. She was exhibited again to all who were willing to pay three francs. She became an even greater attraction in the French capital than she had been in London. A prurient public flocked to see her and buy her portrait and she was featured in satirical cartoons. In November 1814, a one-act farce, 'The Hottentot Venus, or the Hatred to French Women', began a long and popular run at the Vaudeville Theatre in Paris. In March the following year, a commission of biologists and physiologists, consisting of Baron George Cuvier, Geoffroy St Hilaire and Henri de Blainville, examined Sarah over a three-day period.

In a back street of Paris on New Year's Day in 1816, Sarah died of an unknown disease, without ever again seeing the beloved home that she had left six years earlier.

But a further indignity was heaped on her after her death. Her body was cast and then dissected. Her brain, genitalia and full skeleton were preserved and placed on public display in the Musee de l'Homme in Paris, and her remains kept on display there until 1974. Now, at last, after a period of 189 years, she has made the return journey she so desperately longed for. Sarah Baartman has come home to her country, and to the people she loved so much.

In a very moving ceremony, attended by the State President, she was laid to rest in the foothills of the Grootwinterhoekberge, just outside the small town of Hankey.

The following poem was written by Diana Ferrus:

I have come to take you home – remember the veld?
the lush green grass beneath the big oak trees?
the air is cool there, and the sun does not burn.
I have made your bed at the foot of the hill,
your blankets are covered in buchu and mint,
the proteas stand in yellow and white
and the water in the stream chuckles sing-songs
as it hobbles over the little stones.

I have come to wrench you away – away from the poking eyes
of the man-made monster who lives in the dark
with his clutches of imperialism, who dissects your body bit by bit
who likens your soul to that of Satan
and declares himself the ultimate god!

I have come to soothe your heavy heart
I offer my bosom to your weary soul
I will cover your face with the palms of my hands
I will run my lips over lines in your neck
I will feast my eyes on the beauty of you
and I will sing for you
for I have come to bring you peace.

THE CATTLE DROVERS

The far Western Transvaal, or North West province, has always been a special place for me. With its many battles over the years against the Zulus under Mzilikazi, the handing out of the konsessieplase or 'concession farms', to the men who fought for the land and the constant battle against drought. Life in that area has never been easy, and the little towns that dot the map are rich in history.

Swartruggens, meaning 'black ridges', still bears the scars of those Frontier Wars. It was on those very same ridges that the brilliant Boer War General, Koos de la Rey, led the British such a merry dance when he appeared suddenly, hit quickly and then disappeared into the hills, never to be found. It earned him the name 'The Lion of the North'. Quick was his attack, lightning-fast his disappearance.

It was in this area that the now famous Afrikaans writer Herman Charles Bosman, immortalised as 'Oom Schalk Lourens', served his time in the little schoolhouse at the foot of the Huimveeberg. After a tragic life, he left behind remarkable stories that give us such insight into the workings of the simple but hospitable farming folk of that area.

It was just outside the little Free State town of Zeerust, established 20 years before Johannesburg, that the famous missionary David Livingstone had his first South African posting at Gopane, a little village just 35 km outside of Zeerust. On the ground, where the magistrate's court now stands, Kasper Coetzee built the first fort in 1860, to protect the people of the district against what they termed 'the marauding local Bechuana'.

It was in this town that all the elephant hunters used to gather, prior to going up to the Tati District. It was also in this area that the first white woman in the Transvaal died in 1836. She was Mrs Wilson, the wife of the American missionary David Wilson. Her tombstone was rediscovered in 1914 by a doctor named John Gubbins. The town also boasts the infamous characters of Coenraad de Buys, and the cattle-thieving Scotty Smith, the highwayman and filibuster of the legendary Boer Republics of Stellaland and Goshen in the 1880s.

It was just outside this town that the Malmani Goldfields were discovered, which led to the famed gold rush, and overnight the settlement grew out of the Western Transvaal dust, promising to be the South African equivalent of the Klondike. The town streets bore the names Commissioner Street, Eloff Street and Rissik Street. The names were soon stolen by Johannesburg in the Witwatersrand gold rush, and the booming little town died a quick death. The sounds of the honky-tonk pianos and the dance-hall girls faded down the road to Johannesburg, where the pickings were much greater. All that remained was the little farming hamlet of Ottoshoop. There is still gold in those hills, but the water table put paid to the deposit.

However, this is not all the area is famous for. Its other claim to fame, or notoriety, was cattle rustling – the curse of the west. The cattle rustling in and out of Botswana was a weekly occurrence. There was no hope of the police ever patrolling the huge expanse of fencing demarcating the boundary between Botswana and South Africa, and the drovers were a hard and wily bunch. Most of them were never caught, as they were too smart by half. One of their tricks was to tie branches to the tails of the cattle, thereby obliterating all traces of footprints left in the wake of the trek. There would be no spoor to follow. Another was to burn the veld afterwards, thereby destroying the last remaining traces of cattle movement. There were poor men who became very rich in a short space of time in those days, but the dangers were many and very real. Cattle stampeding occurred regularly and men were often trampled to death. The herds were regularly stalked by lion and you had to be a good marksman to take care of that threat.

Legend tells us of Adrian Lewis, who was the best lion killer in the whole of the Kalahari district, and knew no fear of the big cats at all. The age of massive herds being driven by horsemen are all but gone now, but there was a time when thousands of cattle would be driven from the Ghanzi district of Botswana down the 800 km road to Lobatse and the Botswana Meat Commission on horseback.

The trek was a nightmare, and water was a constant problem. There was once a man who lost 650 cattle out of 800. The well that he was depending upon turned up dry, and there was no alternative source. It took him five years to repay the debt. In those days, a drover was paid for every head he brought through, but if cattle were lost through negligence, he was charged accordingly. The drovers on that route had to travel a total of 1 600 km, 800 there, and 800 back. They were in the saddle for weeks on end.

I was lucky enough to experience one of the last big drives of cattle. It went past just south of the town of Jwaneng. The herd was over 2 000 strong, and the main drover was the husband of Angela Hardwater the half-Bushman, half-European daughter of the legendary Colonel Hardwater, who had married a Khoe woman and settled down to farm in the Ghanzi district of Botswana.

The romance of the drover is gone now. There is a tarred road, the Trans-Kalahari highway, and the horses have been replaced with the cattle truck. In some ways, it's a pity.

OF KwaZulu-Natal's flying
AND FISHING

From the initially modest settlement of Durban, the old road snaked its way up into the vast unknown interior, and as it climbed out of the scenic village of Howick, it passed through a river and a mountain range named the Karkloof. The name dates back to 1845, when a local Dutch farmer was travelling along this road with a heavily laden Cape cart. He crossed the valley and started up the pass, but near to the top his horses took fright and swerved. The Cape cart overturned and all of the goods tumbled down the hillside. Fortunately, nobody was injured, but the wreck of the cart lay there for years for all to see. To this day, the area remains one of the most beautiful and scenic parts of our country.

It is this beauty that was partly responsible for the settlement of people in the Natal Midlands – and one such young settler was the young John Goodman Household. He was one of the sons of a British 1850 Settler in the area, and was eventually to leave his mark as a prospector in the Tugela area of Natal. But prior to this, he had other ideas.

In the early 1870s, Household conceived the idea of flying. Roaming around the hills and valleys, he studied the flight patterns of all the soarers – the eagles, vultures and other raptors that soar and glide so effortlessly in that neck of the woods. He shot a vulture, and recorded all of its measurements and proportions, paying particular attention to the weight-to-span ratio.

He then designed a glider, with proportions big enough to carry the weight of a fully-grown man. He constructed this contraption using a centre of lightweight steel tubing, with stout bamboo emanating from it, as well as oiled silk and heavy gauge paper. It had a pilot's seat resembling a swing that was suspended below four ropes off the inner-wing area. *Prototype 1* was completed in 1871, but try as he may, he could never get the unwieldy machine to fly.

However, being a determined sort of chap, he designed yet another glider, called *Mark 2*. When this sleek contrivance was eventually completed, Household, accompanied by his brother Archer and assisted by a few Zulus from the farm who were sworn to secrecy, trundled it out one moonlit night, to the very top of the ravine. Everything to date had been executed in complete and utter secrecy, for fear of his parents' wrath, and moreover, public ridicule.

After much effort, balancing and swearing, the glider was run off the top of the ravine into a good updraft. Away, into the evening shadows soared the intrepid young John Household. Managing a turn and skimming the tops of the trees, he caught the updraft again, and climbed to almost 120 m. Out, over and across the valley he glided, for over one and a half km, and then he attempted to land the crude craft.

Unfortunately, the controls of this craft were rather basic, and it side-slipped. Over-correcting, he went into a stall and crashed into the treetops. Household was catapulted from his seat and landed in a pool of water, earning himself a broken leg for his trouble!

The glider was a complete write-off, and Household's brother and the Zulus carried him home. Naturally, when his parents heard the complete story, they were furious, and whilst the first ever glider pilot in Natal was confined to bed, the heap of twisted metal, wood and fabric was assigned to the loft of an unused barn. His parents saw to it that it was never repaired, and, after a while, it was thrown on the rubbish heap and forgotten. Thus ended what was certainly man's earliest attempt to fly in South Africa. What a pity they had not had more foresight and preserved it for all to see.

Another rather interesting fact that many are not aware of is that it was in this scenic area of the Midlands, that trout fishing was first introduced. In

1882, an individual called John Parker wrote away to *The Field* magazine in England, asking for advice on the possible introduction of trout into the Natal rivers. The man in charge of the Howick town fisheries was Sir James Maitland, and he responded with a gift of a couple of thousand ova. John Parker's farm, Tetworth, was some distance north of Howick, but all of the ova died. The following year, Sir Maitland sent more ova, but they met with the same fate.

Nonetheless, interest had been aroused and a three-man committee was formed, comprising Parker, Younge and Colonel Vaughan, who selected the farm Boschfontein, near the present day Balgowan, as a hatchery. With a grant from the legislative council of Pietermaritzburg, the necessary equipment was purchased and installed, and in 1890, 30 000 ova were imported from Dumfries in Scotland. The experiment turned out to be a success, and each year following, more ova were hatched, and the Mooi, Umgeni and Bushman's Rivers were stocked. For the first time, Natalians were able to experience the tranquil joy of trout fishing in their rivers, a pastime that grew to be loved throughout South Africa.

THE HILLS OF MAPUNGUBWE
AND BAMBANDYANALO

One of the many aspects of the disciplines of history and archaeology that fascinates me, is that in many respects, archaeology becomes the verifier of history. Let me explain what I mean by this.

For hundreds of years, the African folktales and mythologies of the people of the Limpopo told of the Babahole people, 'The Men of the Rhinoceros', who were massacred by a marauding tribe. They told of the existence of a hill, with a treasure of gold buried on the summit. Mapunguwbe, they called it – 'The Hill of the Jackal'. And there, for almost 900 years, it remained – a golden rhinoceros, bowl and spiralled sceptre, buried and shrouded in the mists of mythology and time, safely hidden away from the eyes of the non-believers.

There was a hermit by the name of Lottering, or 'Lotrie', who lived in a shack at the base of the hill. It is said that he discovered some gold artefacts and buried them, not wanting the nearby settlers to find them. It strikes me as strange, that this is said to have happened in 1933, when I know, from the records that there was a family of Lotterings living in the now-deserted town of Schoemansdal, as early as 1859. Schoemansdal is not too far from Mapungubwe, and I wonder whether he was not one of the descendants of that family.

In 1932, a local farmer, one E.S.J. van Graan, managed to persuade a local tribesman to take him to the site – revered by the local people. Mowena led the party, walking backwards all the way, for it was taboo to approach such a holy place with your eyes gazing directly upon it. You had to constantly look over your shoulder out of respect.

He directed them to the gully, with its famous *Ficus* tree guarding the entrance. Climbing up the gully and emerging on the plateau, the white people found Mapungubwe. Thus, the mists of time, and the shrouds of mythology were removed, and the site moved into the books of history.

I must say that I sometimes pity archaeologists, for theirs is a strict discipline, pertaining to discovered facts. Their experiences must be akin to those of Alice in Wonderland, who discovered a small crack in the door, and, gazing through the narrow aperture, could see only an extremely reduced portion of that which lay on the other side of the wall of time. Archaeologists can only see the blades of grass, they cannot see the complete lawn. They cannot speculate on the vastness of the other side – they can only report on the little that they see and find.

To me, the discovery of those gold artefacts, and all the related finds, ask more questions than they give answers. Why would they mine gold, unless they knew that it had an intrinsic value? Who taught them, on the southern tip of Africa, to mine gold at least 800 years ago, and why? And how? All the surrounding gold mines in that entire area, stretching right up into Zimbabwe, are known to have been worked by an ancient people. Is it normal for a civilisation to mine and beneficiate gold and iron ore before they learn to write in their own language?

Why is it that the tales speak clearly of the Arabs, who came there from the Lowveld? They called them 'Mapalakata'. These were people with big noses, piercing eyes and heavy hands, for they bore in those hands, the chains, not only of trade, but of slavery as well. Their trade beads have been found in their thousands.

Why is it that the beautiful golden sceptre is fashioned in the shape of a spiral, not dissimilar to the two entwined snakes we find in the medical emblem? It is also similar to the spiral of the human DNA structure. Is this a coincidence? I sometimes wonder. What about the Chinese pottery shards found in the middens? They are also present in the related site of Thulamela, in the northern extremity of the Kruger National Park.

Contrary to popular belief, I do not believe that we have even started to unravel the pictures of this country's ancient past. I believe that in time to come, as technology improves, we will uncover stupendous tales about our past.

THE STORY OF
MARIA OOSTHUIZEN

During the Anglo-Boer War there lived in the eastern Free State near the town of Zastron, a young woman named Maria, whose farmer husband was away on commando. Maria and her maid Sabina were living alone when they heard of the impending arrival of the British troops, coming to burn their farm. They took refuge in a freshly dug pit under some corrugated iron and remained there until the conflagration had passed and night had fallen. Under the cover of night, they ran for the Maluti Mountains.

At daybreak a British search party scoured the area and it is said that a Scottish soldier found them hiding in a cave. Maria begged him to leave them alone and he turned around, walked out of the cave and reported that it was empty. Thus they made good their escape into Lesotho and eventually arrived in the small town of Matatiele.

Maria, with help of Sabina who was a trained inyanga, started to eke out a living by curing illnesses with natural herbs and medicines, and soon became renowned for her healing powers. Sadly, it was at this time that she learnt that her husband had been killed while fighting in the war.

The local Dutch Reformed Church (NGK) Minister in Matatiele, Dominee Oosthuizen, preached against her from the pulpit, declaring that her cures were unnatural and the work of the devil, and that the people must cease consulting her. Then, when he himself fell ill and was tended by her and nursed back to health, he fell in love with her and they were married.

Shortly after this, Oosthuizen was transferred to the district of Greytown in Natal, to preach amongst the Zulus. One Friday evening in 1918 he came back from visiting an outlying district and fell from his horse, desperately ill. He told Maria that the Zulus were dying in their hundreds from an unknown disease, and he himself died the following day.

Maria retired to her room and scoured her books to seek a cure. After three days she mounted her horse and rode off into Zululand. From kraal to kraal she rode, telling the Chiefs to instruct their people to drink their own urine as an antidote to the illness. So great was her name amongst the Zulu people that nobody questioned her. And so it was that the Zulu nation was saved from the tragic influenza pandemic that killed so many millions of people during the years 1918 to 1919. However, Maria was so devastated by her husband's death that she sold the farm and moved to Johannesburg, still accompanied by the faithful Sabina.

In her old age she wrote how bitterly disappointed she was that Sabina had deserted her in her time of need. What she did not know was that Sabina had walked all the way back to Zululand and had informed the Chiefs that the old woman was dying. An impi was despatched at once to bring Maria back to Zululand. They arrived in Johannesburg but her door at the boarding house was locked. They broke it down and found her there, lying dead in her bed.

That impi gently gathered up the body of the old woman and carried her all the way back to Zululand. The Chiefs, at the direct orders of the King, gave her a royal Zulu burial in eMakhosini, also known as the Place of Kings. So it is there that the mortal remains of a brave Afrikaans woman, who won the undying respect of that proud people, lies buried in the place most sacred to the Zulus.

BIBLIOGRAPHY

Anderson, K. *Heroes of South Africa.* Purnell and Sons, Johannesburg.

Aylward, A. 1878. *The Transvaal of Today.* W. Blackwood & Sons, London.

Balfour, A.B. 1970. *Twelve hundred miles in a wagon.* Pioneer Head, Salisbury.

Becker, Peter. 1967. *The Path of Blood.* Longman, London.

Becker, Peter. 1969. *Hill of Destiny.* Longman, London.

Becker, Peter. 1970. *Rule of Fear.* Longman, London.

Beinart, Delius & Trapido. 1986. *Putting a plough to the ground.* Raven Press, Johannesburg.

Bevan, D. 1972. *Drums of the Birkenhead.* Purnell & Sons, Cape Town.

Binns, C.T. 1974. *The Warrior People.* Howard B. Timmins, Cape Town.

Blackburn, Douglas. 1908. *The Prinsloo of Prinsloosdorp.* Alston Rivers, London.

Bloomhill, Greta. 1962. *Witchcraft in Africa.* Howard B. Timmins, Cape Town.

Bulpin, Tom. V. 1952. *Shaka's Country.* Howard B. Timmins, Cape Town.

Bulpin, Tom. V. 1953. *The Golden Republic.* Howard B. Timmins, Cape Town.

Bulpin, Tom. V. 1954. *To the Shores of Natal.* Howard B. Timmins, Cape Town.

Bulpin, Tom. V. 1955. *Storms over the Transvaal.* Howard B. Timmins, Cape Town.

Bulpin, Tom. V. 1957. *Islands in a Forgotten Sea.* Howard B. Timmins, Cape Town.

Bulpin, Tom. V. 1957. *Lost Trails of the Transvaal.* Howard B. Timmins, Cape Town.

Bulpin, Tom. V. 1959. *Trail of the Copper King.* Howard B. Timmins, Cape Town.

Bulpin, Tom. V. 1966. *Natal and Zulu Country.* Books of Africa, Cape Town.

Bundy, C. 1988. *The Rise and fall of South African Peasantry.* David Philip, Cape Town.

Burman, J. 1971. *Disaster struck South Africa.* Struik, Cape Town.

Burton, A.W. 1935. *Sparks from the Border Anvil.* David Philip, Cape Town.

Carruthers, Vincent. 1990. *The Magaliesberg.* Protea Book House, Pretoria.

Chapman, J. 1971. *Travels in the interior of South Africa.* Balkema, Cape Town.

Churchill, Lord R. 1994. *Men, Mines & Animals in South Africa.* Books of Rhodesia, Bulawayo.

Cloete, S. 1958. *The Mask.* Collins, London.

Cloete, Stuart. 1963. *Rags of Glory.* Collins, London.

Cloete, Stuart. 1969. *African Portraits.* Constantia Publications, Cape Town.

Coetzer, J.P. [1960's]. *Tales of Veld & Vlei.* Maskew Miller, Cape Town.

Colenso, F. 1994. *My chief and I.* University of Natal Press, Pietermaritzburg.

Colenso, J.W. 1982. *Bringing forth the Light.* University of Natal Press, Pietermaritzburg.

Conan Doyle, A. 1903. *The Great Boer War.* Thomas Nielson & Sons, London.

Cope, John. 1967. *The King of the Hottentots.* Howard B. Timmins, Cape Town.

Dapper, Ten Rhyne, De Gravenbrock. 1933, *The Early Cape Hottentots.* Van Riebeeck Society, Cape Town.

De Klerk, W. A. 1977. *The Thirst Land.* Rex Collings, London 1977.

De Wet, C.R. 1902. *Three years War.* A. Constable & Co., London.

Delegorge, A. 1990. *Travels in South Africa.* Vol 1 & 2. University of Natal Press, Pietermaritzburg.

Duminy, A. & Guest B. 1989. *Natal & Zululand from the earliest times.* University of Natal Press, Pietermaritzburg.

Fuller, B. 1953. *Call back yesterday.* N.V. Drukkerij, Amsterdam.

Goldie, F. 1963. *Lost City of the Kalahari.* Balkema, Cape Town.

Green, Lawrence G. 1932. *The Coast of Treasure.* Howard B. Timmins, Cape Town.

Green, Lawrence G. 1945. *Where Men Still Dream.* Howard B. Timmins, Cape Town.

Green, Lawrence G. 1949. *Land in the Afternoon.* Howard B. Timmins, Cape Town.

Green, Lawrence G. 1952. *Lords of the Last Frontier.* Howard B. Timmins, Cape Town.

Green, Lawrence G. 1959. *To the River's End.* Howard B. Timmins, Cape Town.

Green, Lawrence G. 1961. *The Great North Road.* Howard B. Timmins, Cape Town.

Green, Lawrence G. 1966. *Thunder on the Blaauberg.* Howard B. Timmins, Cape Town.

Green, Lawrence G. 1975. *Karoo.* Howard B. Timmins, Cape Town.

Guest, H.M. 1902. *With Lord Methuen & the 1st Division.* H.M. Guest, Klerksdorp.

Guy, J. 2001. *The view across the River.* David Philip, Cape Town.

Harrington, A.L. 1980. *Sir Harry Smith.* Tafelberg Publishers, Cape Town.

Isaacs, Nathaniel. 1971. *Travels and Adventures.* Killie Campbell, Durban.

Johnson, Frank. 1940. *Great Days.* Books of Rhodesia, Bulawayo.

Klein, Harry. 1951. *Land of the Silver Mists.* Howard B. Timmins, Cape Town.

Kruger, Rayne. 1959. *Goodbye Dolly Gray.* Cassell, London.

Lehman, Joseph. 1972. *The First Boer War.* Jonathan Cape, London.

Lowe, S. 1967. *The Hungry Veld.* Shuter & Shooter, Pietermaritzburg.

Mackeurtan, Graham. 1930. *Cradle Days of Natal,* Longman Green & Co. London.

Manfred, N.H. 1960. *Voortrekkers of South Africa.* Tafelberg Publishers, Cape Town.

Marais, Eugene. 1928. *Sketse uit die Lewe van Mens en Diere.* Nasionale Pers, Cape Town.

McNeile, Michael. 1958. *More True Stories from this Africa.* McAlan, Cape Town.

Mendelsohn, R. 1991. *Sammy Marks.* David Philip, Cape Town.

Metrowich, F. 1956. *The Valiant but Once.* Standard Press, Cape Town.

Metrowich, F. 1968. *Frontier Flames.* Books of Africa, Cape Town.

Metrowich, Frank. 1953. *Assegai over the Hills.* Howard B. Timmins, Cape Town.

Metrowich, Frank. 1962. *Scotty Smith.* Books of Africa, Cape Town.

Meyer, Prof. Adrie. 1998. *The Archaeological Sites of Greefswald.* University of Pretoria.

Millin, S.G. 1951. *The peoples of South Africa.* CNA, Johannesburg.

Milne, Robin. 2000. *Anecdotes of the Anglo Boer War.* Covos Day, Johannesburg.

Morris, David. 1966. *The Washing of the Spears.* Sphere Books, London.

Morton, Henry. 1948. *In Search of South Africa.* Methuen & Co., London.

Mostert, Noel. 1992. *Frontiers.* Pimlico, Johannesburg.

Packenham, Thomas. 1982. *The Boer War.* Futura, London.

Plaatje, Solomon. 1973. *The Boer War Diary.* Macmillan, Johannesburg.

Pringle, Eric. 1963. *Mankazana.* Eric Pringle, East London.

Rosenthal, Eric. 1951. *The Hinges Creaked.* Howard B. Timmins, Cape Town.

Rosenthal, Eric. 1955. *Cutlass and Yard-arm.* Howard B. Timmins, Cape Town.

Rosenthal, Eric. 1958. *Other Men's Millions.* Howard B. Timmins, Cape Town.

Rosenthal, Eric. 1959. *Shovel and Sieve.* Howard B. Timmins, Cape Town.

Rosenthal, Eric. 1961. *Encyclopaedia of South Africa.* Frederick Warne, London.

Rosenthal, Eric. 1979. *Memories and Sketches.* AD Donker, London.

Russell, R. 1911. *Natal, the Land and its Story.* D. Dries & Sons, Pietermaritzburg.

SA Archaeological Bulletin, 2002

Samuelson, R.C. 1974. *Long Long Ago.* T.W. Griggs, Durban.

Schapera, I. 1930. *The Khoisan peoples of South Africa.* Routledge & Kegan Ltd, London.

Schoeman, P.J. 1957. *Hunters of the desert land.* Howard Timmins, Cape Town.

Scoble, John & Abercrombie, H.R. 1900. *The Rise and Fall of Krugerism.* W. Heinemann, London.

Scully, W.C. [19—]. *Between Sun and Sand.* Juta & Co, Johannesburg.

Scully, W.C. 1984. *Transkei Stories.* David Philip, Cape Town.

Shapera, I. 1953. *The Bantu speaking peoples of South Africa.* Maskew Miller, Cape Town.

Shaw, C.S. 1990. *The Karkloof Hills.* Shuter & Shooter Pietermaritzburg.

Turner, Malcolm. 1988. *Shipwrecks and Salvages.* Struik, Cape Town.

Van Warmelo, D. 1977. *On Commando.* A.D. Donker, Johannesburg.

Wannenbergh, Alf. *Forgotten Frontiers.* Howard B. Timmins, Cape Town.

Williams, Alpheos F. 1948. *Some Dreams Come True.* Howard B. Timmins, Cape Town.

Wilson, David M. 1901. *Behind the Scenes in the Transvaal.* Cassell, London.

Wulfson, Lionel. 1987. *Rustenburg at War.* L. Wulfson, Rustenburg.

Wylder, Atherton. 1994. *My Chief and I.* University of Natal Press.

asian vegetables

A Guide to Growing Fruit, Vegetables and Spices from the Indian Subcontinent

Sally Cunningh

This book is dedicated to my husband, and to the people of Leicester, without whom it wouldn't have been written

eco-logic books

First Published in 2009 by
eco-logic books
Mulberry House
19 Maple Grove
Bath BA2 3AF
www.eco-logicbooks.com

ISBN 978 1 899233 16 8

Editing by Alethea Doran
Book and Cover Design by Steve Palmer, The Design Co-operative
Printed and bound in the UK by Cambrian Printers of Aberystwyth
Printed on Greencoat Velvet – 80% recycled post consumer waste

All Photographs by Sally Cunningham except where otherwise attributed to:
Peter Andrews of eco-logic books
Manji Kerai of tropicalfruitandveg.co.uk
Penny Turner

Sally Cunningham would like to thank the following for their generous help and assistance: Chelsea Physic Garden; Belgrave Hall Museum, Leicester; Garden Organic, Ryton Organic Gardens; Harold Martin Leicester University Botanic Gardens: Jepson Gardens, Leamington Spa; Leicester Guildhall Museum.

Further copies of the book may be ordered from eco-logic books. They also sell, by mail order, books that promote practical solutions to environmental problems, organic gardening, sustainable development, permaculture, peak oil, transport and related topics.
Visit their web site at **www.eco-logicbooks.com** for a complete list.

The Small Print
Whilst every effort has been made to ensure the accuracy of the information in this book the publisher and author accept no responsibility for any errors and omissions or personal injury that may arise as a result of actions inspired by this book.

CONTENTS

Spices 77

Ornamentals 95

Suppliers index 121

Appendix I: Plant names 124

Appendix II: Additional banana varieties 129

INTRODUCTION

The seeds of this book were sown when I first came to Leicester in the early years of my career as a professional gardener, over 25 years ago. I ventured into a local Asian supermarket, looking for spices, but instead my attention was caught by an array of exotic vegetables. What, I wondered, was that spiky thing that looked like a cross between a cucumber and a crocodile? And what did you do with it to make it edible?

Later, when I worked at Ryton Organic Gardens, I grew a range of unusual and peculiar produce from the seeds and plants that were available in the UK at the time. However, I found to my surprise that the fruits and vegetables I saw in our market or in the Asian shops were even more unusual. Later still, I worked with Leicester Museums and Kew Gardens for the Plantcultures project, a government-sponsored website describing Asian plants and their importance throughout history among different races, and came across more exotic vegetables I could not identify. I investigated further, but could find relatively few reference books to enlighten me, and none that helped me identify a plant by its Hindi or Gujerati name. Some plants had different names according to where they came from, and I quickly realised just how many languages there are on the Indian subcontinent. I have tried to compile as many names as possible for the fruits and vegetables included in this book, but I am sure there are some that

are lacking. For simplicity, only one Indian name, as well as the English and Latin, is given in each individual chapter: the full listing is provided in Appendix I. In most cases the Indian name given in the chapter is Hindi, but there are a few exceptions, where the vegetable is better known here by its name in a different language.

Originally, this book was planned as a brief guide to identifying vegetables and fruits from the Indian subcontinent, designed as an aid to other interested cooks and gardeners. Knowing the plants at first only by their Asian names, the only way I could find out about them was to talk to as many people as possible about what they grew, and how they cooked and ate it. I became fascinated. There was a vast breadth of knowledge, especially among the older Asian generation, about these plants – medicine, folk tales and a history of cultivation going back centuries – which was completely unknown or ignored by mainstream English horticulture. As the population of Leicester became more racially diverse, but also more homogenised, I was aware that this knowledge was gradually being lost by the younger generation – many of whom wanted to retain their heritage but didn't have the time to learn the traditions. I felt it was important that the cultural expertise was recorded before it died along with those who possessed it.

Being a gardener, the next thing I wanted to know was, could you grow these unusual vegetables in the UK? What did the plants look like? Could you get a reasonable crop? I tried selecting over-ripe fruits or vegetables to obtain seeds, and talked to yet more people. Kind friends brought me seeds from India to try, and others suggested what treatments might be beneficial to encourage germination and improved cropping, and how to cook the result. Space does not permit the inclusion of culinary advice in these pages, but recipes can be obtained by contacting the publisher eco-logic books.

Most of the plants in this book wont give huge yields when grown in the UK, and many of them require protection. However, all those described in the five main sections of this book – Leaves, Beans, Roots, Fruits and Spices – can be grown productively in this country. (I have used 'fruits' as a botanical classification which includes fruiting vegetables).

It is worth mentioning that the cultivation of this produce may become more relevant in our changing times. Air travel will surely soon be less viable than it is today, and it will become prohibitively expensive to fly fresh produce halfway across the world. And, as climate change alters our growing seasons, maybe we will all be raising chick peas on our allotments in 20 years time, and the sigh of lablab growing will become more familiar than that of runner beans.

The sixth section of this book, Ornamentals, covers plants that wont yield a crop in this climate but can still be grown successfully for novelty value. After all, it's an almost universal urge to plant a pip –and you may have wondered whether you could grow a mango in your sitting room from that huge stone. By trying out the seeds of some of these fruits or vegetables you could achieve a very unusual set of houseplants..

A few words about growing conditions

There are various ways of assessing how much cold a particular plant will stand before it dies, but these are never very satisfactory. A number of factors affect the hardiness of an individual plant: the inherent genetic variability of a species, the location from which the seed was sourced (e.g. from higher altitudes or otherwise climatically challenged individuals), and the microclimate of the particular garden. Finally, there are always the vagaries of the British weather to bear in mind. But it is worth remembering that, as a general rule, plants that are kept dry in winter, or those that have good drainage at their roots, will withstand lower temperatures and remain in better condition than those that have become waterlogged.

I refer in many cases to the 'minimum growing temperature', and sometimes give a 'hardiness temperature', which may be different. The former refers to the degree of

warmth required for the plant to actively grow. The latter indicates the minimum temperature a well-grown healthy plant may tolerate: such a plant can often survive adverse conditions for a short time, often at temperatures below those that would be expected to kill a younger or infirm specimen. I have also used the term 'half hardy annual' in the sense in which most gardeners understand it, namely to refer to a plant that requires a longer growing season than our weather will allow, and therefore needs to be started off under heated protection in order to achieve the minimum size to reach flowering (and fruiting) stage before autumn. This may apply to plants which, on strictly botanic grounds, are actually perennial.

Only for a few species have I referred to the required pH: unless otherwise indicated this should be taken as 6.5–7.5, i.e. more or less neutral.

Sourcing seed or plants

Many of the plants in this book can be grown from the seed or root of a suitable specimen sold as food in the shops. For those where this is not the case, or where a wider choice of cultivar may be preferable, a list of suggested suppliers is given in the Suppliers index. Many species are offered by UK suppliers, although in some cases it may be necessary to use international sources. For some vegetables I have indicated the relevant suppliers to try: this information is correct at time of writing although, of course, companies do change their stock listings from year to year.

Always try growing some plants outside, and some inside as well. You never know what sort of growing season you are going to get – and if some enthusiastic gardener hadn't tried (and kept trying) in the past, we wouldn't be growing celery, tomatoes or plums today in the UK. If a plant does well, leave a pod or fruit to ripen fully and save the seed for next year. Saving and resowing seed from crops that originally came from a hotter country will gradually self-select for plants that are better adapted to this climate – and the more generations of seed come from plants that have succeeded here, the better acclimatised the plants will be!

LEAVES

Chauli, amaranth

Haak, mustard greens

Kela na patti and kela phulm, banana leaves and flowers

Methi, fenugreek

Pan, betel leaf

CHAULI, AMARANTH

(Amaranthus gangeticus, A. lividus, A. spinosus, A. viridis and hybrids)

Family Chenopodiaceae

The vegetable

Chauli, or amaranth, is sold in bunches like spinach, but unlike spinach it can be almost any shade of green, and sometimes has a red or purple tinge. Some people prefer different colours of leaf – many Indians consider that the white or pale green forms have a superior taste, but personally I can't detect much difference. The leaves are fairly soft and thin in texture, so they wilt quickly once picked: they may be sold in plastic bags to keep them fresher. They vary in shape and size, from small, short oblongs to broadly elongated forms around 15cm (6in) long.

At the junction of the leaf stem and stalk is often another small tuft of leaves, which may have traces of flower spikes nestling within them. If the flowers are very obvious, the leaves will be tough and the bunch should be rejected. The younger the plants are the better, although older leaves can have more taste – they'll just need a bit more preparation as you'll have to remove them from the tough stem.

There are a number of related species of amaranth, and it is known by various names. Bangladeshis have a number of names for the different species: 'katanotey', 'danta' and 'noteyshak'. However, they all taste similar and cook the same, to a fairly gloopy green vegetable – self-destructing to a fraction of the uncooked volume, just like spinach.

The plant

Many of the sixty or so Amaranthus species are common weeds throughout the tropics, but all are edible. They are cultivated worldwide for leaves as well as seeds – especially for seeds in the Americas – as well as for their medicinal qualities. Although very tolerant of adverse conditions, including poor soils and low night temperatures, they grow best in high temperatures, bright sun and dry soils.

Amaranths are annuals, and can range in height from just a few inches to over 1.2m (4ft). They have an awkward habit of hybridising and forming local cultivars, so although it's relatively easy to recognise an amaranth, it's a lot harder to tell which one it is. Botanists seem to delight in regularly changing the names, but for the moment the following descriptions still apply.

A. lividus has a creeping habit and very small leaves, usually with a darker central blotch. A. spinosus is much taller, and can reach 75cm (30in) or more under cover or on a good site. The stems have small, thin, brittle spines that have a nasty habit of sticking in the back of your hand, and the broad leaves are tipped with spines too. A. viridis and A. gangeticus are comparatively short in stature, with small, smooth leaves.

The foliage of all types of amaranths can be very brightly coloured, and this has been selected for in the types grown as decorative bedding plants, such as 'Illumination', which has golden, green and raspberry-red to purple leaf markings. Indian cultivars include 'Pusa Early Bunching', 'Bari Chaulai' and the CO series, which (at the time of writing) can be obtained as seed from the US via the Internet.

One of my favourite names for amaranth is the 'caterpillar bhajee plant', because the long spikes of flowers look as if they'd wriggle away when your back's turned.

Nutritional value

There is much regional variation in the nutrient content of amaranth. The best-tasting and most nutritious leaves are from fast-growing plants, although this isn't really a characteristic of any particular species.

Leafy amaranth is generally a good source of protein, iron and zinc. The leaves are also a good source of lysine, an important amino acid. The seeds can contain up to 15 per cent protein, and are said to have the one of the most richly varied amino-acid contents of any vegetarian protein source.

Other uses

Amaranth is an astringent, soothing and cooling herb. The leaves are applied as a poultice for boils and burns, while a decoction is given for excessive menstruation and dysentery. Red-leaved amaranth produces a permanent red dye and is used in food colourings. The ashes of burnt amaranth plants have also been used as a salt substitute.

Certain species of amaranth are used for grain production, particularly in Mexico and Africa. In some parts of northern India the seeds are used to make laddu – little gooey sweetmeats. The seeds of A. polygamus, an Indian native species, are claimed to be an aphrodisiac and improve fertility. The grains are free of gluten so are ideal for coeliacs, but need washing first because of their saponin content. To do this, put the grain in a bowl of water and soak overnight, then rinse, holding the seeds in an old tea towel, until the rinse water is free of suds.

Cultivation

Amaranth is surprisingly easy to grow and can be found in most inner-city allotments. It is hardy to around 10°C (50°F). Seeds are available commercially, although there is not a great deal of choice of cultivar, except for leaf colour or seed production. If you can obtain seed from local Asian growers, it may be of an improved form selected for leaf production.

Really fresh leaves from bunches sold for food can be propagated by taking softwood cuttings from any non-flowering shoots. They will need some sort of protection to keep the humidity high while rooting – use a propagator or put a plastic bag over the top of the pot. Heating from below also helps: the rooting temperature is around 20°C (68°F). Success or otherwise will be evident after about ten days.

If you are growing from seed, the minimum germination temperature is around 13°C (55°F), but best results come from sowing a bit warmer, at 18°C (65°F). It's best to sow in April – if you sow too early the plants will bolt as the day length starts to shorten. Amaranth responds well to module sowings, but don't panic if the plants seem to grow very slowly at first, as they'll soon make up for it. Harden them off slowly and plant out

when you feel it's safe to put out summer bedding. They like an open sunny site, with good drainage and a pH of 6 or above, and are surprisingly wind tolerant, particularly the shorter forms. Water in well and keep them moist until established.

Later in summer, from June to mid-August, you can sow direct. Sow thinly in rows 30cm (12in) apart, or at their final spacing, at 15cm (6in) intervals, but with the same spacing between the rows. If you sow in a continuous line, thin plants to 15cm apart and use the thinnings in salads or stir-fries. Pick as soon as there are enough leaves to eat, as plants exposed to stress will run to seed. Harvest by either pulling up by the roots or cutting the plants down to within a couple of leaves – they will often resprout to provide a second cutting, if watered well.

You will probably need to protect late sowings with horticultural fleece on chilly nights, but the plants grow so fast it's worth the gamble. Expect a crop from spring sowings within two to three months; slightly quicker from summer sowings. If your plants bolt, it's worth letting them go to seed – they make an excellent source of food late in winter for wild birds. They may self-set after mild winters.

HAAK, MUSTARD GREENS

(Brassica juncea)

Family Brassicaceae

The vegetable

Indian mustard greens are usually found in Asian shops in the late winter and spring, although smaller quantities are also sold in autumn. Like most leafy vegetables they are sold by the bunch, rather than by weight. The leaves are like grey-green, oblong-shaped, slightly lobed cabbage leaves with a prominent midrib, 15–30cm (6–12in) long. If not very fresh they may have an unpleasant odour of rotting cabbage.

Each bunch of greens holds a few leafy shoots, which sometimes has a small head of pale yellow flowers on it, rather like those of tenderstem or purple sprouting broccoli. Unlike with broccoli, open flowers are not considered detrimental to the plants' use as a vegetable, unless the shoots are very old and withered.

The fresh leaves have a hot, peppery cabbage taste if chewed – a flavour that mellows on cooking.

side shoots, to a height of almost 1.2m (4ft) before the clusters of four-petalled primrose-yellow flowers open. Some mustard cultivars, particularly those grown as dual purpose for oil and leaf, have double flowers. The flowers are followed by beaked pods containing dark reddish-brown round seeds.

The plant

Indian mustard greens are an annual, sometimes biennial brassica from the colder parts of Asia. The plants are large, up to 1m (3ft) across, and look remarkably like the familiar UK crop oil-seed rape, except that they have paler flowers and (usually) smooth leaves. Oil-seed rape has hairy leaves, as do Chinese mustard greens and the similar but distinct Texel greens. Indian mustard as sold in the UK is not generally very hardy, although other cultivars can be grown in severe weather: in general, those with hairy leaves seem to be tougher.

The young plants form a central rosette, then a tall central shoot erupts, covered with leafy

Nutritional value

Mustard greens are rich in iron. As with other members of the Cruciferaceae family, eating them regularly is said to inhibit cancer.

Other uses

Mustard seed is used in all types of spicy recipes, and is ground and mixed with vinegar or water to make the familiar yellow-brown condiment. Brassica juncea seed is usually mixed with other species, such as black or white mustard, for maximum bite and aroma, as it's not as hot as either of these.

Cultivation

Easily grown from seed in the summer months, mustard greens

are just about frost hardy, to 4°C (39°F), but dislike the wet of UK winters so are best treated as a late-summer to autumn crop. They will overwinter in mild conditions, especially in city gardens, but need a well-drained site and perhaps a little fleece protection on cold nights.

Seeds are widely available (try Suffolk Herbs), although there's not much choice of cultivar. Brassicas readily outcross, but if you have a good strain it may be worth trying to save your own seed, as this is one way of improving hardiness. Even if your plants from saved seed aren't quite what you expected, it shouldn't be too difficult to select the best types to grow on, and, as all brassica greens are edible, you can still eat the others.

Sow direct, thinly, in drills 2.5cm (1in) deep, allowing 45–60cm (18in–2ft) between rows. Water well until plants are established to reduce attacks from flea beetle, and keep weed free. You may need to provide protection from pigeons or cabbage white butterflies using netting supported on sticks.

Make small successional sowings every three or four weeks if you have room, from late April to August: mustard greens are a quick-growing filler for gaps where other crops have failed or you've just removed something. They will take six weeks to four months to be ready for eating, depending on the sowing date.

To harvest, either pull out individual plants as soon as the leaves are large enough to eat, gradually thinning to leave plants 20cm (8in) apart, or allow them to reach 15cm (6in) or so

tall, and cut off just above the lowest leaves. Mustard greens don't always respond well to the cut-and-come-again method in UK conditions.

Like all brassicas, mustard greens prefer a fertile soil with a pH of 6.5 or more. In acidic soil they can be prone to clubroot, which shows itself in dry conditions when the plants look blue- or yellow-leaved and miserable: when pulled up, their roots are found to be grossly distorted and swollen. Put any such plants in the dustbin and wash any tools used, don't grow brassicas in that patch again for at least four years, and top-dress the area with lime. Repeated applications of compost (separated from the lime by either 60cm (2ft) or six weeks!) will often reduce the clubroot problem, not by removing the organism responsible but by increasing the number of microbes in the soil that fight it.

KELA NA PATTI, BANANA LEAVES AND KELA PHULM, BANANA FLOWERS

(Musa spp.)

Family Musaceae

The vegetable

Although the fruit of the banana plant is now highly familiar in the West, and needs no description here, the uses for banana leaves and flowers are less well known.

Banana leaves are usually sold as a cylinder of concentrically folded, slightly glossy, thin, light-green material, which looks almost like a roll of fabric. Once removed from the bundle the leaves are huge, anything up to 1.2m (4ft) long. They have no scent, and feel greasily smooth. They store well in the fridge and can be kept in good condition for over ten days. Although not edible in themselves, they are used to add flavour, as well as being a biodegradable alternative to aluminium foil.

Banana flowers are often sold wrapped in cellophane to keep them fresh. They are in fact the sterile male bracts surrounding the true male flower. The elongated cone shapes vary in colour from pale creamy-rose to bright buff-

pink. As the flowers age or if they are exposed to cold, they sometimes develop brown discolouration and sunken patches or withered edges. This is generally confined to the top few layers of petals, and shouldn't be a reason for automatically rejecting the produce. However, banana flowers are permanently frost damaged if kept below freezing for any length of time.

When a banana flower is cut it weeps a thin, white, sticky sap, which clings with remarkable tenacity to anything and everything it comes into contact with.

The plant

The world's edible banana fruits come from a single sterile hybrid, selected in prehistoric times for its absence of seeds and sweet flavour, which is propagated only vegetatively. Wild banana species are native to a large area of South-east Asia, from northern India to northern Australia: their natural habitat is the woodland edge. The banana leaves and flowers found on sale come from a variety of species, although most imported banana leaves are the by-products of large commercial banana plantations dedicated to growing for fruit.

The growth habit of the banana is more like

that of a grass or a palm than a tree, since it is technically a stoloniferous perennial plant – producing suckers from underground stems. Bananas have no true trunk, just a collection of old leaves and leaf stems, so never reach a great height.

Banana leaves emerge in a succession of spiral sheaths to form the trunk, and from the topmost sheath a large, drooping flower spike appears. At the tip, suspended on a naked, vulture-like neck, hangs the male flower, protected by a series of bracts that vary in colour according to the species, from green through yellow to a bright purple or pinkish-red. The female flowers hang in groups some distance behind the male bracts and are tubular, creamy coloured or yellow.

It takes 12 to 18 months from the flowers' first opening until the fruit develops. After fruiting, an individual trunk will die, but meanwhile new suckers, or offsets, spring from the base of the plant to repeat the process.

Nutritional value

Banana fruits, which can be eaten ripe or unripe, are high in carbohydrates, with some fat and protein. The flowers are astringent, mucilaginous and high in carbohydrates.

Other uses

The banana leaf is extremely versatile: leaf-sheath fibres are used as temporary string, and portions of the leaf are used as plates, thatching material and high-quality animal fodder. Because the banana leaf is an asexual organ coming from a sterile and seedless plant, it is used as an offering in religious ceremonies when a virgin material is required. Milk-based sweets offered to Ganesh, the elephant-headed Hindu god, at Diwali are often served on platters of banana leaves.

Cultivation

There are no bananas that will survive all year round in all parts of the UK, but several of the

Musa species are coming into favour as spectacular bedding to give a tropical feel, especially in city gardens. Some species are hardier than others, however, and are worth trying to overwinter, well wrapped against the cold – either in situ or in a frost-free shelter. Banana plants can now be obtained from garden centres as well as by mail order from specialist growers. The number of species available is growing all the time, and there is plenty of scope for the amateur gardener to experiment in finding the best-flavoured leaf or flower, as no members of the genus are poisonous. Some suggested species are listed at the end of this chapter.

Although the common banana is sterile, seeds of other species are available from catalogues and this range too is increasing every year. Some of the most promising bananas for growing under British conditions include the hardier *Ensete* species, which tolerate temperatures as low as 7°C (45°F), and *Musa basjoo*, which is said to withstand a few degrees of frost if well wrapped around the trunk. Perhaps the most reliable species for UK growers who can offer the plants some protection are *M. Thomsonii* and the extra-dwarf strain of the Canary Islands banana, *M. cavendishii*, which produces flowers while still comparatively small.

All bananas like warmth, fertile soil, space and water, but they don't all require a great deal of heat. They will take up a lot of room if allowed to – though many will stay a respectable size if kept in a fairly small pot. To protect banana plants left outdoors over winter, wrap up the trunk carefully with fleece, straw and sacking, or any other covering that will allow the stem to breathe but keep water out. For root protection, mulch heavily with straw or bracken, then cover with fleece, bubble wrap or old carpet. One option for overwintering a large plant is to dig it up, cut back the leaf stems as far as the tightly folded terminal bud, as well as some of the roots, put it into a big pot and plunge it into a dustbin filled with straw. Keep it somewhere cool but frost free over winter, then in late April take it out of the bin and move it to a heated porch or conservatory. Plant out in May or June when the leaves are already growing well.

If you want to try growing from seed, soak the seed for 24 hours as this improves germination rates. Fresh seed should germinate rapidly. Sow in a large pot using a loam-based potting compost, and keep slightly moist at 27–30°C (80–86°F). For flower production the

plants really need to have a huge pot – I look round local factory yards to see if they have large wooden crates that can be bargained for – or planted out into greenhouse soil, again using a loam-based compost.

If *M. cavendishii* is kept at a minimum of 15–18°C (59–65°F) it should produce flowers and fruits all year round. In a greenhouse the fruits will achieve edible ripeness. A single clump will produce only one flush of flowers, and sucker production should be limited to a single replacement plant to encourage flowering. Leaves can be removed whenever they're too big. For cooking it's better to select middle-aged leaves, as they're more flexible and less likely to be damaged than older foliage.

If you want to split a banana clump up, remove a piece of root with what looks like a big bulb emerging from it, as this is most likely to be a successful offset.

In Appendix 2 there is a comprehensive list of the best banana species and varieties to try for leaves and flowers.

METHI, FENUGREEK

(Trigonella foenum-graecum)

Family Leguminosae

The vegetable

Methi, or fenugreek, is one of the most commonly seen Asian vegetables, and I've found it for sale in some surprising places in Britain, from city post offices to major supermarkets.

It's sold in large bunches, and has long-stemmed, mid-green, trifoliate leaves like clover. The leaves are about 5cm (2in) long and have shallow teeth along the edges. Fenugreek is soft to touch and, like clover, wilts rapidly once cut. Sometimes it may have small flower buds among the leaf stems, but if it's got open flowers on it, reject the bunch as the plants will be poor quality as a vegetable.

The fresh plant, especially when bruised or handled, has a pleasant spicy scent but not a particularly strong taste, but the flavour is brought out when it's combined with other ingredients. Dried fenugreek has a powerful, sweet fragrance like freshly made hay.

The plant

Cultivated since 7000 BC in Assyria, and native to Europe and South-east Asia, fenugreek has a long and well-documented history as a cultivated plant. It grows to knee height or slightly taller, has an upright habit and loves poor, stony, well-drained soils. It's not hardy (although sometimes well-established crops will tolerate a very light frost), so can be grown only as an annual crop in the UK.

The flowers are small and similar to pea flowers: they are white to yellowish and often have a violet stain at the base of the keel. Flowers are quickly followed by the narrow pods, which are up to 10cm (4in) long, have sharp edges and, when ripe, contain up to twenty more-or-less rectangular tawny-yellow seeds. The dried seeds have a distinctive scent and are an important ingredient in many curry mixtures.

Nutritional value

Fresh fenugreek contains quite high levels of protein for a leafy vegetable, in particular lecithin, as well as vitamins B, C, phosphates and iron.

Other uses

Fenugreek is a valuable nitrogen-fixing green manure and the flowers are excellent attractants for bees. The whole plant is used

as a fodder crop. Because of their strong scent, the dried leaves and stems have historically been used to adulterate musty or damaged hay. The Ancient Greeks complained of unscrupulous hay merchants using fenugreek to sell poor-quality fodder at top prices.

The plant has a long history of use in Ayurvedic and Chinese medicine, being used in the treatment of ailments from TB to diabetes, painful menstruation and digestive disturbances. Fenugreek is known to stimulate the womb, has a mildly soothing laxative and diuretic effect, and and is reported to reduce the growth of certain types of cancer cell.

The sprouted seeds are eaten and are considered to be beneficial for problems of the male reproductive and urinary systems. The dried seeds, soaked, boiled and eaten as a spicy pulse, are held to cure fevers and all sorts of stomach problems.

Cultivation

Fenugreek is easy to grow provided the soil is sufficiently warm, and thrives in a well-drained, fertile soil and a sunny position. It is a very useful catch crop that stands the heat of summer and can fit in almost anywhere, taking only six weeks to achieve cropping size. Established plants are hardy to perhaps -4°C (25°F).

Broadcast-sow from the end of April to

mid-August, covering the seeds with their own depth of soil. Germination usually takes two to three weeks, but in the height of summer (after a thunderstorm, when the soil was in perfect condition) I've known it take only three days. The plants grow quite rapidly and suppress most if not all weeds, and can be thinned out to 10–15cm (4–6in) apart, cut off an inch above the ground (when they will resprout) or just plucked as required.

If plants are allowed to go to seed the leaves will deteriorate in quality, becoming tough and rather strong, so as soon as flowers appear either harvest the whole crop, dig it in for its nitrogen-fixing properties, or simply leave it for the bees and sow another patch.

Fenugreek rarely self-sets, as the winter frosts usually destroy the seeds, but you may see the odd plant popping up after you've grown it in previous years.

PAN, BETEL LEAF

(Piper betle)

Family Piperaceae

The leaf

Pan leaves are often found near the sweet section in Asian shops, as they are not eaten as a vegetable but are used in Hindu ceremonies and for making betel quids. These are composed of pan leaves wrapped around finely ground betel nut, with ground shell lime and flavourings such as saffron or other spices, and are traditionally chewed at the end of an Indian meal or at other times of social exchange. Pan leaves are also found in specialist pan shops, which sell betel quids made freshly to the customer's requirements. Red splattery markings on city pavements are generally a sign you're not far from a source of fresh pan leaves!

The leaves are shiny, leathery and heart-shaped, 10–15cm (4–6in) long, of a soft mid-green colour with prominent veins and short stalks. They have a characteristic spicy, slightly clove-like scent when bruised. Small sweetmeats or savouries are sometimes served on plates covered with pan leaves, especially at festivals, because of their non-stick surface and glossy good looks.

The plant

Pan is a member of the tropical pepper family, of which the best-known species is black pepper. It is a shrubby, climbing vine with semi-woody stems, which clings to rough-trunked trees, and is believed to have originated in Malaysia or Sumatra but is no longer found in the wild. Traditionally it is often grown around areca palms, which supply the betel nut. Tiny flowers hang in greenish-yellow catkins, male and female on separate plants. The male flowers are about 15cm (6in) long; the female clusters are slightly shorter and are followed by long chains of small red berries.

Pan loves heavy shade and fertile, well-watered soil, and tolerates heavy clays and deep river muds. It is cultivated wherever betel is chewed, especially in the Tamil Nadu region of India. There are a number of cultivars, including the slow-growing 'Calcutta' and the faster 'Mitha' and 'Bangla', although these are available as named varieties only in the tropics.

An Indian legend tells of a pair of lovers, forbidden to meet, who fled to the jungle together to escape their families. Eventually their relatives caught up with them and the young man's brother shot him with an arrow from across a river, killing him instantly. Clinging to his bleeding body, the girl cried to the gods for protection and leapt into the raging torrent. The gods took pity on them and turned him into a betel palm and her into a pan vine, so they hold each other tightly for eternity.

Nutritional value

Pan is consumed only in small quantities. The spicy taste is due to small amounts of essential oils, including eugenol, the same compound that is found in cloves and nutmeg.

The leaves are antibacterial and antiparasitic. Chewing them increases the secretions of the salivary glands, so promoting digestion and leaving the mouth feeling clean. The active ingredient, arecoline, is a stimulant to the lungs and brain, and generates a nice relaxed feeling.

Chewing betel quids has been implicated as a cause of mouth cancer, although betel and tobacco (which is sometimes used in betel quids) are both known carcinogens and it is not known exactly which part of the quid is the most powerful trigger.

Other uses

In Asian country medicine, pan leaves are used as a decoction for coughs, colds and other lung conditions, and to soothe inflamed wounds and arthritis. Pan roots are used to make a toothache remedy in China.

Pan leaves contain a volatile oil, which is useful as a natural pesticide and fungicide. Diluted and sprayed on cotton plants it destroys many pests, including cotton aphids, bollworm and whitefly, both at adult and egg stages. The extract has toxic effects on various groups of plant-pathogenic fungi, but seems relatively harmless to humans and other creatures.

At certain Hindu festivals and holy days a

string of pan leaves may be seen suspended above the door of homes and always above the door of a Hindu temple, to bring good fortune. Afterwards the leaves are left to wither and fall away rather than being removed, as to do so would be to throw out the luck.

Cultivation

At the time of writing there is only one commercial source of pan in the UK, Salley Gardens, although it shouldn't be difficult to grow once you've got hold of a plant. It is hardy

to only 16°C (60°F) and so requires a heated greenhouse or a conservatory.

Like most of the tropical pepper family, pan is easily raised from seed or from semi-ripe cuttings taken in summer, in a greenhouse or in covered pots to retain humidity, with bottom heat. If you find somebody who already has a plant, the best berries are those that are fully red and squishy. Extract the seed from its red pulpy fruit and sow in pots at 21–24°C (70–75°F) in spring. Separate seedlings once they are large enough to handle. Use a loam-based compost to pot on, and feed fortnightly during the growing season with a balanced liquid feed, or equal amounts of comfrey liquid and manure tea with a dash of seaweed extract.

Keep warm, at a minimum of 16–18°C (60–65°F), as well as moist and humid by misting regularly and standing the pot in a tray of damp pebbles. Provide support or some sort of frame for the plant to grow up: a moss-covered pole does very well, and helps keep the humidity levels up. Pinch back weekly during the growing season, to keep the plants bushy and within bounds. Harvest leaves as required. As the days shorten, stop watering so frequently and reduce the misting, but keep the moss pole or pebbles moist. Prune back in the spring. If you are lucky you will be rewarded with flowers and fruit in late summer.

Pan is almost totally free of pests because of its powerful chemical content, although scale insects can occasionally be a nuisance. Organic gardeners have a choice of several methods: the rather laborious option of washing leaves with a solution of insecticidal soap, or the quicker way – spraying with lukewarm water containing the nematode Steinernema (also used to treat vine weevil) and enclosing the plant in a plastic bag for 24 hours, keeping above 13°C (55°F). The nematodes will swim through surface water on the leaves and devour the pests. Non-organic gardeners can use a systemic insecticide, but should avoid culinary use of the leaves for the period stated on the container.

BEANS

Chairi, yard-long bean

Guar, cluster bean

Kacha channa, green chick pea

Liva, papri and valoor; lablab bean

Toovar, pigeon pea

CHAIRI, YARD-LONG BEAN

(Vigna sesquipedalis, syn. V. unguiculata subsp. sesquipedalis)

Family Leguminosae

The vegetable

Chairi are found in both Asian and Afro-Caribbean shops, usually in bundles. They resemble elongated French beans – over 30cm (12in) long or considerably more but, sadly, they don't often grow to a full yard long. The beans are very thin and smooth, without the bulges you usually get on the sides of over-mature runner or French beans: they have a softer texture and bend more easily. They are often sold coiled up so they'll fit in a grocery bag! Unlike French beans, the pods are blunt rather than sharply pointed at their far ends.

Chairi sold in the UK are usually green, and are in season for most of the summer months, though may be available almost all year round. There is a very pale green or white form grown in Africa, which is harvested during the spring, and a dark-red-podded cultivar from India, but I haven't yet seen either of these for sale in the UK.

The plant

Wild chairi probably originated in tropical Africa, but the bean is now grown throughout the tropics and is a valuable crop in Asia and Africa. Traditionally it is grown with sweet potatoes and taro or yams to make the best possible use of field space while providing nitrogen to enrich the soil. It is a useful crop in the tropics as it tolerates high temperatures and poor, dry soil conditions when other beans won't set.

Chairi climbs vigorously to a height of some 5m (16ft). The leaves are typically bean-like, trifoliate and plain green, but rather smaller and more pointed than those of French or runner beans. The plant climbs by twisting stems, in the same manner as a runner bean, rather than by tendrils. Its flowers are shaped like pea flowers,

in pairs, and are as big as sweet peas. When first open they are yellow with pale violet markings, but fade to pale blue once fertilised. They rapidly flag to close tightly by midday. Most forms of the bean are short-day crops, so seeds from Indian plants will probably set pods in the UK only after midsummer.

Nutritional value

Chairi is high in vitamin A and iron but has little other nutrient content, being mostly water and fibre: the cooked beans contain only 2–3 per cent protein and slightly higher quantities of fat.

Other uses

As with other legumes, chairi fixes nitrogen from the soil and so reduces the need for fertiliser inputs, making it an important part of the small grower's economy. The beans are also sometimes eaten as a dried pulse. The stems and leaves are used as animal fodder.

Cultivation

Chairi needs warmth and a fairly long growing season to succeed, so it's really worth attempting as a serious edible crop only if you live in the extreme south of Britain, or have a greenhouse or a conservatory with a high roof! On the other hand, it's a fun thing to have a go at growing, and you may get a sizeable crop of beans as a bonus.

In the hot summer of 2006 it did very well in Leicestershire with minimum protection, when more conventional beans failed to set.

The pods sold in shops for eating are immature, so seeds taken from them won't grow, although you may find dried red or brown chairi seeds in Indian grocer's shops, which will probably germinate. But you can also buy seeds from a variety of UK suppliers, and these are often selections of cultivars that are slightly better adapted to growing conditions here.

Chairi can be quite tricky to grow – it's prone to red spider mite if too dry, and readily contracts Botrytis in conditions of high humidity. Capsids certainly made a bee-line (or should that be a bug-line?) for my plants when grown in a polytunnel, but the resultant distorted leaves didn't seem to upset the plants unduly.

Sow two or three seeds to a 9cm (3in) pot, in late April to May, at a temperature of around 18°C (65°F). Once the true leaves have unfolded, plant out in rows, allowing 15–20cm (6–8in) between plants and 2ft (60cm) between rows. If you're going to try growing plants outside, don't plant while there's any risk of frost, even in a sheltered garden. Cover with fleece if the temperature shows any signs of dropping below 12°C (54°F). Although established plants will survive surprisingly low temperatures, even coping with a touch of frost in the autumn, the young, soft growth is easily destroyed in May or June. Ideally night temperatures shouldn't drop below 18°C.

In the US a root innoculant is recommended

when growing chairi, especially on alkaline soils, because the bacteria that fix nitrogen on the roots in its native region are different from those found on beans and peas elsewhere.

Provide a framework for the plants to grow up: this can be string or a net suspended from the hoops of a polytunnel, or a row of bamboo sticks (as for runner beans) if you're growing against a wall. If you want to use a growbag instead of planting directly into soil, you'll just about be able to squeeze six plants in, but four will give you an equally good yield and not require as much watering, and they will also be less likely to suffer from red spider mite. Once the plants are growing, encourage them to climb by bending the tips towards the supports, pinch out any stray stems, and generally try to keep them within their allotted space.

With low soil moisture the pods are short and fibrous, so once the flowers appear keep watering. You may want to feed the plants using a high-potash fertiliser weekly when the pods have started to set. Regular misting will help prevent the spread of red spider mite, as will occasional thinning out of foliage in the centre of the plants.

Pick when the pods are still soft and about 30cm (12in) long. If you accidentally miss one lurking beneath the leaves it's amazing how quickly it will lengthen, and after a long weekend away you may indeed have (almost) yard-long beans, although they tend to be a bit tough by that stage.

To save seed leave a few pods on the plant to ripen, stop watering and wait till the pods are rattling dry. If the plants develop grey mould or excessive spider mite, the pods can be cut off and dried separately.

GUAR, CLUSTER BEAN

(Cyamopsis tetragonoloba)

Family Leguminosae

The vegetable

Guar looks, to the unaccustomed eye, like a
pea pod or French bean that has been
steamrollered. The pods are about as long as a
man's finger, light green and slightly shiny in
appearance, with a satin-matt finish that feels
faintly slippery. Each pod tapers to a sharp
point at one end and has flattened sides
divided by a short hinge-like structure, giving a
triangular cross-section when the pod is cut.
Inside the thick-ribbed outer husk are five to
seven pale green, flattened oblong beans. If a
raw pod is chewed it has a slippery texture and
a distinctive taste.

When choosing guar, select fresh-looking
beans that are firm, bright in colour and
slippery skinned.

The plant

A straggling, scrawny annual, guar can reach 1–
3m (3–10ft) tall. The pale green, very glossy
leaves are trifoliate, slightly toothed, long and
thin with long stalks, and are quite tough to the
touch. They look more akin to a bramble than a
bean. When the young leaves are crushed
between the fingers the sap feels slightly
slippery. The plant has pea-like flowers in dense
clusters carried at the top of the stalks, ranging
in colour from white through pinks to purple.
The seeds are white, grey or black and round;
the size of a red lentil.

The cultivated form of guar may possibly
have originated from Cyamopsis senegalensis,
but it has been grown for so long that wild
plants are unknown.

Indian cultivars include 'Navbahar',
'Sharadbahar', 'Aharadbahar' and P28.

Guar grows best in sandy soils, with high
sunshine levels and occasional intermittent

rainfall: it can thrive in dry conditions where
other plants wither and die. Rain after the
flowers open can make the plants become too
leafy and produce fewer pods with fewer seeds
– but if the pods are meant for eating fresh this
isn't a drawback, because the plants will crop
continually provided they are watered and the
pods are being picked. Most cultivars are short-
day crops, but 'Brooks', 'Mills' and 'Pusa Bada
Baka' are day neutral and more likely to be
worth cultivating in high latitudes. Guar shares
the same microfungi that fix nitrogen on the
roots with chairi (yard-long bean), which are
different from those found on French or runner
beans.

Nutritional value

The dried beans contain 30 per cent protein
and 46 per cent carbohydrate, but the
immature ones rather less, with only 4 per cent
protein and 10 per cent carbohydrate, as well
as some iron and vitamins A and C. Guar is a
good source of dietary fibre, and the colloids it
contains are beneficial to the bowels.

Other uses

The seeds of guar contain in their endosperm a
natural hydrocolloid that expands when in

contact with cold water to produce a thick solution – guar gum. This is used commercially for everything from ice-cream thickener to shampoo ingredients. Only the immature pods are eaten by humans, but the stems and leaves, as well as the by-products of guar gum production, are useful fodder crops. The crop residue can also be incorporated into the soil as a green manure. Like all legumes, guar is an important crop for building soil fertility.

The dried beans are sold for medicine, as an antacid and for urinary tract problems. Because of their hydrocolloid properties, ground guar beans are useful for people with digestive problems, as they help regulate the frequency and consistency of bowel movements.

Cultivation

Guar isn't really suitable for growing in the uncertain climate of the UK, being hardy to only 9°C (48°F), although it would be OK in a greenhouse. It grows best with a soil temperature of 25–30°C (77–86°F), while the minimum temperature needed to induce flowering is 21°C (70°F). It will provide only low yields here, but the flowers are pretty, the flowerbuds starting white, becoming pink as they open and turning purple or blueish as they fade. It is an interesting subject to try out, if only as a pot plant – once established it copes well with neglect!

Seeds are occasionally sold by the more adventurous seed merchants (Suffolk Herbs, Thomas Etty and Chiltern Seeds have all sold it in the past), and are available from foreign seed suppliers via the Internet. You may occasionally see dried guar seeds sold in Indian shops as food or medicine. The pods sold here for food very rarely contain useable seeds, but you might find one or two older pods with big enough seeds to try sowing.

Sow in late March if you can provide at least 16°C (60°F). Plant two or three seeds to a 9cm (3in) pot, in a very gritty compost, and grow on in a bright position but away from direct sun.

Repot as required: they grow slowly until the days are quite long, when they put on a sudden spurt. A single plant will grow happily in a 27cm (10in) pot all summer. If you want to risk them outside, plant out in late May to early June somewhere very warm, open and sunny, and provide pea sticks for support. Young plants will need a lot of weeding until they are quite advanced.

Guar cultivars vary in height, and plants grown in this country are likely to be much shorter than those in their native clime, but potted plants will probably become leggy because of lower light levels here. Pinch out the tips to keep them bushy, and provide twigs to keep plants supported if necessary. Keep fairly dry, watering only when the top of the pot feels dry, and then give the pot a good soaking. Site on a bright windowsill, as guar doesn't suffer from scorching in the sunlight once established. The plants shouldn't require much feeding, but a seaweed feed may be beneficial when the flowers start to open. Plants kept inside may need hand-pollinating.

Pods can be picked from around late August with luck, and should be harvested when young and tender. Keep picking to ensure continuity of supply, but don't expect many – you'll probably be lucky to get more than twelve pods per plant.

KACHA CHANNA, GREEN CHICK PEA

(Cicer arietinum)

Family Leguminosae

The vegetable

Green chick peas are immature versions of the more familiar dried chick peas, and are sold in their pods. They are indeed green – vibrant and delicious-looking in the dark days of winter, which is when they are found in the shops here. Each oval-shaped plump pod is about the length of a man's thumbnail. At one end is a sharp point, which tapers to a whisker; at the other end is long-sepalled six-pointed calyx, often papery and brown.

The pod divides into two with a thin, dark stripe down the middle, and encloses one or two, occasionally three, fat, pale green wrinkled seeds. These can be eaten raw, when they taste a bit like a mealy, over-mature garden pea (but with a much nicer texture), or roasted or boiled.

The plant

Chick peas are an ancient vegetable, grown for at least 5000 years and probably for longer. The plants are small-leaved annual legumes, reaching about 60cm (2ft) tall. They have many-divided, ferny, silver to grey-green leaves and small white, lilac or blue flowers, similar to tares. The pods dangle from long stems like tiny pointy balloons. The peas inside the pods may be red, white or black when they ripen.

In the right conditions a crop of green chick peas can be ready in three to four months from seed and will continue to produce pods, provided they are picked regularly, as long as there is sufficient water. Over 80 per cent of the world's chick peas are grown in India, almost all of them in the semi-desert areas of Rajasthan. Chick peas are said to need only four rains to grow them – one just before sowing, another when the seed germinates, one while growing and one just before the flowers open.

Like garden peas, chick peas come in two types. 'Desai' is wrinkle seeded and is the sort seen for sale fresh, while 'kabuli', which is round seeded, is more commonly seen dried, although it can also be eaten fresh. Desai is more drought and heat tolerant so is grown in India and the drier areas of Africa. It has coloured flowers – lilac to bluish – and the dried peas have a thick, dark skin. Desai strains have greater resistance to seed-carried diseases, because the tannins in the seed's coat inhibit fungal attack.

Kabuli is grown in cooler, wetter climates. It has white or purplish flowers and the dried pulse has a thinner, white skin. Plants have survived -25°C (-13°F) under snow cover. Occasionally some kabuli cultivars have all the leaflets fused to form a single leaf, similar to that of a garden pea.

The whole chick pea plant is covered with minute glands, usually developed into tiny hairs, which exude malic acid – if you have sensitive skin, take care especially when harvesting. Some cultivars are hairier than others, and the mature pods are the hairiest part of the plant.

Nutritional value

Chick peas are a valuable source of protein, though less so in the green stage than as a dried pea. They also contain appreciable amounts of Vitamins C and B group, as well as iron and potassium.

Other uses

Chick-pea haulm (the stalks) is a useful fodder for cattle and donkeys throughout Asia, and is enjoyed by poultry – including budgerigars – in the UK. The plant is said to be injurious to cattle if they eat too much of it.

In Kashmir and Nepal, rubbing the juice of the fresh leaves into the scalp is said to encourage hair growth in the balding. Chick-pea leaves may also be boiled to make a warm poultice for sprains. In parts of India and Kenya the leaves are laid in water overnight and the resulting acidic solution is used as a vinegar substitute. Young chick-pea leaves have a slight twang to the taste, and could perhaps be usefully employed in salads if chopped finely.

Cultivation

Both forms of chick pea are hardy to around 9°C (48°F), so are a feasible crop in the UK, although in theory kabuli types would do better in our climate. They are worth growing as a luxury crop, as they're not easy to find fresh in the shops and are also quite pricy!

According to Simon Hickmott, who runs Future Foods, a breeding programme for chick

peas adapted to colder climates is currently in progress. In his book *Growing Unusual Vegetables*, he recommends using the cultivars 'Calia' and 'Kabuli Black' for growing in this country.

Some seed companies sell chick-pea seed, but you can get quite respectable results from sowing dried channa from an Indian supermarket. (Desai are big fat white seeds, while kabuli are smaller with a black seed coat.) Another useful source is chick peas sold for sprouting, as these will be freshest and will have been preselected for good germination rates.

A colleague of mine has had good results from sowing chickpeas in shallow trays in late November in a cool greenhouse with minimal heat, later transferring the plants to 15cm (6in) pots: these plants cropped in late March to April. Don't expect high yields from plants grown indoors, however – they take up a lot of space for only a handful of peas.

If grown outside, success depends on a good summer, but chick peas are useful for hot, dry gardens: the hot summer of 2006 was exceptionally good and plants sown outside in May cropped until August. Chick peas require a sunny spot, sheltered from strong winds, and good drainage. Fertile soil helps, although it doesn't have to have been manured for the previous crop.

Either sow in trays or pots on a windowsill in early April, and move the plants outside when the danger of frost is passed, or sow outside in May in rows about 25cm (10in) apart. The peas can be quite close-spaced or broadcast, as this helps them support each other – about 7cm (3in) between seeds is fine. If you've started them off under cover, plant out in double or even triple rows, allowing 7–10cm (3–4in) between plants and 22–30cm (9–12in) between each multiple row. You can provide a few sticks or a string mesh to give the plants some support, but they don't need to be propped up as much as many legumes, and

once established are an excellent ground cover. They may need netting against birds.

If you have mice in the garden, sprinkle the seeds with a little paraffin or neem powder to make them taste unpleasant – it won't hurt the seeds. When transplanting, don't put the plants out till they've grown at least three pairs of true leaves, or the mice will find the remnants of the germinating seed a tasty treat.

Keep the plants weed free until established, as they are initially rather frail. Pick once you can feel the peas inside the pod as large as a garden pea, and keep picking. The plants don't need much other care and, because they have a deep taproot, won't need regular watering.

Chick peas are generally trouble free, although they can suffer all the problems associated with garden peas, particularly the Ascochyta root rots, so keep them apart from other legumes or grow as a normal legume in a rotation. If grown in very damp climates the plants often develop mildew, as they collect dew too easily.

Sparrows can be irritating when they peck off (but don't eat) young succulent shoots for no apparent reason. There doesn't seem to be a cure for this behaviour, except perhaps getting a cat… although, as sparrow numbers are declining, perhaps we gardeners just have to be

PAPRI, LIVA AND VALOOR, LABLAB BEAN

(Dolichos lablab syn. Lablab purpureus)

Family Leguminosae

The vegetable

Lablab is an incredibly variable vegetable, and comes in innumerable forms. The types sold in the UK are usually called 'papri', 'liva' or 'valoor', but other names include 'val', 'bonavista bean' or 'hyacinth bean'. Although these different types are the same species they don't taste the same.

Both papri and liva are usually eaten as fresh seeds (like garden peas) rather than pods, unless the pods are extremely young and tender. Valoor is usually eaten as a whole pod. All three types are sold frozen in packs, like frozen peas, in Indian supermarkets.

Papri pods are papery in texture, about 5–8cm (2–3in) long, tightly curved in a scimitar shape, flattened and very thin. The beans inside show lumpily through the skin. The pods may be pale green to greyish or almost white, and sometimes have splashes of dark purple or grey-blue across them. They have short stalks, often with a remnant of calyx still showing, giving each bean a little pixie hat. At the opposite end of the pod is a sharp point, but this tends to get knocked off in well-travelled vegetables. One of the best signs of whether papri are stale or fresh is the presence of the little hat and spike at either end of the pod.

Even very fresh papri can look a bit sad and limp externally.

Young papri can be eaten whole, or cut in pieces, if very fresh. Over-mature papri pods are sometimes found for sale, and these are best podded, although this is time-consuming as each pod holds only about five beans. When the pod is peeled, the beans inside are slightly flattened, round and have a distinct hilum (that's the little stripe down one side where the bean attaches to the pod.)

Dried papri beans can be a range of colours from very dark grey to pure white, but papri beans sold freshly podded are usually some shade of green. They taste similar to papri in pod but are a bit mealier.

Liva too has scimitar-liked curled pods, grey to green, with a more matt finish than papri. The seeds are shinier and a more olive green than papri, larger and more rounded; usually three to six in a pod. Liva are sometimes sold podded and ready to cook. Like papri, the fresh beans show a distinctive hilum down one side.

Valoor superficially looks like a French bean but has pointed sides, which give it a sword-blade outline, and a pointed spike at the tail. This spike is harder than the one on the end of a papri pod and tends to stay in place no matter how old or knocked about the pod gets. Valoor are a bright green colour, although as they

become older they may take on a yellowish tint. There are said to be spotted cultivars in India.

Valoor flesh is less succulent and slightly more fibrous than that of a classical or 'true' bean, and inside are up to eight small flattened oval seeds. In the pods exported to the UK these seeds are usually too small to pick out individually, but sometimes you can find some with beans inside, and can occasionally grow them on.

The plant

Lablab was probably originally a native of India or Africa, but has been cultivated throughout the tropics for possibly as long as 3000 years – hence the many and varied cultivated strains. In many places, including much of south-eastern US and parts of Africa, it has escaped and naturalised very happily.

All types of lablab are very drought tolerant once established, and almost pest free. They cope well with many different soil conditions, from poor, stony, arid soils to levels of aluminium that are toxic to many other plants, and are a very useful crop for small organic farmers.

An annual or a short-lived perennial, lablab has two forms. One is a vigorous climbing vine that can reach 5m (16ft) or more in a single season; the other is dwarf, 60–120cm (2–4ft) tall. Some species of valoor have a dwarf, bushy habit, while others climb. Liva is usually short and bushy, but most cultivars are a little taller than dwarf valoor. There are short- and long-day cultivars of lablab, although not all are photosensitive. The earliest will ripen in 60 days from sowing, while others haven't even begun flowering after 140 days.

Lablab leaves are similar to those of a runner bean but are smooth above and slightly hairy below. They are usually light green but may have a purple tint. Lablab flowers look like a larger version of sweet peas or runner-bean blossoms and come in a gorgeous translucent shade of hippy purple ('Ruby Moon'), an equally delicious shell-pink to flame-magenta, or white, and have a sweet, light perfume. Papri often has large, white flowers, and valoor white or a reddish cerise-pink blooms, but there is an almost infinite variety of flower colour, seed marking and pod shape throughout the tropics. The flowers are carried in long, upright spikes from top to bottom of the plant and a vine is a striking sight when in full bloom. They are edible too, tasting vaguely pea-like – something like the scent of a field of broad beans translated into a taste, with an extra dollop of pollen – and look very pretty in salads.

'Ruby Moon', which is very decorative, with deep purple pods as well as flowers, is usually the only cultivar available from UK suppliers. It is also fairly cold tolerant. Other Indian cultivars include 'Early Prolific', 'Arka Jay', and 'Arka Vija'. Commercially grown varieties include 'Highworth', an early type selected for frost tolerance and high yields, and 'Rongai', a white-flowered late form more suited to lowland culture. 'Highworth' has dark markings on the leaves near the stems, purple flowers and black seed. Those clones of lablab with dark-coloured flowers and seeds generally seem to be hardier.

Nutritional value

Dried lablab beans contain 20–28 per cent protein, while those eaten young as a whole pod contain 4.5 per cent protein and 10 per cent carbohydrate.

The young seeds of lalab are edible and good, but in some strains the fully developed seeds are toxic, containing cyanogenic glycosides, although as with many other legumes these are destroyed by boiling hard for at least ten minutes.

Other uses

Lablab is grown for animal fodder as well as human food and is of major economic importance in most tropical countries. The leaves can be eaten safely by all types of livestock except horses and donkeys. Young, tender green leaves are also eaten by people as a form of spinach.

Because of its deep roots, lablab helps prevent soil erosion, and the dense leaf cover shelters the soil in violent tropical rainstorms. It can be grown as a companion crop with maize to provide support, reaching maximum growth after the maize has been harvested, or as a shade provider and

weed-suppressing vine (with the bonus of nitrogen-fixing qualities) for tropical fruit orchards. Dwarf cultivars have been grown as green manures and seeded into pasture to provide a dry-season feed crop.

Dried lablab seeds are fermented to make tempeh.

Cultivation

Lablab is hardy to 4°C (39°F) once established, but not quite hardy enough to do well outside north of Oxford unless in a very sheltered position or an exceptional summer. However, it will thrive in a greenhouse with only minimal heat, or in a conservatory. It climbs vigorously and will make a beautiful half-hardy display as well as providing a small- to moderate-sized crop.

Fresh seed is vital to ensure good germination: if buying seed, store it in its foil packet inside a sealed container in the salad tray of the fridge to ensure maximum freshness before sowing. You may be able to find mature seeds – or even ones that are already sprouting – in produce sold as food. If the beans inside the pods are hard and plump they're worth a try.

Lablab seed is sold for growing in the UK (Suffolk Herbs is one supplier), but these are not the same strains as the papri, liva or valoor sold here for food. However, there are seed companies in other countries that sell these strains: try B & T World Seeds.

Sow two or three seeds to a 9cm (3in) pot, as you would for runner beans. Seed germinates at around 21°C (70°F), so start them off in an airing cupboard, mid-March to early April, moving them to a warm sunny windowsill once seedlings emerge. Sow earlier if you have a heated greenhouse or propagator, in mid-February to early March. Remove the weaker seedling once true leaves develop. Young plants resent cold draughts and can be slow to recover once chilled, so coddle them by bringing the plants inside the curtains on cold nights if you're raising them on a windowsill. The minimum temperature at this stage is about 7°C (45°F).

By mid-May plants can be transferred to a greenhouse or a large tub or growbag. You'll need a strong support – I used stout twine attached to a glazing bar – as the plants are rapid climbers. In the right conditions they can put on 25cm (10in) a day!

Once established, lablab is very drought tolerant and grows well at 18–27°C (65–80°F). It does best on a slightly acid soil, pH 5–7. It shows considerable resistance to red spider mite but has the potential to develop diseases that seem common to all legumes. Bacterial blight (Xanthomonas) can be a problem, especially in long periods of high humidity and wet summer weather, so avoid growing lablab closely with French beans, which occasionally develop this disease.

Several 'val' plants grown by myself and colleagues had beans with a rough, almost serrated upper surface to the pods, especially when young. This may possibly have been a reaction to being grown in the UK, or was perhaps a varietal characteristic.

If any of your plants set seed, it's well worth saving some – they are much more likely to germinate the following season than those sourced elsewhere. Saving your own seed over successive generations is a tried-and-tested method of improving hardiness and other adaptations to local conditions. Allow the pods to remain on the plants as long as possible, until they are so dry they begin to split and feel like a paper bag. If heavy rain or frost is forecast, snip the pods from the plants, lay them on slatted trays – old wooded cauliflower boxes are ideal – and turn them regularly until the pods are rattling dry. Remove the seeds, spread them out on newspaper in a layer one bean thick and store in a warm, dry place, stirring them round regularly until they feel like the dry beans you buy for cooking. Keep them in a sealed container, ideally in the fridge, until next season's sowing.

TOOVAR, PIGEON PEA

(Cajanus cajan syn. Cajanus indicus)

Family Leguminosae

The vegetable

Toovar are about the size of a sugar snap pea, as long as a forefinger but not as fat. They have prominent oblique ribs, looking almost as if plaited. The pods are quite hard to the touch, unlike garden peas, and are greenish to yellowish-brown in colour. They have a coating of fine brownish hairs over a smooth skin.

Inside the papery-textured pods are small, smooth, pale green seeds, smaller and flatter than garden peas. Sometimes the seeds are reddish or spotted, and the cut pods may exude a reddish-orange juice.

In shops in large cities you might find ready-podded fresh toovar seeds sold in small plastic bags.

The plant

Toovar is a short-lived, scraggly shrub, sometimes reaching 3m (10ft) tall but generally shorter. It is grown throughout the hot regions of Asia, often as a boundary hedge along rice paddies or dividing smallholders' fields. It is also used to provide shade for vanilla crops.

Along the dark stems are alternate stalks bearing elliptical trifoliate leaves, about 10cm (4in) long. The leaves are smooth on their upper surface but have a fine fringe of silvery-grey hairs around the edge. On the underside of the leaves are oil glands, which emit a faint scent when the plant is disturbed.

The flowers, which can be yellow, yellow with brownish-red markings, or occasionally whiteish, are carried on stalks in loose clusters of two or three. The pods are covered in a fine down, and turn brown when ripe. As with chick peas, the pod hairs can irritate sensitive skin.

A large number of different races of toovar

derive from the various regions of India, exhibiting a wide range of flower colours, seed colours, heights, earliness of pod formation and productivity. The shortest cultivars are less than 1m (3ft) tall. 'Arhar' has yellow flowers and short pods, is annual and almost unresponsive to day length, while 'tur' has yellow flowers with violet or red markings and longer pods, is perennial and is very sensitive to day length.

Toovar are still grown in India and Pakistan with mustard and wheat, giving three crops from the same area of land, which ripen at different intervals through a single season. Traditional older cultivars are low-input, long-lasting crops, which enable them to be easily intercropped but prevent any form of mechanisation. Modern breeds have been selected for dwarfness and early maturity, but growing these continuously depends on an independent water supply in addition to the monsoon rains.

Nutritional value

Toovar pods are high in protein, iron and carbohydrates. The young shoots and leaves, which can also be eaten, contain 9 per cent protein.

Other uses

The leaves of toovar are used for animal fodder, and plants are also used to make brooms or for thatching. The dried stems are made into baskets. The roots and young leaves are boiled to form poultices to treat wounds. As with other legumes, toovar fixes nitrogen – up to 40kg per hectare if the crop haulm is ploughed in – so is a valuable crop for the organic farmer.

Cultivation

Toovar will grow in the UK but doesn't flower well. Although established plants are hardy to 10°C (50°F), the minimum growing temperature is 13°C (55°F), so it will need some protection. It also usually takes several months, sometimes over a year, to reach flowering size, so it's not really worth cultivating as a serious crop. However, it does make an unusual sort of houseplant, if a rather leggy-looking one. If you had enough, you could also try eating the young shoots as a boiled vegetable. The plant can be easily grown from the dried peas found in Asian and Afro-Caribbean supermarkets (sold as gungo peas in the latter), and seeds can also be obtained from some seed merchants.

If buying the peas from a shop, it may help to soak them for four to five hours prior to sowing, as they become dry with age, but viability is quite good even in older seed.

Sow in March to April, in 2cm (1in) deep large modules, or two or three seeds to an individual pot, and cover the pots with clingfilm or glass to increase humidity. Germination should take around three weeks at about 16°C (60°F). As soon as the seeds emerge, remove the film or glass from the pots and keep in a bright position out of direct sunlight.

As the plants grow they can be potted up and either hardened off for planting out in late May, or grown on in a 30cm (12in) pot as a houseplant. If growing outside, allow at least 30cm between plants, in a staggered double row. The young plants will probably need pea sticks or a cane and string to stop them flopping over. However, unless you know which cultivar you have it won't be possible to predict the ultimate height, flowering time or fruiting potential.

Keep the plants well watered and weed free. With luck the flowers should start to open from August and pods will develop shortly afterwards. Harvest when the peas are visible through the sides of the pods. Take care when picking the pods (if you have delicate skin you may need to wear gloves) because of their irritant hairs.

ROOTS

Arvi, taro, and patra, elephant's ears

Garmar, Indian coleus

Mooli, white radish

Sakurkund, sweet potato

ARVI, TARO, AND PATRA, ELEPHANT'S EARS

(Colocasia esculenta)

Family Araceae

The vegetable

Arvi, or taro, is the group name for a population of edible arums, of which there are at least 1000 cultivars bearing countless regional names. There are two main types recognised, normally sold in the UK under their Afro-Caribbean names: dasheen and eddoe.

Dasheen (*Colocasia esculenta var. esculenta*) is a large root (technically a corm), which may be round or elongated, with a slightly roughened hairy surface. The tubers can be huge, but those seen in the UK are usually football sized or smaller. Their skin colour ranges from yellow or brown to almost purple, and the flesh may be pink, white or yellowish. The pale patches on each corm are where the new plant will germinate from. There may be little lumpy dots present too: these are adventitious buds, similar to the 'eyes' on a potato.

Eddoe (*Colocasia esculenta var. antiquorum*), is a smaller, oval-round tuber, about the size of a goose egg. It is hairy all over and usually some shade of brown. The flesh can be white, yellow, pink or orange.

Old and past-it tubers are sunken, with shrivelled patches, and feel light for their size. When choosing arvi look for plump, firm roots that feel heavy and have no external damage.

Patra refers to the leaves of both Colocasia and Xanthosoma, a similar aroid, and may be seen for sale fresh in bunches of five or ten. The leaves are sometimes called elephant's ears, for obvious reasons: they are huge and triangular, nearly 1m (3ft) long. Borne on long, stout stems, they have glossy green tops and much paler undersides, with a bloom underneath that is easily rubbed off. Patra is most often seen for

sale around the times of the big Hindu festivals such as Holi or Diwali, as it perishes rapidly and is quite expensive.

Some Colocasia esculenta tubers and leaves contain calcium oxalate, which causes an unpleasant burning sensation (any gardener who has pulled up borage or comfrey bare-handed will recognise the feeling), but fortunately this is not too long lasting. However, it is important not to eat patra raw, as the calcium oxalate crystals can lodge painfully in the throat and stomach. They are destroyed by cooking, particularly if steamed.

The plant

Taro has been cultivated in Asia for around 7000 years, making it one of the earliest vegetables ever to be farmed. The wild plant probably originated in India but has spread throughout the tropics. Although it's not a complete food source it is a vital part of many tropical diets – one square kilometre of taro will feed 5000 people for 12 months! Cropping the leaves once or twice a season doesn't seem to affect the quantity of roots harvested, provided not all the leaves are removed and the plant is well watered afterwards.

Taro will typically grow to around 1m (3ft) tall. The leaves, which are held at an angle of 45 degrees to help them shed heavy tropical rain, can be up to 50cm (20in) long. A giant form of the plant exists, grown mostly in the US. Some cultivars have a reddish blotch in the leaf centre, where the leaf joins the stem; others may be marbled with purple in various patterns. The leaf stems vary greatly in colour – they may be pink or almost black on some cultivars. The more attractive varieties are available as ornamental plants.

Some cultivars have never been known to flower, and, even among those that do, seed is rarely produced. The flowers are insignificant but have a delicious fruity scent, something similar to a ripe mango. They look like elongated, squashed arum lilies of papery yellow, pinched at the base with a twisted top

Nutritional value

The tubers are mostly carbohydrate, containing 13–30 per cent starch, less than 2 per cent sugar, and no more than 3 per cent protein. They also have significant levels of vitamin C and B groups, with some minerals. The leaves are richer in protein (over 4 per cent), and contain appreciable levels of iron, calcium, potassium, and vitamins C and A.

Other uses

Taro starch is high in calories, exceptionally fine grained (each starch grain is only a tenth the size of a maize starch grain) and is easily absorbed by the gut, so slurry of ground taro has been used as a substitute food for patients who can't eat normally, or have to be fed by tube. It's also been used for making pharmaceutical powders, and in the manufacture of starch-based surgical gloves, particularly valuable for use by people who can't tolerate latex. Taro starch is also added to biodegradable plastics to help them break down.

The juice from cut taro stalks is said to stop bleeding, even from an severed artery: this is possibly due to its tannin content.

Cultivation

Let's face it, you are not going to be self-sufficient in taro in the UK. The plant is frost tender, so although it may be OK outdoors in summer it will require a heated conservatory or greenhouse in winter. It needs a minimum temperature of 16°C (60°F), although it can survive colder spells for short periods if kept dry, or if dormant.

However, it does make a nice houseplant, and even if you have just a large steamy bathroom in which to house it, within a couple

of years you'll be able to tuck into your very own tropical foodstuff. From a single large pot, with good conditions, you can harvest one crop of leaves every growing season, plus a couple of meal-portions of roots after two to three years – leaving you with one tuber to start again.

If you're lucky you may find taro sold with shoots already present, but usually you will have to select your own small tubers and hope they will break dormancy. Eddoe is usually easier than dasheen to get going, and is often hardier. Keep the temperature high, about 21°C (70°F), water generously, and maintain humidity by misting the plants daily or by standing the pot on a tray of pebbles covered with water. Leaves that grow too big or just get in the way can be snipped off at the base and used as patra.

A well-grown plant will reach 1–1.2m (3–4ft) or more, so you will need plenty of space. They don't need very high light levels, however, so are happy to sit on the floor in a large pot, which is just as well. Try to site the pots away from cold draughts as this often causes browning of the leaves. Other possible problems include scale insects and red spider mite.

Don't worry if the plants lose leaves in the winter – simply reduce watering to keep them barely moist, and with luck they will resprout as the light improves.

GARMAR, INDIAN COLEUS

(Plectranthus barbatus var. barbatus, syn. P. forskohlii, Coleus barbatus, C. forskohlii)

Family Lamiaceae

The vegetable

When I first saw garmar roots for sale in a local store I thought they were a rather superior form of salsify. It was only as I picked a few up that I realised they were something different, and I wondered whether they were akin to another member of the Compositae family, burdock, which I knew was eaten in Japan.

The slightly hairy roots are not much thicker than a man's thumb but as long as a forearm, mid- to light brown in colour, with a thin rind that doesn't rub off easily. The diagnostic factor that I'd missed in my mental classification is the absence of dried latex on damaged parts of the root. It's the lack of white juice when broken, unlike that which exudes from dandelion roots, which marks garmar as something different.

If a root is snapped there are visible starburst rays in the white to pale grey flesh, but no thick core. And then there's the scent! Delicious, somewhat spicy, undetermined... not ginger but

evocative of it; not chilli-hot but with a subtle warmth at the back of the nose after sniffing hard. It seems to become more elusive the more you smell it.

Look for firm, plump roots that are not limp, bruised or shrivelled. If your garmar is really fresh you may notice small leaves still attached to the root tops, or lying in the bottom of the box. These are small, tightly round-folded and downy-soft like a mouse's ears.

Garmar can be hard to find, and is not always called garmar: furthermore, two of its alternative names, pattur chur and pashan bhedi, are also used for its close relative Plectranthus amboinicus, country borage. It's a very seasonal vegetable, sold fresh in the UK only from January to early March, although pickled garmar is available all year round. The taste is distinctive: a warm spiciness, like potatoes or parsnips cooked with a lot of fresh galangal, with a lingering, garlic-like intensity that most Western palates find hard to manage in any quantity at first. It grows on you, however, and becomes quite compelling.

The plant

Garmar as it grows in India is an upright plant, variable in height, habit, flower colour and leaf size and shape. It reaches anything up to 1.5m (5ft) and is generally bushy and many branched. It has round to oval, small-toothed leaves of a furry, silvery grey-green, which turn bright silver when the plant is suffering from drought. The plant has an aromatic scent, not unpleasant but not immediately attractive, unlike the delightful scent of the roots. In warm and wet places it grows all year round and is a long-lived perennial. The upright racemes of typical two-lipped salvia-type flowers can be any colour from a very faded lavender to a strong blue, sometimes deeper coloured on the flower lips, and may have pale bee-markings on the throat. The bracts surrounding the flowers are puffy and distinctive, apple-silvery to grey-green, with a small tip narrowing to a hair-point. The flowers are attractive to bees and, if you're lucky enough to live where they do, hummingbirds.

Garmar is cultivated in the hillier parts of India, including Rajasthan and Maharashtra, and is propagated by stem cuttings planted about 20cm (8in) apart. The roots reach a harvestable size in about five months, and yields of up to 1000kg of dried roots per acre are claimed.

Garmar roots – photograph by Peter Andrews

Nutritional value

Garmar is eaten in fairly small quantities, so its constituents aren't of particular nutritional significance. It does, however, contain essential oils, principally borneol and bergamotene in the roots, and others in the leaves, including the powerful diterpenoid forskolin. There has been a report of a medicinal preparation (presumably concentrated) of garmar root causing acute irritation of the anus after ingestion, so it is perhaps advisable to try only a small quantity at first if it's new to you, to avoid any chilli-type afterburn.

Other uses

The roots and leaves of garmar have a number of important uses. In traditional Indian household medicine garmar has been held to be very useful for digestive problems, heart trouble and clearing up bad skin, and it's interesting how many of its possible 72 active chemical properties seem to echo these. It is currently under investigation for treatment of a range of conditions, from oral thrush and stomach ulcers to developing a natural-looking artificial tan by stimulating melanin formation in fair skins.

Garmar is often eaten after a meal as an aid to digestion, and is particularly good for people who don't want to chew pan but feel the need to nibble something so as not to be left out or (importantly), not to insult their host's hospitality.

Perhaps one of the most interesting developments for the gardener is its use as an aphid antifeedant (it makes leaves unattractive to greenfly), possibly due to the high terpene content. Garmar has been used in this way in India for centuries, although it is not legally approved as a pesticide in the UK.

Cultivation

When I first came across garmar and started making enquiries to identify it, it soon became apparent that, although it was known and used in almost every Indian household, nobody had ever heard of an English name. According to the books and the Internet, garmar did not exist. As I couldn't place it, I planted a root in a pot on the kitchen windowsill. Thus began a project which took over eighteen months to track down the plant's Latin name. Garmar grows readily from a fresh root, potted into a mixture of equal parts of general-purpose potting compost, fine-grade composted bark (passed through a ½-inch gardener's sieve) and grit, with a little bottom heat. It doesn't seem to require very high temperatures to develop roots, only around 14°C (57°F). Once established, like many other Plectranthus species, garmar can be easily propagated from stem cuttings. In Asia it's also grown from seed, but as yet it's too little-known in the UK to be available as seed here. If grown in large pots or in the soil in a greenhouse, you should be able to get a small but useful crop of roots.

Garmar is said to perform best under subtropical conditions and require a hot, humid climate, but I found my plants grew as happily as a common coleus when kept on a windowsill, pinched back occasionally to keep them within bounds, and formed a neat globe of leaves around 38cm (15in) across within a few months. Flowers developed when the plants were about 25cm (10in) high, having being fed at weekly intervals with a tomato feed during the growing season, but when I left the spent flowers on in the hope they might set seed, the plants became rather straggly. A plant kept dry on an unheated bedroom windowsill coped quite well with normal UK winter conditions, and was removed from the glass only on nights when outside temperatures fell below -5°C (23°F). Fertile well-drained soil of pH 5–6 is recommended in an Indian government publication, but my compost mix was not particularly acidic, and regular watering with alkaline tap water didn't produce ill effects. The only problem appeared to be whitefly, which made repeated attacks throughout the growing period.

I think garmar should manage quite well as a half-hardy annual outside in a sheltered border. It should be possible to dry off roots and store them like dahlia tubers to grow on next year, which will enable you to select for desired characteristics such as quicker root formation, hardiness or better flower colour. The dormant roots should be hardy to perhaps 5°C (41°F) if stored in a pot or box of almost-dry compost or leaf mould.

MOOLI, WHITE RADISH

(Raphanus sativus 'Longipinnatus'

Family Brassicaceae

The vegetable

Mooli is generally sold in two forms. The first is recognisably a radish: a tapering, pearly-white root topped by a tuft of fresh green leaves, no bigger than a young carrot. These are picked young, while the other sort is picked when older: these are smooth, thin, cylindrical, sugar-white and very long – 60cm (2ft) or more. At one end they taper to a point with a few root hairs attached, at the other is a short remnant of green stems where the leaves have been chopped off.

If a mooli is cut in half there is hardly any visible difference between the white marble-like skin and the white flesh, although older, stale specimens may show a pattern inside like a star radiating to the skin, indicating that the flesh is becoming tough. If sniffed at hard, the pungent, horseradish-like aroma may make you sneeze. The flavour is slightly milder than that of smaller types of radish.

Mooli roots should be crisp and firm, with undamaged skins and no holes. When buying young mooli, select those that are bright and fresh with unwilted foliage.

The plant

Mooli is a biennial member of the cabbage family and has been grown in southern China for over a thousand years. As its popularity increased it gradually spread through much of Asia. It is a cool-weather crop, grown in the more northerly or high-altitude regions or during the Indian winter. Although it was unknown as a commercial crop in Europe until as late as 1975, a large proportion of the mooli used in the UK today is grown here, and more is grown in Holland or Spain.

Like many crucifers, mooli has bright green, slightly hairy leaves, broad and long with irregular rounded lobes, clustered together in a basal rosette in the plant's first year. Mooli grown for eating are harvested at this stage. They can become quite large even in a single season, spreading to 25–30cm (10–12in) across. Some cultivars have floppy leaves, while others are more upright in habit.

In the second year the plant rapidly changes shape and develops a long shoot with smaller leaves, topped by clusters of creamy, dark-veined four-petalled flowers. These turn into long, thin seed pods, turning downwards as they dry out, until they finally split in half and, by twisting at the same time, fling the small round seeds a considerable distance.

There are a number of cultivars of mooli, which have been developed for different soils and climates. Those seen in the UK are generally of the long, thin type, but they can also be round with most of the root showing above ground, like a khol rabi, or short and fat with only a little root protruding from the soil. For those interested in the development of the radish in Japanese and Chinese cultures, Joy Larkcom's book Oriental Vegetables is an informative and enjoyable read.

Nutritional value
Mooli contains Vitamin C, a little iron and some protein.

Other uses
Claimed to improve digestion if eaten regularly, mooli is less 'windy' than European radish. It is also ideal for the make-a-monster-from-vegetables children's class in village shows!

Cultivation
Mooli seeds are offered by most of the larger seed suppliers, although there is not usually much choice of variety. For the longest, straightest roots, 'Minowase' types are best. They tend to run to seed if exposed to cold temperatures early on, so don't sow until midsummer in cold areas. The plant requires a fertile, well-drained soil with an open position and plenty of regular watering to encourage tender roots. The soil should be manured for the previous crop, and if necessary lime should be applied to bring the pH to 7 or slightly higher.

Sow direct in well-watered rows, 34cm (14in) apart, or sow pinches of seed at 10–15cm (4–6in) intervals – you won't need very many plants at once, so stagger sowing from June to late August at three-week intervals. Cover the seed to its own depth, no more, and thin out to one or two plants at 10cm (4in) intervals at first, then 20cm (8in) and finally 30cm (12in) as the

seedlings grow, to obtain the largest roots but still provide a crop in the meantime.

Keep the plants weeded and water regularly. Roots may split after a sudden summer rain or plants may run to seed during prolonged hot dry spells, so sow little and often to give you best chances of success. Pull soil around the root tops to cover them, or they will become green and hard.

Flea beetle may be a problem, and first shows as tiny shotgun-peppered holes in the leaves. Probably the best method of combating this pest is to grow the plants as rapidly as possible by keeping them warm and moist, as they are susceptible only for a short time, until they have about six leaves. If you expect trouble, invest in some fine-mesh netting or horticultural fleece to cover the seedlings until they are past attack size. Netting will also stave off cabbage white butterflies.

Small, tender roots will be ready to harvest from as early as six to seven weeks after sowing, but the longer ones are best if left in the soil until October or later in mild districts. You may find that the limiting factor is slug damage to the roots rather than plants dying off from cold, as they are fairly hardy, tolerating soil temperatures of a few degrees below freezing

SAKURKUND, SWEET POTATO

(Ipomoea batatas)

Family Convolvulaceae

The vegetable

Sakurkund, or sweet potato, is becoming more and more a part of mainstream British food, and is usually for sale in the larger supermarkets as well as in Asian or Afro-Caribbean greengrocers.

There are two types of sweet potato: the mealy-fleshed or dry, which are usually pale in colour – beige or greyish – and taste floury, rather like sweet chestnuts; and the moist, soft-fleshed types, which are more orange, yellow, or rosy-purple to red-chestnut, and taste sweeter. The tubers are usually elongated and pointed at one end, although I have seen a cultivar, probably of Afro-Caribbean origin, which has almost-round tubers of a glowing rose-violet colour. The orange forms are high in beta-carotene, which is converted to Vitamin A in the body.

When choosing sweet potato, beware of soft or blackened spots on otherwise sound tubers, as these frequently have patches of brown rot beneath the surface. This spreads in store and quickly makes the tubers useless. In late summer, tubers often have small adventitious buds starting to sprout from the eyes, but this doesn't affect their eating qualities unless the sprouts are very long.

The plant

Sweet potato probably originated in South America, but the plant was grown in eastern Asia for a long time before it made the journey to Polynesia and finally reached New Zealand around 1350. It was introduced to Europe in about 1550. It is a trailing vine that lollops happily to lengths of 2m (6ft) or more – it will scrabble at a support but isn't very inclined to climb unless you are very strict about tying it in every couple of days. Left unattended it roots all too easily at the leaf axils, so a patch can rapidly become

overgrown and incredibly entangled. For children brought up in tropical Asia, tending the sakurkund vines can be a very tedious chore!

There is a huge variety of leaf shapes and colours. The leaves can vary from palmate or deeply lobed to almost completely entire, and from heart shaped to elongate or oval. Normally they are some shade of green, but bronze, near-black, brilliant golden and variegated forms are known. A range of brilliantly coloured decorative-leaved types, 'Sweet Caroline', is available for hanging baskets.

Some types never flower (those suited to UK conditions seldom do), but others bloom prolifically. Many of the Indian cultivars flower well, with pale pink, saucer-shaped blossoms with a dark raspberry-pink centre, similar to bindweed flowers, in clusters of three or four. Seeds are rarely formed, but when they do they are small and round in pointed seed capsules.

As a native of the tropics, sweet potato likes high temperatures and a good supply of water when the tubers are forming, followed by dry weather to maximise production. The original form has a short-day requirement for inducing tuber production, but again there is great variation: in other types, tubers are formed fastest and are also highest in sugars when the day length is over 14 hours.

Nutritional value

Sweet potato is high in calories as well as carbohydrates – it is about one-and-a-half times as fattening as an ordinary potato. It is also a good source of Vitamin E, C and A (the latter is highest in yellow- or orange-fleshed cultivars.) The leaves are extremely high in antioxidants and are also rich in iron. Boiled for a few seconds they make a pleasant if rather chewy and gloopy green leafy vegetable.

Other uses

Sweet potato is popular in hot climates to make a rapidly growing green screen. The plants will grow to a remarkable size without soil, feeding

on the starch contained in the tuber, provided the foliage is misted daily. The foliage and skins, as well as the tubers, are used for animal fodder.

Cultivation

Although you can sometimes successfully sprout sweet potatoes from tubers sold in the UK as food, the chances of being able to harvest anything grown from them apart from the foliage are very slim, because of the short growing season and low temperatures here. It has been done, and is worth a try if you have a stray tuber that starts sprouting, but don't expect miracles. Fortunately, however, there are a few cultivars adapted to UK conditions, thanks to a great deal of work by NIAB at Wellesbourne: among these are 'Beauregarde' and the virus-free 'Beauregarde improved', which are richly orange-fleshed; 'Georgia Jet', also orange; and T65, which has white flesh. Minimum growing temperatures for these cultivars are around 7°C (45°F).

As it is a root crop, sweet potato does better with a free range, so open ground is preferable to a pot, but it grows reasonably well in very large containers. Anything over 34cm (14in) diameter will do, but the bigger the pot the better the crop.

During the growing season plants will need a minimum of 20°C (68°F), so they're much happier with some form of protection. Sweet potato is well suited to a polytunnel or a large coldframe, and ideal growing conditions are similar to those for cucumbers or melons: warm and humid. However, established plants can tolerate surprisingly wide swings in temperature, so don't be put off even if your conditions are less than perfect. Fleece or plastic can be useful on cold summer nights.

Sweet potato is not propagated by planting individual tubers but by 'slips' or cuttings from the shoots that arise from the eyes on the tuber. Several seed companies offer these unrooted cuttings. When they arrive, carefully unpack them (they can be annoyingly fragile) and plant around the edge of a wide pan pot containing equal parts of sharp sand and a loam-based compost or, if you have any, some well-rotted leaf mould. Keep warm, with bottom heat, and roots will soon develop. When you see white shoots emerging from the base of the pot, remove and separate the plants into individual 15cm (6in) pots filled with a loam-based general-purpose compost.

Soil temperatures need to be at least 12°C (54°F) before planting out into the ground, which in most of the UK means planting no earlier than late May. In the tropics sweet potatoes are traditionally grown on ridges, although this may simply be for ease of harvesting or weeding. Plant about 30–35cm (12–14in) apart, with slightly less distance, say 23–30cm (9–12in) between plants. Bury the plants deeply, with at least half of the stems covered, to encourage tuber formation.

The soil should be fertile but not over-rich in nitrogen, as this encourages excess foliage at the expense of tubers. Sweet potatoes like a slightly acidic soil but are not too fussy up to a pH of about 8. You may find that you need to pinch out wandering shoots as they get too enthusiastic. Organic gardeners should feed growing plants regularly using comfrey liquid, while others can sprinkle a little sulphate of potash around them once established. Slugs

don't bother the plants much but whitefly does, so keep your eyes open for pests.

Water well and in hot weather you'll almost be able to see the plants growing. Unlike ordinary potatoes, tubers form where the stems touch the ground. They will begin to form from around August but, if you can, wait until plants have been touched by the frost before harvesting, to achieve maximum cropping. The tubers won't survive frost in the soil, so lift them as soon as the leaves show signs of cold damage.

Once lifted, rub as much soil as you can from the tubers and allow the skins to set by storing them in a warm place, around 25°C (77°F), for about a week, then keep them somewhat cooler, at the temperature of a normal living room. They easily become chilled and suffer if kept cold, and rapidly shrivel as they dry out, so it's best to eat them fairly soon after lifting. The usual advice is that you're unlikely to be able to store them for longer than a month, and that for best results you should bury the tubers in a pot or tray of slightly damp soil or silver sand and keep above 10°C (50°F). They don't need to be stored in the dark, just away from draughts and anything likely to nibble them. Having said that, I have met someone who successfully overwinters his sweet potatoes every year in a cardboard box topped with newspaper in the back bedroom.

FRUITS

Bhindi, okra

Brinjal, aubergine

Chichingga, snake gourd, and parwal, pointed gourd

Dudhi, bottle gourd

Karalla, bitter melon

Khali turai and ghia turai, angled and smooth luffa

Kontola, spiny cucumber

Mandanmast, passionfruit

Papaya and babaco

Tinda, Indian round melon

Tindora, ivy gourd

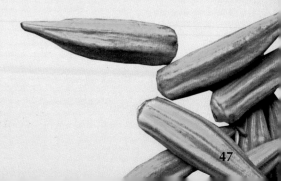

BHINDI, OKRA

(Abelmoschus esculentus syn. Hibiscus esculentus)

Family Malvaceae

The vegetable

Bhindi, or okra, is becoming more common in Western shops, and can now be found in most major supermarkets. The pods are pale green to mid-green in colour and wedge shaped in cross section, typically as long as a man's middle finger, and taper to a point at one end. Inside a bhindi there are a number of small seeds and several membranes, surrounded by a gelatinous flesh.

The plant

Perhaps surprisingly, bhindi was being grown in Spain as early as 1216, but its lack of hardiness meant it was never much cultivated in the colder climes of northern Europe. Originally the plant came from North Africa, but it has spread extensively throughout hot regions of the world.

Bhindi is an attractive but very cold-sensitive garden plant, with creamy-primrose, dark-eyed flowers like baby hollyhocks, which last just one day (or even less in hot weather) before shrivelling. It reaches a height of 1–1.3m (3–4ft) in the UK, but grows much larger, as tall as runner beans, in the tropics. It is very drought tolerant once established.

The leaves are slightly downy, scallop-shaped or palmate according to cultivar, and, like many other members of the Malvaceae family (such as the hollyhock), prone to rust diseases. Rust is usually treated as a cosmetic problem in mature plants, but can cause losses at the seedling stage

or in older, stressed individuals.

A red-leaved form of bhindi is known, which is even more striking than the common green and has beautiful blood-red pods that not only turn cooking liquids crimson but retain most of their colour when cooked. Sadly, this variety is even less cold tolerant than the green type, and is certainly suitable only for protected cultivation in the UK. It has pale cream flowers just like its green cousin.

Nutritional value

Bhindi is a good source of fibre, Vitamin C, iron, calcium and potassium. The ripe seeds contain up to 25 per cent oil.

Other uses

Ripe bhindi seeds may be eaten roasted, or ground and used as a coffee substitute. Infusions of the pods have been used to treat coughs and urinary problems. The slimy, sticky substance produced when bhindi pods are boiled has been incorporated into artificial blood to give it the correct viscosity.

Cultivation

Bhindi is a problem child for high-latitude climates with fluctuating temperatures: it needs long days, warm temperatures and a stable

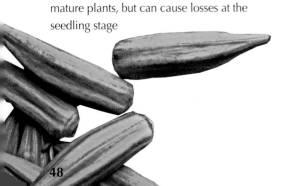

sunlight supply, but in Britain gets stuck with the vagaries of our summer. Some growers claim success every year, but bhindi should really be treated as a maybe, rather than a staple crop anywhere further north than Coventry. I am told it is possible to achieve a outdoor crop from the green variety, from an indoor sowing, in central London and Cornwall, but in most parts of the country the plant must be grown under protection. It is hardy to perhaps 16°C (60°F), although the ideal growing temperature is similar to that for cucumbers, at around 21°C (70°F).

Most seed merchants sell one or two cultivars – normally 'F1 Pure Luck'! However, I have known much better results from imported Caribbean seeds, so it is possible that the choice of varieties in the UK is partly to blame for cultivation problems here. 'Clemson's Spineless', a heirloom or heritage variety, has done better than 'F1 Pure Luck' grown under glass at Ryton. The only red cultivar sold here is 'Burgundy'. Both of these varieties are available from Chiltern Seeds and Chase Organics.

Germination can be erratic and take two to four weeks or more. Soaking the seed overnight, pouring boiling water over it or even rinsing it in bleach have all been recommended to induce the process. Sow in large modules, or two or three seeds in individual 9cm (3in) pots

in early April to May, at temperatures of 18°C (65°F). Pot the plants up as they grow, and try not to allow the seedlings to suffer a check in growth. They will need staking at some stage, but encourage the plants to bush out by regular pinching of the tips. Bhindi hates confined roots. You can fit three plants comfortably in a growbag, and they will tolerate a 30cm (12in) pot, but never do as well in pots as in greenhouse or polytunnel soil. Plants in the ground should be 30cm (12in) apart, with 45cm (18in) between rows.

The final growing medium should be high in organic matter and well drained. Feed using a high-potash liquid fertiliser every two weeks as soon as flower buds form, and continue to feed throughout the summer. Hand-pollination is not required, as the flowers are frequently visited by small insects and hoverflies – although putting a known attractant plant such as single French marigolds or coriander next to the bhindi will help bring insects along.

Regular watering and frequent dampening down of greenhouse paths or misting of plants will help keep the humidity to the desired level. Pick the pods when small, otherwise further production will stop. They will keep for over a week in the salad tray of the fridge. Each plant should produce between 15 and 50 pods over a season, depending on the site and cultivar.

Okra - photograph by Manji Kerai

BRINJAL, AUBERGINE

(Solanum melongena)

Family Solanaceae

The vegetable

Brinjal, or aubergines, come in all shapes and sizes, from the tiny little clusters of green berries sometimes called pea aubergines, through the round, pure white, dappled green, or occasionally orange-and-purple globes, to the more familiar long, purple or stripy fruits and the purple-black, oval variety seen in supermarkets everywhere.

When buying brinjal, choose those with a shiny skin as they will not be over-mature – fruits that are too old often turn bitter. Because of their tough skins, brinjal travel well and will keep for up to ten days in the salad tray of the fridge.

The plant

Brinjal were first cultivated in China in 500BC, and have long been grown in India. The different forms and colours of the vegetable now in existence appear to have been recorded in the mid fifteenth century, with no further refinements being developed since, other than in terms of fruiting earlier or more plentifully.

Brinjal is a short-lived perennial (in sufficiently warm conditions), stiffly upright in habit. It needs long, hot summers and regular water supplies, and does best on a well-drained, fertile soil. The plants reach a height of 1–1.6m (3–5ft), although their habit and size vary greatly. They have broad, dark-green, irregularly lobed leaves a bit like a potato leaflet. Some cultivars are almost spineless, while others are quite savagely armed with spines on the underside of the leaves and on the stems.

The flowers range in colour from purple-pink through pale lilac to dirty white, with five petals bent sharply backward, and a cluster of central yellow stamens. They are shaped like potato flowers, as are many other members of the Solanaceae family. The fruits have a star-shaped calyx enveloping the top, which again is often prickly. Small-fruited types – the 'pea aubergines' – which are used more in Thailand and Mexico, carry clusters of five to seven fruits like bunches of grapes and tend to become invasive, sprawling over a square metre or more.

Nutritional value

Brinjal is rich in vitamins C and the B group. The flesh also contains appreciable quantities of iron and calcium, and just 3 per cent carbohydrate.

Other uses

Brinjal leaves and skins are used fresh in India to place around the base of other plants as a mulch, as they are said to inhibit caterpillars – which is perhaps because of the spines. Regular eating of white brinjal is held to be beneficial for diabetics, and is also said to help control bean-induced flatulence.

Cultivation

Growing brinjal under cover in the UK is relatively easy if you can keep the temperatures high enough. They need a warmer place than peppers or tomatoes, so are ideal for a heated greenhouse or a conservatory, but will crop in a polytunnel or cool greenhouse if started off somewhere warmer. Unless you live in the south or have a very sheltered garden they're not good plants for outdoors.

You will need to buy seed, as the UK season isn't long enough to develop fruits to full ripeness, and the vegetables sold for eating are immature. In recent years the more flamboyant cultivars

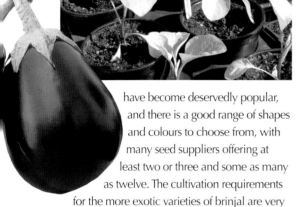

have become deservedly popular, and there is a good range of shapes and colours to choose from, with many seed suppliers offering at least two or three and some as many as twelve. The cultivation requirements for the more exotic varieties of brinjal are very similar to those for the more familiar types, although they do tend to be untidier plants.

Round green varieties include 'Thai Dark Round Green' and 'Thai Green Pea' (Chiltern Seeds), while 'Mohican F1' (Thompson & Morgan) and 'Snowy' (Chilterns) are white and more or less conical. 'Turkish Orange' (Chilterns) is green, turning eventually orange, quite small and round, and strong tasting. 'Calliope' (Thompson & Morgan) is a reddish pinky-purple fruit splashed over with cream, while 'Fairy Tale F1' and 'Graffiti' (commercial seed quantities only) and 'Listada di Gandia' (Thompson & Morgan) are all blue-purple splashed with white. 'Lousinana Long Green' (Chilterns) is pale green with darker green stripes, and banana shaped. 'Long Purple' (Chilterns, Kings and Chase Organics) is more interesting looking than the supermarket fruits, being long, skinny and very purple (though when very ripe it does turn blackish-maroon). 'Violetta di Firenze', a widely available Italian cultivar, is round and purple with creamy splashes and is an excellent and reliable cropper.

Sow early on, in late March or even sooner if you can, two or three seeds to a 9cm (3in) pot at 18–21°C (65–70°F), and repot as necessary. If growing in containers, the plants will eventually need a 30cm (12in) pot; or you can fit three to a growbag. Planted in greenhouse or polytunnel soil, brinjal should be spaced 60cm (2ft) apart, with plenty of headroom.

Pinch out plants at 30–45cm (12–18in) and support with a string or bamboo cane , tying in as required. Minimum temperatures are around 16°C (60°F), but for optimum growth they should be 21°C (70°F) or more. If temperatures drop too low the plants will stop growing and remain in a state of suspended animation until conditions change.

Keep the plants well watered. Misting or dampening down greenhouse paths will help to maintain humidity. A high-potash fertiliser every two weeks will be beneficial, as will regular doses of seaweed-based feed.

The plants shouldn't require hand-pollination even in a greenhouse, as they attract small insects, but if in doubt you can brush your fingers from one flower to another to transfer pollen. Individual flowers contain both male and female parts, but the male parts develop pollen before the female part of the flower is receptive, so fertilisation is more successful if pollen from a neighbouring flower is used. Harvest the fruits as soon as they are large enough and are shiny skinned. Remove dead leaves, as they can rapidly become infected with Botrytis.

Like many other indoor plants, brinjal can, and often does, suffer from red spider mite, whitefly and aphids.

Photograph by Penny Turner

CHICHINGGA, SNAKE GOURD

(Trichosanthes cucumerina var. anguina)

PARWAL, POINTED GOURD

(T. dioica)

Family Cucurbitaceae)

The vegetable

The more conventional forms of chichingga found in shops look similar to a small elongated marrow, with a firm, pale greenish surface and a slight swelling at the far end. Others are twisted in shape. Older chichingga can be much bigger, over 1.5m (5ft) long! They sometimes have vestigial stripes, which are most noticeable near the stalk end. Inside, the juicy flesh is pale coloured and similar in texture to that of a courgette or cucumber, depending on the stage of ripeness and cultivar. There are sometimes immature seeds present, which are oval-oblong and slightly bean-like.

Parwal is smaller than chichingga, with a less angled surface, and has distinctly pointy ends. It sometimes has four or five paler stripes running stalk- to tail-end, and the skin can become glossy, especially when polished – as it sometimes is to make the fruits look more enticing to prospective purchasers. Parwal are often a darker green than chichingga, but this varies according to cultivar.

Both vegetables have a fine, white, wax-like coating, similar to the bloom on a grape, which is rubbed off with handling to show the green skin below.

The plant

Chichingga grows wild throughout most of Asia and Australasia, and has long been cultivated in India. It is an annual herbaceous plant; a useful crop with harvestable fruits in as little as three months after sowing.

The deeply lobed leaves, which may have three or seven segments, are slightly prickly

LEFT: The Snake Gourd plant

BELOW: The Parwal, or Pointed Gourd

and look similar to those of a courgette. They have a faint, musky odour when bruised. Chichingga flowers are 10cm (4inch) wide and pure white, with fancy, finely cut frilly bits around the edges, like a rather superior lace doily. They open in the late afternoon and on dull days stay open for a while the next morning, but are usually hanging limp by noon.

Mature chichingga can reach 2m (6ft) long. At first the fruits hang straight, but as soon as they encounter the least obstacle they twist and twine into very weird shapes – hence the name 'snake gourd'. When ripe, at about 1.5m, they turn orange.

Indian cultivars include the CO series, TA19, and the recently released variety from Kerala Agricultural University, 'Manusaree', which is claimed to be the heaviest-cropping plant yet.

Parwal is grown in the hotter regions of Asia. It is a perennial, also a herbaceous climber, and produces fruit for eight months of the year, from the rains until late December. The woolly, slender stems are more deeply angled than those of chichingga, and the heart-shaped, very rigid leaves are rough to the touch. The pure white flowers

are beautifully fringed, with fantastic knotted dangly bits hanging from their edges.

Like chichingga, the small oval fruits are bright orange-coloured when ripe, but reach only about 10cm (4in) long. They aren't fit to eat at this stage, and turn very soft.

Indian cultivars include 'Swarna Alaukik', 'Swarna Rekha' and the FP series.

Nutritional value

Chichingga aren't really high in any nutrients as they are mostly water, though if you eat enough of them you do gain a little vitamin C. They are good for slimmers, as the cellulose and other fibres in them makes you feel full and helps the digestion.

Parwal are rich in protein (for a cucurbit) and Vitamin A.

Other uses

The roots of chichingga have been used as an abortificant, although there is no risk to pregnant women from eating the fruits. They contain beta-trichosanthin, a complex protein that has excited interest in the US recently because it has been shown to have the capacity to stop the AIDS virus from growing.

Parwal has ulcer-healing properties and, like a number of other Indian cucurbits, has been shown to lower both blood sugar and fatty acid levels.

Cultivation

Chichingga and parwal are fast-growing and easily raised from seed, but are unlikely to thrive outdoors in all but the most sheltered of UK gardens. They like growing in a cool greenhouse or polytunnel, as most conservatories get a bit too hot for them and usually lack humidity. Hardy to perhaps 7°C (45°F), they need around 18°C (65°F) to really grow. The plants don't need full sun (I've seen a very happy chichingga growing under white polythene on a Birmingham allotment), but do appreciate lots of deep, well-mucked soil and plenty of water during the growing season.

Chichingga or parwal sold in the UK are immature, so won't contain viable seeds; however, various seed companies sell the seeds as snake gourd or club gourd. You may not necessarily get a Trichosanthes species under this name though, so check which gourd it is! Seeds in India tend to produce an over-abundance of male plants, but this hasn't been a problem among people I've talked to who've grown them here. The plants can also be grown from root or shoot cuttings.

Germination temperature is around 22°C (72°F). Sow the seeds quite late, as they rapidly outgrow a windowsill. Plant out into greenhouse soil or a very large tub; alternatively, allow no more than two to a growbag.

Male and female flowers are carried on separate plants. The male flowers appear first; female ones open a little later. In cold seasons you may need to hand-pollinate the flowers, although they usually manage quite well on their own: they seem very popular with hoverflies.

The plants will do better if you give them something to climb up, and the chichingga fruits will tend to grow straighter this way. In India, little weights are tied to the ends of chichingga gourds to help them grow straight down – you can use anything to weight them, from bottles to bits of old iron.

Potted or growbag-grown plants benefit from a regular high potash feed, and the more you water the plants the larger your fruit will grow, just like a pumpkin. If you find that a fruit has touched the ground, put a bit of slate or board under it to stop it rotting, as you would with a pumpkin or marrow. Expect chichingga to grow into unusual shapes.

Pick fruits when they are 15–30cm (6–12in) long, as they rapidly go tough once over-mature. If you want to save seed for next year, leave a fruit or two to turn orangey-red and squishy. Pick the seeds from the gloopy flesh, wash them in a sieve and dry on kitchen paper, then store somewhere cool till next spring. A word of warning, however – like all the cucurbit family Trichosanthes don't always breed true and can be promiscuous with it, gaily crossing with pumpkins, cucumbers and melons… so you may have a surprise in store.

DUDHI, BOTTLE GOURD

(Lagenaria siceraria)

Family Cucurbitaceae

The vegetable

Dudhi are similar to a small marrow but have a much sleeker skin. They can be pale yellow to cream in colour, or a pale to pea green. Eaten as immature fruits, they vary quite widely in shape at this stage – sometimes they are long, thin and somewhat club shaped, sometimes more swollen at the base, and occasionally round. As the fruits get bigger and mature (when they become too stringy to eat) they become oval or round.

Even a young dudhi on sale may be as much as 60cm (2ft) long and weigh over 3kg (6lb), but fully mature ones can be much bigger. Inside a baby dudhi is porous white flesh and sometimes a few immature seeds. More mature dudhi are meatier than young ones, and up to a point they will improve with keeping, as the skin gradually allows the moisture within to evaporate through the pores and intensify the flavour. Older specimens may contain a central hollow, but the flesh is still well flavoured and juicy. When buying dudhi to eat, look for bright-skinned, firm and heavy fruit. The seeds of a more mature dudhi in the shops, though more developed than in a younger one, will still not be viable.

The plant

Dudhi originally came from Africa but has travelled very widely over the millennia. Remains found in Peru have been dated from 12,000 BC. One of the reasons dudhi may have become so adventurous is the remarkable tenacity of the hard, lightweight and waterproof fruit – they are capable of floating for over a year on salt water without loss of viability of the seeds.

The modern dudhi is a very vigorous climbing vine, with softly furry, rounded to heart-shaped leaves, often three- or five-lobed, and strong tendrils that clutch anything in their grasp. The

foliage has a heavy, persistent scent, which some say is like musk. The plant grows well during the rainy season in the tropics, or if irrigated in hot, dry climates.

Dudhi have attractive, large white flowers, both male and female on the same plant, which last only 24 hours. They open at night and in the wild are pollinated by moths. Unlike those of most other cucurbits, the flowers can be entire or beautifully striated and fringed – the most elaborate ones look like an complex crocheted hanky or a sort of passionflower.

There are a number of cultivars, including the Indian 'Summer Prolific Long' and 'Summer Prolific Round', 'Punjab Komal', NDBG1 and KBG1. Some cultivars have a distinct indented waist, while others are more rounded. Dudhi of various other colours are available in India or imported as seed for ornamental gourds in the UK, including a rather marvellous striped and dappled, dark green and silver, long-necked inedible cultivar called 'Amphore'. As with other marrow family members, the young shoots and leaves can be cooked. The seeds are also edible.

Nutritional value

Dudhi are not a very rich source of nutrients, but they do contain a little calcium, potassium and Vitamin C. Ripe dudhi seeds can be used in soups, and are sometimes sold as melon seed, spiced or salted and roasted.

Other uses

Most dudhi are used for their hard, waterproof skins rather than for food: these are usually round in shape, taste very bitter and have even been said to be poisonous when fully ripe. They may be made into kitchen utensils, fishing floats, toys or musical instruments. A design scratched on to a young fruit will remain as a scar when it is dried. The pulp of the ripe fruit is emetic and purgative: small quantities of the juice may be administered as a folk remedy for indigestion.

Cultivation

Dudhi is easy to grow under cover or on a sheltered fence or wall. Like many of the other tropical cucurbits it grows extremely rapidly, so it's probably just as well it's not fully hardy. It will survive temperatures as low as 7°C (45°F), though needs around 13°C (55°F) to grow.

Getting hold of the seed of so-called 'non-edible' varieties is relatively easy, as many seed suppliers sell them for growing your own ornaments, but finding seed of the better-quality edible types is less so. However, all cultivars can be eaten when young, before the skin has hardened, and they are quite prolific if continually picked. The appearance of a cultivar in the 'ornamental' section of a seed catalogue does not necessarily mean that it is inedible, only that it has not been formally classified as a vegetable. Cultivars include 'Canteen', 'Dipper' and 'Large Bottle', but if you can find it the one to select is 'Snake', which has a long, straight habit if allowed to hang from a trellis but curls up if grown on the ground. This is the closest variety to the Indian vegetable.

Start the seed off in the same way as marrows or courgettes: sow two to a 9cm (3in) pot in late April to May, depending on the likely date of the last frost in your area, at a temperature of 18–21°C (65–70°F), and remove the weaker seedling once germinated. Start to harden off the plants once they have three or four truc leaves, and plant out as soon as conditions permit.

Dudhi enjoy a rich, well-manured soil and a sunny site. They need much more room than you think, and plenty of water in dry weather! If grown under glass, they will need as much root space as you can give, so plant only one to a growbag. The fruit will grow to their fullest length if the plants are kept upright – this is one of those plants that really does look good growing from a pergola or archway covered in coarse mesh netting. In India, a small stone is often tied to a string at the base of the flower bud to keep the young fruits growing straight and true. Support the plants with sticks, string or netting and keep your secateurs ready to snip off any octopus-like tendrils threatening to throttle other vegetation nearby.

Hand-pollination is often recommended but I've never found it necessary, as the flowers seem to be favourites with hoverflies and others. If, however, you want to save your own seed, you will need to make sure that the flies don't bring in foreign pollen, so carefully wrap a little masking tape round the tips of one female and two male flower buds when they're almost ready to open early in the morning. In late evening, open the male flower buds first and remove the petals, leaving a brush-like stamen tuft laden with pollen. Open the female flower and dust pollen on to the stigma, then tie string or coloured wool around the stem so you'll know which fruit to save. The plant won't produce more fruit once existing fruits are ripe, so make sure you have enough plants for food before you sacrifice one for seed.

Pick dudhi when still tender and soft to the fingernail, at anything from 25–35cm (10–14in) long, or even less. Like courgettes, dudhi plants will crop more or less continually until the frosts arrive if the young fruits keep being picked.

KARELLA, BITTER MELON

(Momordica charantia)

Family Cucurbitacae

The vegetable

Two forms of karella are usually imported into the UK: one (called 'jungli karella') has pronounced spines, while the other is smoother and has a ridged appearance. Karella range in colour from dark to pale green; if they're turning yellow it means they're over-ripe. Excessively ripe fruits feel soft when pressed and develop a slight smell. Don't squish too hard or you'll break the skin – they turn very gluey inside. Avoid fruit with dark, sunken patches, which are usually caused by over-zealous refrigeration or virus diseases (which can be transmitted to other cucurbits growing in your garden).

Karella should be eaten young, when fresh and tender, about the size of a courgette. The skin is quite thick, and inside is a creamy-green flesh with small, undeveloped, flattened seeds similar to those of a cucumber. The fruits seem very bitter to Western tastes, although much of the bitterness is removed by parboiling or salting when the vegetable is prepared. As with many cucurbits, the young shoots and tendrils can be eaten as a vegetable: these are not at all bitter but have a pleasant, almost nutty flavour.

Karella will keep for a couple of weeks in the salad tray of the fridge, or for a few days in the cool and dark of a pantry.

The plant

A vigorous climbing plant, karella has been cultivated in Asia for at least 2000 years. It was introduced to Europe in 1710 but has never really caught on here, perhaps because Europeans didn't like the taste – or just didn't know how to cook it.

The plant can grow huge in the tropics,

TOP: Jungli Karella
ABOVE: Smooth KArella

sprawling over other vegetation. It clings by small tendrils that coil tightly round anything within reach, and can happily climb to 4m (12ft). In a greenhouse it tends to be slightly less of a thug, but can still take up much more space than you anticipated.

The deeply divided leaves are smooth, non-spiny, light green and five- to seven-lobed. Karella has small yellow flowers with a distinct fragrance: some say of vanilla, but I find it's more complex – a combination of dust, chalkiness, faded perfume and worn kid-glove leather. The male flowers are much more fragrant than the females, and open early in the morning. They are the size of pound coins, long stalked and golden-yellow with five petals, while the females are much less spectacular. Male and female flowers are carried on the same plant.

The fruit develops into a spiny cylinder up to 25cm (10in) long. When ripe it turns first golden, then bright orange, then quickly mushy, splaying open like a three-pointed starfish to display its vibrant red seeds, flattened with crinkled edges. The seeds themselves are poisonous, though not their seed coat is not. Not all cultivars have red seeds, but those generally available in the UK do. Great variation is possible, as karella, in typical cucurbit style, can easily cross-fertilise with related species.

Although only two forms are generally available as fruit in this country, there are also white-skinned cultivars, long thin forms and an extra-wide type, popular in China and Japan. In China and Thailand a smooth-skinned, pale green form is preferred, which is milder in taste.

Indian heritage landraces include 'Mithi', 'Kuruvithalai', 'Periyakai' and 'Nettai'. I have not yet found these to be available from UK seed merchants, but it may be possible to obtain them via the Internet.

Nutritional value

Karella is high in iron and vitamin C compared with other cucurbits, but is still mostly water so is very low in calories. The iron in karella is more easily absorbed by the body than that in other vegetables.

Other uses

The bitter taste of this vegetable is due to momordicin, which has been used medicinally in the East for generations. In the West it has recently been investigated for its use in diabetes. Eating karella regularly has been long been claimed to cure or lessen the impact of diabetes in India, and people who eat it at lot are advised to inform their GP if they are taking anti-diabetic medicines. Momordicin or other alkaloids in karella also reduce levels of blood cholesterol if the fruit is eaten regularly.

Poultices of karella leaves have been used for generations as a folk remedy for burns or chapped hands. An infusion of the leaves is a very gentle laxative, which soothes inflamed tissues and is traditionally used to treat dysentery and other inflammations of the gut. It is antihelmetic (used to kill parasitic worms), a uterine tonic and kidney cleansing, as well as antibiotic. Karella, particularly the root, has been used as an abortifacient, so excessive consumption should perhaps be avoided for pregnant women.

Cultivation

Karella is hardy to around 11°C (53°F), and mature plants may survive lower temperatures for a night or two, but the minimum growing temperature is 16–18°C (60–65°F), so unless you have a very sheltered garden you will need a polytunnel or a greenhouse.

As the fruit is imported when immature, it's unlikely that you'll be able to find one that is sufficiently ripe to harvest viable seeds (although I have found them in a few, so it is worth looking). Fortunately, there are a number of UK seed suppliers (e.g. Chiltern Seeds, Suffolk Herbs tropicalfruitandveg. co.uk), although the choice of cultivars is generally limited. Indian cultivars include 'Pusha Vishesh', 'Priya', 'Coimbatore Long' and 'Arka Harit' (try Kokopelli). Seed is also available from international mail-order suppliers.

Buy fresh seed every year, as it doesn't keep well, or better still save your own.

For best results, it shouldn't be sown too

early in the season – late April is fine if you have a heated greenhouse. If you don't, or if you live north of Oxford, wait until May. Germination takes 10–21 days and requires a temperature of around 18–21°C (65–70°F). Sow a few seeds in pots, discarding the weakest as they grow. Once the seedlings have three true leaves, plant out into greenhouse or polytunnel soil, or a couple to a growbag.

Karella prefers fertile, well-drained soil and sunny conditions. Support will be necessary, as it can easily take over a polytunnel. Given normal growing conditions, expect flowers to form on plants within about a month of the emergence of the first two true leaves. Train the plants along the supports, as with cucumbers. They require the same level of humidity as cucumbers, and benefit from regular dampening down of the greenhouse floor or daily misting with water in hot dry weather.

Pollination in Asia is usually performed by small flies, but may need to be done by hand if you don't have many insects around in your protected cropping area: use a soft brush to transfer pollen as soon as the female flowers start to open. Try not to grow karella next to other cucurbits if you plan to save your own

seed – or protect designated female flowers from open pollination and pollinate them by hand (see dudhi for how to do this). Fruits should reach harvesting size about three weeks after flowering: pick them when they're about 15–22cm (6–9in) long.

In some areas fruit flies and birds may attack the young fruits – sparrows seem to find them particularly attractive. If this happens it is suggested that you protect the fruits by enclosing them in a paper bag fastened to the stem above them, which apparently fools the birds completely. However, this hasn't been a problem in the UK so far as I know, possibly because of the falling population of sparrows or their dislike of the fruits' bitter taste. Slugs and snails are not too much of a pest.

When saving seed, allow the fruit to go almost rotten before removing the seed, then wash off the slimy red coating and allow them to dry on kitchen towel over several days before storing in envelopes. The seeds are a golden dark brown colour and look as if they have been intricately etched with pretty patterns on their flat sides. Viable seeds are thicker, plumper-looking and feel solid when pinched, while non-fertile ones are very flat and pinch hollow, like an empty drinks can.

59

KALI TURAI, ANGLED LUFFA

(Luffa acutangula)

GHIA TURAI, SMOOTH LUFFA

(L. aegyptiaca syn. L. cylindrica)

Family Cucurbitaceae

The vegetable

Kali turai, or angled luffa, is easily recognised by its ten thick ribs running from end to end, a bit like an umbrella folded with the struts outside. The hard, dark green skins have a matt appearance. Inside, the flesh is cream or white, similar to that of a courgette. The fruits in the shops are usually about the same size as a cucumber.

Ghia turai, or smooth luffas don't have such big ribs, just faint lines or stripes, and are not so hard to the touch. They are paler skinned, usually an anaemic greenish colour; sometimes rather yellow or white tinged, and with a slightly shinier surface. They're often thicker at one end than the other. Should you be tempted by their rounders-bat-like appearance to pick one up and whirl it around, remember that smooth luffas are much heavier than angled ones – though they're not really hard enough to be a useful blunt instrument.

Only the immature fruit is sold, as it rapidly becomes fibrous and inedible: mature luffas can reach nearly 3m (10ft) long! Neither sort of luffa keeps well, and they suffer cold injury if stored in the fridge. Ideally you should eat them at once, or store for no more than two or three days in a plastic bag in a cool dark place, above 10ºC (50ºF).

The plant

Wild luffa grows throughout tropical Asia but is very bitter to the taste. Cultivated varieties are much better tasting and usually come true from seed, especially if grown in isolation.

Both types of luffa are grown all over Asia as climbing annuals, often scrambling over the roof of a barn or village hut. Plants can reach 15m (50ft) in just a few months and make an attractive splash of green as well as producing a useful crop.

Angled luffa has smooth-sided, square or five-angled stems in cross section. Its leaves are plain green and have five or seven lobes with deep central veins. The plant climbs by tendrils, which are split into three, twining from the leaf axils. Its flowers are golden-yellow, 5cm (2in) across, opening in the late afternoon or evening. They have a delicious fragrance, which is one of the glories of an Indian vegetable garden, but sadly this is short-lived: the flowers are faded like limp dusters by morning. The variety used for eating is usually distinct from that grown for fibre and sponge production.

Smooth luffa has four-sided stems with distinct ridges or ribs. The irregularly lobed, roundish leaves, with deeply divided indentations (sometimes even the seed leaves are divided), have silvery or white markings and are a paler green than those of the angled

luffa. They may be smooth or bristly in different cultivars. When held up to the light, a smooth luffa leaf shows minute pinpricks like St John's Wort, due to the presence of tiny oil glands. The tendrils may be in twos or threes.

The large, yellowish flowers are 5–10cm (2–4 in) across, covered with a thick, white or grey/buff-coloured wool, and open in the early morning. Each flower lasts at least 24 hours and sometimes longer in cool conditions, but they have no scent. The seeds are slightly winged, and when ripe are roasted for eating or pressed for oil, used for cooking and lighting.

Nutritional value

The fresh leaves and tendrils of luffa contain some vitamin C and minerals. The immature fruits have less than 3 per cent protein, though slightly more carbohydrate.

Other uses

The internal skeletons of mature smooth luffas are the sort generally sold as back scrubbers, the best quality coming from Japan. Angled luffas can also be used, but the fibres aren't quite as firm. Luffas have a remarkable capacity to resist mould growth despite frequent wetting, and the particles are incorporated into a range of scrubbing products, from skin exfoliants to pan cleaners. Ripe, cleaned luffas are also used in India for shock-proof headgear. In the eighteenth century the US navy used luffas as filters to separate water from oil in ships' boilers.

In Chinese medicine, a strong infusion from the boiled ripe fruits of smooth luffa is said to benefit circulation and improve the function of lungs, liver and stomach. Mature luffas contain purgative chemicals, and the seeds of angled luffa are emetic and purgative.

Cultivation

In the UK luffa is best grown indoors with some heat. It is hardy to 13°C (55°F), but the minimum growing temperature is around 18°C (65°F). If you can grow a cucumber in your greenhouse, you should be able to grow a luffa just as easily. Unlike many cucurbits, luffas are not very gross feeders, preferring a fertile but sandy soil, although angled luffa prefers slightly richer soil. The site should be in good light for at least six hours a day.

Luffas sold for food are not mature enough to have produced seed. Seeds of smooth luffa are relatively easy to obtain – Chiltern Seeds,

Suffolk Herbs and tropicalfruitandveg.co.uk sell them – but angled luffa is more of a challenge: those usually available here are selected for their skeletons, as bath luffas, rather than their edible qualities. Try B & T World Seeds or Tokita Seed.

The seed is quite hard, so either soak it overnight or for even longer before sowing, or carefully chip it with a penknife. Germination temperatures are high, 27–35°C (80–95°F), although the temperature can be lowered gradually to around 21°C (70°F) once the seedlings have emerged. Sow as for other cucurbits – two or three to a 9cm (3in) pot in late April or May, discarding the weaker seedlings, and planting out once they have at least three true leaves. Don't expect great germination rates, however: emergence seems to be low even with fresh seed.

Plants should be at least 60cm (2ft) apart, with 2m (6ft) between the rows. They will need support from the earliest stages. Pinch out exuberant young shoots when the plants have filled their allotted space, and keep the atmosphere well ventilated but humid, either by misting the plants daily or by dampening down the greenhouse floor.

Plants that are kept too cold often drop their flower buds or the very young fruits. Another cause of fruit drop is lack of pollination. Hand-pollination is recommended for both types of luffa, especially for night-flowering angled luffas – moths and other night-flying insects in India have longer tongues than similar species in the UK, which can't reach into the depths of the flower to fertilise it even if they visit the plant for nectar.

As with marrows, luffas will grow faster and be more tender if kept well watered. And, like marrow plants, luffas grown hot and happy produce more female flowers and hence fruits than cold-stressed

plants, which produce mostly males: this sexual imbalance in the flowers also happens as the days shorten.

Plants from seed sown in late April will produce their first edible fruits by August. Pick fruits for eating when young and tender as required, since they don't keep well. If you keep picking you should get about 20 or more fruits from each plant.

Remember to save at least one fruit to mature – not only for a home-grown back-scratcher, but for seed for next year. It should be allowed to hang on the vine for as long as possible, when the skin will turn hard and golden brown. If frosts intervene before this has happened, you can usually rescue fruits once the skin has set by cutting them off and keeping them somewhere warm and airy for a couple of weeks.

Peel off the hard outside skin – it comes off with a knife fairly easily once the skin has been cracked – and remove the ripe flesh from the skeletal cellulose beneath by holding it under a running tap. The seeds should wash out at this stage and can be collected in a sieve if you want to save it. If the fruit is starting to rot, which makes removal of surplus flesh much easier, you may need to do this outside: it's a smelly job. The luffa can be soaked overnight in a weak solution of bleach to remove any lingering odours. Once your bath luffa is extracted, hang it up to dry somewhere warm. It should last for several months, maybe longer.

KONTOLA, SPINY CUCUMBER

(Momordica cochinchinensis)

Family Cucurbitacae

The vegetable

Two Kontola is a small oval fruit, 8–12cm (3–5in) long, closely related to karella. The skin is covered with minute spines with a warty base, thin as horsehair, which don't rub off easily. The stalks are at least as long as the fruit.

Green at first, the ripening skin turns first a pale yellow then brighter gold, and finally scarlet orange. Kontola as sold are usually at the pale green to lemon-yellow stage. They get sweeter as they turn orange, but it's best to buy them before they're too ripe and keep them for a few days as they travel better – like kiwi fruits, they squash very easily when over-ripe. Avoid bruised or obviously damaged fruits, or ones with dark bits or those showing any hint of mildew, as they taint rapidly. The seeds inside are first a gaudy orange but then turn dark brown, with complex indented patterns on their skin. Unlike many other members of the Cucurbitaceae family, kontola seeds are toxic, so don't be tempted to try them!

Kontola flesh is very juicy and sharply fragranced – a bit like sour plums, perhaps. To European tastes it may seem quite bitter, but it is relished for its refreshing properties. The fruits can be eaten either cooked or raw, but in the UK they are generally cooked as they often don't develop their full flavour because they've been picked unripe. Ripe fruits have a sweeter, more spicy flavour than unripe ones, with a nutty aftertaste – and they colour the mouth and lips orange.

Kontola will keep for five to seven days in the salad tray of the fridge if you buy them yellow; a bit longer if you buy them green.

The plant

Kontola is rarely cultivated, as it grows wild throughout most of Asia, from India and Pakistan through Japan to New Guinea. It's a perennial plant, and a herbaceous scrambler rather than a climber, although it can reach into trees and over houses if it finds something to cling on to with its long, winding tendrils. It has large, deeply divided leaves, with three to nine lobes, coarsely hairy stems and cup-shaped flowers. Each white flower has five petals with intricate gold and black markings inside, presumably to guide tropical insects to the deeply set nectaries. They are mildly fragrant but not as much as karalla flowers. The male flowers have more prominent, dark basal markings.

The fruit are particularly attractive, and sometimes kontola weed seedlings are allowed to grow just to act as a green

Ripe Kontola – photograph by Peter Andrews

Cultivation

Kontola is less hardy than karalla, to around 16°C (60°F), so you will need a polytunnel or a greenhouse. Cultivation guidance is similar to that for karalla. Unlike karalla, however, kontola is very attractive to slugs and snails, so take precautions!

If you are lucky you can find ripe kontola for sale and save the seeds from these, but if not you can ripen them at home, as you would tomatoes: in cool but dry, airy conditions. Positioning next to a ripe banana helps. When over-ripe, the fruits split in three to display the seeds. It is difficult to find commercial suppliers of kontola seed unless you trawl the Internet, although Thompson & Morgan's 'Ornamental Cucumber Mix' may be worth a try.

If using fresh seed, germination is normally rapid at 18°C (65°F). Older seed is very hard and will require chipping or presoaking in an attempt to break its dormancy. Sow seed in threes in 9cm (3in) pots in April or May and discard the weakest seedlings, as they dislike disturbance. Plant out once they have at least three true leaves. You can fit two plants to a growbag quite nicely, but they will need supports. They don't climb quite as well as karella but can still reach 2m (6ft) or more.

Male and female flowers are carried on separate plants, as with ordinary cucumbers, and will require hand-pollination. If the light is poor or the plants are stressed, they won't produce flowers. Pick fruits as soon as they're large enough to eat and keep picking to ensure a continuity of crop. Expect about five or six fruits to a plant under UK conditions.

It's not worth trying to overwinter kontola plants here as they seem to succumb to mildew in winter at the least opportunity.

screen. The wild ripe fruits are apparently sometimes thrown at people by naughty children – they not only make a satisfying splat but are refreshingly cooling to hot skin.

As with many other cucurbits, the young shoots are edible, and they are often eaten curried.

Nutritional value

Kontola contains about as much vitamin C as an apple, and some iron.

Other uses

Although the seeds of kontola are poisonous this has not stopped their use externally as folk remedies for boils, pimples and other skin problems. They are mashed to a pulp and spread on to the affected area as a poultice. Warmed seeds are sometimes wrapped in a piece of clean cotton cloth and wrapped around the throat to treat inflamed lymph glands. Kontola roots of may be pounded to produce a soapy lather for laundry.

MANDANMAST, PASSIONFRUIT

(Passiflora edulis)

Family Passifloraceae

The fruit

Passionfruit sold in the UK are normally of two forms. The most common one is the size of a hen's egg or smaller, with a hard, dark purple shell that becomes more and more crinkled with age. Inside the leathery rind are over 200 small black seeds embedded in a luscious, fragrant, yellowish-green or orangey-yellow pulp, with a refreshing tangy sweet taste.

Less commonly encountered is the golden or mountain passionfruit, which is rather larger and more pyramidal in shape. It often has a long stem attached, which the purple passionfruit lacks, and the skin is a pale orangey-buff colour. The rind has a papery quality to it and is more easily broken than that of the purple fruit, but just as thick. The flesh is similar, but less aromatic and blander tasting.

The plant

The passionfruit originally came from South America, but has been introduced to tropical countries worldwide. It has become naturalised in parts of India, especially Nilgiri, as well as in Africa, Hawaii and Australia.

The two forms of Passiflora edulis are distinguished by the temperature and altitude to which they are suited. Both are vigorous climbers, using tendrils to clamber to a height of 8m (26ft) or more in a single season, and have deeply toothed, three-lobed leaves.

P. edulis f. edulis is the common purple passionfruit, grown in the cool tropical highlands. It has beautiful but unscented fringed white flowers with a purple inner marking, each bloom up to 8cm (3in) across, and is inclined to produce suckers.

P. edulis f. flavicarpa is the golden passionfruit, native of Brazil, now grown in tropical lowlands. It has showier flowers than its purple cousin and is just as vigorous, if not more so. The flowers are sweetly scented, white and purple, and self-sterile. It is resistant to wilt disease and nematode attack, unlike the purple form, and rarely suckers.

There are many cultivars and hybrids of passionfruit. Cultivars of the golden variety include 'Gold Star', 'Golden Nugget' (one of those most commonly imported into the UK as fruit), and 'Norfolk', a large, reddish-fruited form that requires crossing with the purple passionfruit to set.

All forms of passionfruit are easily propagated by heel or semi-ripe cuttings. In recent years viruses have become a problem in plantations, and much research is being done to develop resistant strains.

Nutritional value

Passionfruit are rich in vitamin A, potash and phosphorus, and contain 90 calories per 100g.

Other uses

The vine-like stems of passionfruits may be used for making decorative garlands. A sedative glyoside compound, passiflorine, has been isolated from the leaves. The seeds are rich in oil (22 per cent), which may be of use industrially, although it is unsuitable for animal feed, and the rinds have been used in pectin manufacture. In parts of Asia the purple passionfruit rind is used to produce a dye.

Cultivation

Passionflower is an increasingly popular ornamental plant in the UK. Many of those grown as ornamentals have 'edible' fruits, but this does not mean they taste nice, just that they are not toxic! The species normally grown here is P. caerulea, which has blue or white flowers and is relatively hardy, but its orange fruit are extremely unpleasant. Passiflora edulis is not the only species to produce tasty fruit, however – there are a number of others that have better productive potential under UK conditions, although all need warmer temperatures than P. caerulea. Suggested species are listed at the end of this chapter – try the Passiflora National Collection (see Suppliers index) for plants.

It is fairly easy to get a passionfruit seed to germinate but, having got it growing, not so easy to persuade it to fruit unless you have a very warm sheltered garden, a heated conservatory or a warm greenhouse. It is possible in the warmer parts of the UK to grow fruiting passionflower outside, although the fruit is best treated as a bonus. The best way of ensuring plants survive outside is by burying a soil-warming cable around the roots to keep them from freezing, or by growing the roots inside a warmer building and training the upper growth outside – the reverse of what you would do for a vine.

Passionflowers are thuggish climbers so are best suited to a conservatory or heated greenhouse than a living room. The common purple form will easily reach 6m (20ft) even in this climate, and the golden form even more. If grown in a pot, this will need to be big enough to accommodate them – a barrel 60cm (2ft) in diameter would be about right. The minimum container size needed to produce flowers is about 25cm (10in). Wherever you grow them, they will need some sort of support.

Seed must be sown fresh: viability is retained for a very short time, barely 20 days outside the fruits, so selecting the fruit is important. Choose those that are over-ripe and shrivelled, but not dried up inside. The purple sort should shrivel to less than half their normal size, but the golden ones not as much.

Germination takes two to four weeks at 30°C (86°F). Some people claim greater success with fluctuating temperatures, keeping the seeds at 20°C (68°F) for 16 hours and 30°C for the remaining eight hours each day, or at least allowing the daily temperature to vary by several degrees within these parameters. Once seedlings emerge, lower the heat to 16–21°C (60–70°F) before pricking out.

Plant out the seedlings in a free-draining medium: use a loam-based compost mixed in equal parts with grit or sharp sand. If growing outside, plant amid plenty of rubble. Passionflowers like a sunny position; they should be watered frequently when actively growing and sparingly during winter. The winter minimum temperature is around 4°C (40°F), when plants will lose most of their leaves. Burying the roots deeply, as you would with clematis, can be useful if growing in cold conditions. Try only mature plants outside, not young seedlings.

Keep plants warm during the growing

season if you possibly can – growth is inhibited below 18°C (65°F) and flowering retarded below 15°C (59°F). At temperatures below 20°C (68°F), pollen will not germinate. In the UK the first flowers are unlikely to appear before the plant's second season. Flowering tends to be influenced by photoperiod in some clones more than in others, and seedlings from shop-bought fruit have an infuriating habit of flowering for only a very short period (not long enough to ensure cross-pollination) on their 'birthday' – or at least a very close date in midsummer – year after year! To avoid this behaviour, either invest in a decent form of artificial lighting (shops that stock hydroponic equipment are usually helpful) or a named cultivar that is not so fussy.

Golden passionflowers need hand-pollination, preferably using pollen from a different golden-fruited specimen or the purple form. The purple passionfruit is self-fertile, although you will get a larger crop with hand-pollination (assuming you can reach the flowers).

In the second and subsequent years, pot up in the spring. Once plants have reached the maximum container size you can accommodate, replace the top few inches of compost annually. Prune established plants in February, cutting out any weak shoots and shortening strong ones by about a third, and tie in to supports. Feed regularly during the growing season using a high-potash fertiliser.

Other species of passionflower that may be worth cultivating for their fruits in the UK include the following.

Passiflora alata. Big, dark red, purple and white scented flowers looking like discarded lampshades, carried most of the year, followed by large, sweet, yellowish-orange fruit. Climbs rampantly to 10m (33ft). Minimum temperature 4°C (40°F) if well hardened off, but only for short periods.

P. coccinea (red granadilla). For those with a warm spot! Large, glossy, scarlet star-shaped flowers, with nine petals, May–September; climbs to 4m (13ft)-plus. Minimum temperature 18°C (65°F).

P. x exoniensis. Large, rosy-pink, saucer-sized hanging flowers, June–October. Will fruit in an unheated conservatory. Sweet, finger-sized, yellow banana-shaped fruits. Climbs to 6m (20ft) or over. Minimum temperature 2°C (36°F).

P. herbertiana (rare). Beautiful yellow starfish-shaped flowers, most unlike your typical passionflower, produced May–November. Vigorous climber, to 5m (16ft) and over. Minimum temperature 4°C (40°F).

P. incarnata (maypop, wild passionflower). To only 2m (6ft) in a pot, but is then unlikely to fruit; sprawling to perhaps 5–6m (15–20ft) in the ground. Fragrant white and lilac, pink- or purple-fringed blossoms, and small greenish-yellow fruits that have medicinal uses as well as tasting quite good. Hardy to -7°C (20°F) or less with good drainage. Dislikes confined roots: best buried deeply in a warm spot close to a wall.

P. ligularis (sweet granadilla). Huge, showy, white and lilac flowers, June–September. Best grown outside or moved out for the summer, as it hates being too hot. Climbs to 4m (13ft) or so. Large, golden-green fruit, deliciously aromatic. Minimum temperature 2°C (36°F).

P. mollissima (banana passionflower). Again, best cultivated outside to enable it to fruit well, or will do well in a big greenhouse border. Large, pale pink flowers, June–September, followed by sweet, yellow, banana-shaped fruits. Fast growing, to 5m (16ft). Claimed to withstand a minimum temperature of 1°C (34°F) given adequate drainage.

P. serrulata. Fragrant blue-and-white flowers, April–June, and delicious aromatic fruit. Minimum temperature 10°C (50°F).

passiflora mollissima

passiflora alata

passiflora x exoniensis

passiflora edulis

PAPEETA, PAPAYA

(Carica papaya)

BABACO

(Carica x heilbornii)

Family Caricaceae

Papaya

The fruit

Passionfruit Papayas are seen for sale in two forms: big, orange ripe ones and smaller, dark green unripe ones. Ripe papayas are usually round or elongated, with a pronounced neck, and may weigh up to 3kg (6lb). When fully ripe they are soft and squishy to the touch. Avoid specimens with marked or pitted skins, as the external blemishes are often much less significant than the internal damage.

The flesh of a ripe papaya is a soft, succulent, cream to orange or reddish coloured and of a similar texture to melon, with a rich, perfumed taste. It surrounds a central cavity containing many small, round, black or dark brown seeds. Unripe papayas are more usually oval, only 10–12cm (4–5in) long, and hard skinned. They are firm and green inside, with underdeveloped seeds and taste very sour, rather like unripe mango.

The babaco is a relatively new hybrid of various mountain papayas. Although grown principally in Guernsey and New Zealand, it may be found even in supermarkets in the UK. It has five sides and is pointed at one end and blunt at the other. Like papaya, it is dark green at first, at the stage when it's usually offered for sale, and ripens slowly to a soft golden-orange colour. Unlike papaya, the skin is edible when ripe. Babaco has a powerful, pervasive scent and pale creamy-to-orange flesh, which tastes of the scent and which you'll either love or hate. Babaco have no seeds so are easy to serve up.

The plant

Papaya is native to the tropics of South America. It was introduced to Asia in the eighteenth century, and has never looked back. It's frequently seen as a weed in many warm climates, often growing from bird-sown seed, and is usually tolerated because of its useful fruit and short life.

The plant has large, deeply lobed, palmate leaves of a bright pea green, with irregular slashes and divisions on their edges. These are carried on the top of a bare, scraggledy stem with no branches – it hardly justifies the name of a trunk, which implies density and strength. The whole plant looks like a giant Brussels sprout when it has reached fruiting size, which may be at 6m (20ft) tall. Each leathery leaf may be over 60cm (2ft) across.

The flowers appear in small, pale greenish-yellow clusters underneath the leaves, all year round if the plant is

69

Babaco

well watered, and are very attractive to insects. Male and female flowers are carried on different plants in the wild, but modern hybrids are bisexual.

The fruits develop like small green rugby balls growing flat beneath their leafy hat. As they ripen they droop, and by the time they are ready to pick the tree has a garland of what look like infant hot-water bottles lying close to the trunk beneath the foliage.

Plants can bear fruits within a year of sowing in the tropics, and once they start cropping can produce 50 fruits a year, but they are short-lived and reach only three to five years of age. They are propagated commercially from seed or by cuttings, budding or micropropagation.

Papaya is tolerant of a wide range of conditions and grows in any well-drained soil. Cultivars include 'Red Lady' and 'Solo', a self-fertile hybrid. When wounded, the whole plant produces a white sticky latex.

Babaco is more cold tolerant than papaya and can grow at high altitudes. It is very similar to papaya in appearance – just a bit squatter and shorter, and its leaves are more palmate. It

is seedless because its flowers are all female. Commercial strains of babaco are propagated by budding or cuttings.

Other uses

The latex, fruit skin and leaves of papaya all contain papain, a powerful digestive enzyme that is used to tenderise meat (usually by wrapping the joint in papaya leaves or fruit peel) and to encourage healing of deep wounds and scars, as well as in digestive supplements and for a variety of other purposes – from termite proofing to making sausage skins. Papaya seed is used to treat tapeworms.

Cultivation

If you have a big enough heated greenhouse or conservatory it is quite possible to grow your own papayas, although the plants won't give heavy crops. Papaya seed will remain viable for up to six years if kept cool and slightly damp (e.g. in a film canister in the fridge), so plants can be easily grown from supermarket fruits – although, owing to seed variability, these may not be the most productive. Seed

can also be obtained from seed merchants, e.g. Chilterns. If you want to grow a babaco you will have to buy a young plant, since it's seedless, but plants can be obtained from Unusual Herbs and Edibles. Cultivation advice is the same as for papaya.

Sow four to eight seeds in a pot and thin out the weakest to leave one or two before repotting. Germination is usually quite rapid – between two and four weeks – and seedlings grow pleasingly fast. Germination temperature is around 24–30°C (75–86°F), but once the seedlings emerge they will tolerate cooler conditions.

Young papaya is particularly sensitive to damping off, so water seedlings carefully, using not just clean water but a nice well-washed watering can, and avoid splashing liquid on the leaves. They do best in a rich growing medium, with regular misting for mature plants and plenty of water during the growing season. The minimum temperature for young plants is said to be 16°C(60°F); for mature plants 13°C (55°F), although they have been known to survive lower than this outdoors in Cornwall despite losing foliage. The key to hardiness

appears to be keeping the roots dry: as with so many plants, cold and wet is far more deadly than just cold.

Because of their rapid growth rate, papayas make attractive summer bedding plants to give a real tropical feel to a garden. However, plants grown in the UK usually take two years to flower, so need to be given heated protection for the winter months if they are being kept for fruiting. They can easily develop red spider mite infestation if kept in too dry an atmosphere.

The biggest disadvantage of growing papayas as houseplants is their size – a full-grown plant can reach over 3.5m (12ft) in UK conditions, so they are perhaps best in a stairwell or a very long window. Fortunately, dwarf cultivars are available (Jungle Seeds offers a dwarf strain, called 'Dwarf', said to commence fruiting at 1.2m/ 4ft). Alternatively, plants will tolerate being cut back hard, although this reduces the fruiting capacity over winter. Just lop off the leafy tuft in early spring – the plant will reshoot in three to six weeks. You can still expect some fruits in summer, even if the plant has been cut back severely.

TINDA, INDIAN ROUND MELON

(Praecitrullus fistulosus, syn. Citrullus vulgaris var. fistulosus)

Family Cucurbitaceae

The fruit

Tinda is a pale green fruit the size of a small apple, with a smooth, almost waxy skin with a faint white bloom. It is in season from January to March. Those seen in the UK are usually the cultivars 'Arka' and 'Punjabi Tinda', two of the more productive early varieties.

When cut into, tinda reveals a thick skin and a white, spongy, slightly artificial-looking flesh that has a curious texture, almost like expanded polystyrene. The flesh doesn't turn brown after cutting, unlike an apple. There is no particular scent to it, but a pleasant green-fruit smell to the cut skin. Tinda is usually eaten raw. It should feel firm but slightly yielding to the touch, and be quite juicy and acidic (like a Granny Smith). It's not particularly sour – more a pleasing bite. If the flesh has brown patches or is becoming soft, the fruit is too old for eating.

Embedded in the pale flesh are three to five pale brown to white seeds, which may not be fully formed. Mature seeds are black and shaped similarly to a big fat melon seed, bulging at the sides if fertile. Ripe tinda seeds are sometimes eaten roasted and are occasionally seen for sale (sadly for gardeners, usually preprocessed) as black melon seeds.

The plant

Tinda is an annual plant, and its origin is somewhat obscure. Until recently it was considered to be a subspecies of watermelon, but investigation into its genetics has shown it to be distinct and it has been now allocated to a separate family.

It is a rapidly growing vine that can reach 1m (3ft) or slightly more, and has rather hairy, greenish-grey-coloured, long triangular leaves. The leaves have seven to nine deeply toothed lobes that taper towards the tip, and

are held horizontally, with the edges curling up like a stale sandwich. They alternate along a rounded, grooved and hairy stem.

The solitary flowers are small, about the size of a 50p piece, greenish-yellow to golden, with male and female flowers on the same plant. When the fruits are ripe their green skin darkens. It becomes hard with age, and the flesh becomes inedible.

The cultivated forms of tinda are propagated by seed or occasionally by stem cuttings.

Nutritional value

Tinda is mostly eaten for its cooling properties rather than its nutritional value, but fresh tinda does contain 3 per cent carbohydrate and 1.5 per cent protein, as well as valuable minerals.

Other uses

Tinda is prized in traditional Indian medicine: the unripe seeds are held to be good for the liver, while the rest of the fruit has diuretic qualities. A decoction made from the leaves is drunk to reduce blood pressure, and there is evidence that regularly eating the fresh fruit reduces blood pressure in some people.

Cultivation

You are unlikely to be able to grow tinda outside to fruiting size in the UK. However, if you possess a well-heated greenhouse or a warm conservatory, or perhaps if you live in Cornwall, it is worth a go. The plant is hardy to around 16°C (60°F).

Fruits of tinda imported into this country are usually picked when immature. If you do manage to find a fruit with full, fat seeds, sow them immediately, as the seed needs to be really fresh for best results. Some reports say ripe seed can be kept in a film canister in the salad tray of a fridge for up to three months and still be viable. A number of international firms, including Solana Seeds, supply seed.

Sow in about mid-March to late April, at a temperature of 27°C (80°F), and be patient – germination can take a month, though it's usually much less. Sow in pots, unless you have a large, well-heated greenhouse or conservatory, in which case you can sow direct into a growbag (sow three seeds and discard the weakest two). Once the seed leaves are through the temperature can be reduced to about 24°C (75°F), but at much lower than this the plants just stop growing.

Tinda should be grown like a watermelon – lots of rich soil (if grown in a growbag, plants will need additional feeding), plenty of room to romp about, and lots of water. Train them up a trellis in the same way as cucumbers if you're short of space. They're not as rampant as watermelons, but will still fill a space 2m (6ft) square. Like cucumbers, tinda likes a moist atmosphere, so mist the plants daily.

Hand-pollination will be helpful if the plants are grown under cover. The female flowers have a swelling behind the petals and are usually produced some time after the first male flowers appear. As with many other cucurbits, in very hot or cold conditions (or if the plant is stressed for some other reason), a higher proportion of male flowers will be produced, and in the remaining female flowers fruit setting will be inhibited.

Don't expect a huge number of fruits per plant – even in India it's usually only four or five per vine, so once three fruits have formed remove any extra flowers. Under best growing conditions the plants should produce useable fruits within around 80 days of sowing.

Feed using a commercial tomato fertiliser, or use comfrey liquid and manure water alternately, with a monthly seaweed feed. Heavy watering produces big, less flavoursome fruit, while less produces smaller, tastier crops.

TINDORA, IVY GOURD

(Coccinia grandis)

Family Cucurbitaceae

The fruit

Tindora look something like mini gherkins, and are usually striped green and white. They have smooth, slightly shiny skin, and when cut are obviously a member of the courgette family. The internal flesh is greenish-cream and may contain a number of immature seeds. The fruits are generally eaten when unripe, as the ripe fruits are more bitter tasting, and taste fairly bland but pleasantly fresh – a bit like a courgette, except that they stay crunchy when cooked.

There are various different forms of tindora, but the one most commonly imported into the UK is found in southern India. It is a small, thin fruit, under 5cm (2in) long, with a white-striped green skin. In western India the fruits are a bit bigger, with a dark or light green skin and a few scattered stripes. In the Bihar region they are bigger and fatter, over 5cm long, darker green and not always striped. I have seen this type for sale in the UK as well, although it's not as common.

The plant

Tindora grows wild throughout Asia and has become an invasive species in many parts of the world, from the Canary Islands and Hawaii to Spain. Under the alternative name of ivy gourd it's classed as a noxious weed in many countries. It is a short-lived perennial or half-hardy annual, and remarkably persistent in warm climates, although the British climate is probably too cool for it to be a threat here. It lives through drought and floods with equal enthusiasm, and in northern India and Nepal can grow at high altitudes, though it will not survive prolonged frosts.

Cultivars grown for eating are vegetatively propagated, since plants that are seed raised (including most of the escapees) are usually inedible and extremely bitter. Tindora swarms and clings by tendrils to a height or sprawl of 10m (30ft) or more. The leaves are small and vaguely rounded to ivy-leaf shaped, but always with five recognisable lobes. The five-petalled flowers are white and cup shaped: they open wide for only a short time before fading. In India the flowers are a common sight along hedges and, to the traveller from colder climates, are reminiscent of bindweed.

The small, oblong green fruits turn bright red when ripe, with white flesh inside, and are a favourite with birds.

Tindora, particularly when growing wild, is of concern to vegetable growers as it is a

Tindora fuit - photograph by Manji Kerai

source of ring-spot virus, which affects other cucurbits and papaya. This disease is not yet a threat in the UK, although it is a known problem in the Dutch glasshouse industry. The plant is also an alternative host for the tropical melon fly.

Nutritional value

All parts of the tindora plant are high in iron, and the shoots and young leaves are very high in vitamin A. The immature fruit is low in calories and contains 4.5 per cent protein, as well as being a good source of calcium, Vitamin E and other antioxidants. The ripe fruit, despite its bitter taste, is extremely high in vitamin E.

Other uses

Eating all parts of the plant is considered good for diabetics, as with many of the Cucurbitaceae family. In trials, regular consumption of Coccinia extract has been found to lower blood glucose levels.

Cultivation

As the time of writing there is no commercially available source of tindora in the UK. I hope this will change in the next few years, as several seed companies are looking at the potential for propagating tindora to sell as young plants. Seed is, however, available from B & T World Seeds. The fruits of seed-raised plants are generally very bitter – I await the harvest of fruits from my B & T seeds to find out if that is the case from this source. Since the male and female flowers are carried on separate plants, there is perhaps the potential for raising all-female strains (as with parthenogenetic cucumber plants), which would remove the risk of escapees becoming a troublesome weed.

Tindora needs high humidity and hot conditions, similar to the requirements of karella (see page x) but slightly warmer. In very sheltered southern gardens it may cope

Tindora flower - photograph by Manji Kerai

outside, but otherwise should be grown under cover for the best crops. It is likely to do better in a polytunnel than a greenhouse, because of the higher humidity levels it prefers. Although probably hardy to around 16°C (60°F), it may survive lower temperatures.

If you are able to get hold of a plant for vegetative propagation, take shoot-tip cuttings in late April by breaking off several soft growing tips, about 7–10cm (3–4in) long, with at least two partially developed leaflets. They won't require any rooting powder. Cut them just below a node, and remove any stipules or tendrils from the lower portion. Push the lower part of the cuttings into a pot containing a mixture of equal parts of grit or vermiculite and seed compost, and keep them in a closed coldframe or propagator unit at 18–21°C (65–70°F). This should either be in a brightly lit place but out of direct sunlight, or kept lightly shaded (using plastic netting) to prevent the tender shoots becoming scorched. Maintain humidity and warmth, ideally with bottom heat, for at least three weeks, when the plants should be sufficiently rooted to be repotted into normal potting compost. Grow on in slightly less humid conditions, and gradually move into brighter sunlight.

Keep the cuttings under cover in a warm place until the four-leaf stage, when they can be planted into soil or a growbag (two plants per bag at most). Plants can be moved outside in early June, in very southern areas, or to an unheated polytunnel by late May. You will need to grow several plants to ensure pollination.

Trials in India found that the highest crops came from tindora plants that were allowed to sprawl uncontrolled rather than those that were trained up a trellis or support. However, this may not be possible in a small UK greenhouse! Plants can be trained upwards or the tips regularly pinched to keep them within bounds – this will need to be done every few days, or you may find you have a vegetable octopus rather than a productive plant.

Flowers should be produced within eight to ten weeks from rooting the cuttings, and may require hand-pollination. Pick the young fruits when they're about 5cm (2in) long, and keep picking – they will keep flowering (and fruiting) only while there are no mature fruits on the vine. At the end of the season, it's probably better to take more cuttings than to try to keep the parent plant alive, as overwintering will be difficult except for those with a heated greenhouse or conservatory.

SPICES

Adraku, ginger

Amada, mango ginger, and amb halad, zedoary

Dhania, coriander

Haldi, turmeric

Karri patti, curry leaf

Mirich, chilli

Nimbu ghas, lemongrass

ADRAKU, GINGER

(Zingiber officinale)

Family Zingiberaceae

The spice

Ginger is immediately recognisable to almost everyone in the UK now, although it has been imported in its fresh state only since the 1950s. It is sold as irregularly shaped lumpy roots, called hands, which break into pieces easily. A very large root, such as is obtained from a single plant, is called a race.

The skin of ginger root varies in colour from pale golden-grey to a scaly brown. It is thin and easily peeled to revel first a green cambium and then the creamy-gold, fibrous and very aromatic flesh. Ginger root may be bleached by treating with lime, or peeled ('white ginger') before sale. Fresh ginger is not nearly as hot as the dried root, due to the production of shogoals, one of the active ingredients, when drying.

Fresh ginger will keep in good condition for a month or slightly longer in a cool dry place – a fridge is actually a bit too cold. Alternatively, peeled and chopped ginger freezes well.

The plant

Ginger is native to southern Asia but cultivated worldwide in hot climates, especially in Africa, the Caribbean, China and India. It is an erect perennial herb growing to 1m (3ft) tall, with a spreading tuberous rhizome. There are a number of different races and cultivars.

At the start of each rainy season the plant sends up a long green spike, from which many elongated, spear-shaped leaves unfurl, in pairs on either side of the stem. The leaves have a

slightly spicy taste and scent. The flowers are flattened, cream or white with a deep purple and yellow marking on the lip, and emerge from a persistent spike of oval bracts, carried on a separate, many-sheathed stalk. Ginger seed is rarely produced outside the tropics and some clones don't seed at all. In those that do, the seed forms in three-sided fleshy capsules carried in the bracts.

Growing outdoors in the tropics, ginger needs an ample rainfall, temperatures of 30°C (86°F) or more, a short dry season and a deep fertile soil. It usually takes nine or ten months to produce a crop.

Nutritional value

Ginger is eaten only in small quantities, so isn't nutritionally significant, but does have beneficial effects on the body. It contains at least 12 essential oils, which aid digestion and have antiseptic and antibacterial qualities. It also contains gingerols, complex chemicals that increase the appetite and act as a digestive tonic.

Other uses

Ginger has been used in medicine at least since records began, and is a main ingredient in most Ayurvedic and Chinese prescriptions.

In the UK ginger has traditionally been a hot food, and is used to combat conditions such as colds or rheumatism. It is still a popular ingredient in many British over-the-counter remedies for indigestion, as it is a useful carminative (it assists the release of trapped gas from the gut); and in laxative mixtures, as it reduces spasms, soothes nausea and relieves pain. Eating large helpings of ginger stimulates the immune system.

Ginger tea is a traditional Asian remedy for colds, fever and stomach complaints, especially diarrhoea. A paste of fresh ginger root applied to the skin is sometimes used by hardier Asian elders as a counter-irritant for rheumatism and severe bruising: it causes severe reddening of the skin and pain if left on for too long.

An essential oil obtained from the steam distillation of dried ginger roots is used in flavourings, medicines and perfumes as well as in aromatherapy.

Cultivation

Although hardy to around 10°C (50°F), ginger likes to be much hotter, and can't be grown outdoors in the UK even in summer. However, it may live happily on a windowsill or in a hot steamy bathroom for some years if you can give it house room. Unfortunately, success does seem to depend on the individual plant – some succumb readily to the UK winter because of low light levels. I prefer to grow it as a half-hardy annual, using the fresh leaves in cooking, and buy my root ginger separately. The plant is easily grown from the 'finger' pieces broken off a hand of ginger. Existing ginger plants can also be divided and the roots grown on.

In early spring or late winter, find some fresh ginger in the shops. Choose fingers that have a shoot bud developing – this looks like a small pyramidal horn at the end of the root – and cut the root off at least 5cm (2in) from this bud. To encourage shoot development, store in a warm, light place for a few weeks.

Bury the finger with the bud upwards, 5cm

deep or slightly more, in a small pot of loam-based compost. Keep warm and constantly moist during the growing season. Move to a larger pot as the plant grows (ultimately you might need a 30cm (12in) pot if your ginger is growing very well). Once the plant has started to grow, feed every two to three weeks with a general pot-plant feed. You can snip off excess foliage to add to cooking, and let the root resprout.

The growth habit of ginger is disappointingly straggly compared with that of other tropical plants, and whatever you do it will look rather leggy. Very happy ginger often produces flowers, particularly if potbound or in its second year of growth in UK conditions. If you can bear to harvest them, the flowers make a marvellous addition to a stir-fry.

In the autumn, reduce watering and let the pots dry out, which will encourage the plants to form rhizomes. They can be overwintered at this stage, or the roots used for cooking: under good conditions a plant will form a 13cm (5in) rhizome in two years. The fresh roots are quite strongly flavoured, with a lemony taste and mild heat.

AMADA, MANGO GINGER

(Curcuma amada)

AMB HALAD, ZEDOARY

(C. zedoaria)

Family Zingiberaceae

The spice

Amada, or **mango ginger** is a small, greyish- to buff-skinned root, vaguely reminiscent of both ginger and turmeric but different from both. It is sold in Britain either during late spring to early summer, or in the autumn, according to the country of origin.

Each section of rhizome is about the thickness of a man's middle finger and comes in short pieces, about 4cm (1.5in) long at most. Unlike ginger, the rhizome is rounded rather than flattened. It has a distinctive, fresh, spicy scent: traditionally this is said to be like an unripe mango, hence the English name. Amada can be distinguished from turmeric by the internal colour and the absence of fine encircling lines on the outside of the rhizome.

The flesh inside is firm, crisp and a very pale creamy to primrose colour. It is not as succulent as turmeric, but a juice can be extracted

from it. The taste is mildly spicy, acidic and astringent, making the tongue feel dry, as with sloe berries.

Amb halad, or **zedoary**, is closely related. It is a short, fat, brown-skinned root that looks superficially like ginger but smells different again – some references say camphor-like – with an orange flesh like turmeric. There are numerous different races of zedoary, which were formerly regarded as distinct species but are now classified as regional variations throughout the plant's wide geographical range. One of these, formerly known as *C. zerumet*, is also called amb halad and is occasionally imported. It is a longer, thinner root than ginger, with a yellow flesh. Fortunately all these variants are equally edible and have similar though not identical properties – so from a culinary, if not a botanical, point of view the fact that they are easily confused doesn't matter!

The plant

Native to most of tropical Asia, amada is cultivated in India and Pakistan. Along with the other Curcuma species described above, it has shiny, elongated, broadly oblong-lanceolate leaves, with prominent parallel veins. These look to a European gardener's eye a bit like a hosta, but grow very large indeed – to nearly 1.5m (5ft) – in tropical conditions.

The leaves of amada are much paler green than those of turmeric. Each cluster of leaves leads down to a fragile, swollen root cluster, which can spread slowly by runners if left undisturbed. The plants

Amada root – photograph by Peter Andrews

have small, pale green, star-like flowers with persistent bracts, which interlock one on top of the other like a stack of fraying plastic cups.

Cultivated plants need a rich, fertile, well-drained but moisture-retentive soil, and prefer some shade in the tropics. The small root pieces are planted straight after the rainy season and take over 18 months to produce a profitable crop. The young shoots and leaves are also edible and can be added to curries or stews to give a subdued but spicy taste, used to wrap bite-sized portions of food for easy finger-food, or just steamed as a vegetable.

Zeodary looks very similar to amada when growing, but the principal or type species of C. zedoaria is distinguished by a dark purple or brown stripe down the central midrib of the leaves. The flowers are yellow to white, sometimes with a pink flush, with darker purple-pink bracts.

Nutritional value

Like turmeric, amada isn't eaten in large enough quantities to contribute many nutrients to the diet, as its positive effects are largely medicinal. It is a powerful antioxidant, and eating it regularly is said to be beneficial to those with heart conditions, high blood pressure and diabetes. Used in cooking it adds a spicy flavour but without the heat of ginger – to those who haven't tried it it's a very pleasant surprise!

Other uses

The Curcuma family is well known for having antibacterial, anti-infective and healing properties – turmeric, zedoary and other members of the

genus were known as yu jin in Chinese medicine as early as the seventh century. Eating amada is considered to improve the digestion and general well-being. Fresh amada paste, applied as a poultice to the affected area, is a traditional Indian remedy for bad bruises and sprains.

Zedoary is used in perfumes and, mashed to a paste and mixed with fresh cream or yoghurt, has been used as a face mask or mild abrasive scrub to beautify the skin.

Cultivation

Like their close relative turmeric, amada and zedoary need a hot, damp environment. They make attractive houseplants for a warm bathroom or steamy kitchen, looking a bit like a larger version of an aspidistra, but have the disadvantage of often struggling during the British winter due to poor light levels. They are hardy to 10°C (50°F), or slightly less for short periods.

Choose small pieces of root that are displaying signs of shoot development – these look like little raised bumps on the surface of the skin. If you're lucky you may even find a few with shoots already developed. Shoot formation can be encouraged by keeping the dry roots in a warm, barely light place that is not too dry for a few weeks. An ideal place is a tray under the bench in a greenhouse but, failing that, a thin white paper bag on a kitchen shelf or on top of a bathroom cupboard will do instead.

Once shoots have started to develop, grow the plants on in a warm light place with good humidity and water them well while they are actively growing. Amada and zedoary are quite greedy and benefit from weekly applications of a general-purpose plant feed. If your plant gets too large, simply chop off a few shoots to eat.

As winter approaches, reduce watering but keep the plant warm. It may lose its leaves and die back, in which case you can harvest your roots and save a small piece, or just keep the root slightly damp until spring, when it will resprout. Once the plants are potbound, and if you are very fortunate, they may reward you with flowers.

DHANIA, CORIANDER

(Coriandrum sativum)

Family Umbelliferae

The herb

Coriander is now sold widely in Britain as bunches of fresh leaves. Although the seeds have been used in the UK for centuries, it was not until the arrival of larger numbers of Asian immigrants during the late 1970s that attempts were made to cultivate the plant commercially here. UK varieties already in existence were of borderline hardiness and bolted rapidly, but a series of trials with Loughborough University and the Asian Vegetable Research Project enabled the selection of leafier strains that were better adapted to our weather conditions. Most of the fresh coriander sold in the UK today is home-grown.

The leaves are trifoliate with serrate edges, and have a characteristic, unforgettable scent. Coriander should be bought when fresh and lively, with leaves unwilted and bright green in colour, and with the roots attached. Avoid limp, yellowing specimens or those with the roots cut off. Once harvested, coriander doesn't keep well, so wash the roots carefully and put the bunch in a jar of water, or wash and pick over the whole bunch, dry on a tea towel and store in a plastic bag in the salad tray of the fridge.

Coriander can also be chopped and frozen successfully: it stores well in ice-cube-sized pieces, which are useful for adding to dishes. Remember to keep a special ice-cube tray for this purpose, as the scent taints plastic.

The plant

Coriander is an annual herb, with a long taproot and bright green leaves, which grows up to 60cm (2ft) tall. The whole plant, even the roots, is scented.

As the plant reaches flowering stage the shape of the leaves changes from a large, vaguely oakleaf-like, flattened form to a smaller, feathery, much-divided, carrot-like frond. The broader leaves are best for cooking, but all parts of the plant can be used, including the unripe seeds, although these are unpleasantly chewy. The washed taproot is also occasionally used in place of the leaves, if plants have bolted or been killed off by frosts.

The flowers are typical of an umbelliferous plant, being small and white or pink-tinted in broad, flat-faced clusters, and are popular with hoverflies and other insects. As they fade they are succeeded by the small oval seeds, deeply ridged, which split into two halves when ripe.

Nutritional value

Coriander is high in Vitamins C, A and B group. It also contains a small amount of dietary fibre.

Other uses

Coriander seeds are used in a variety of Indian dishes, from meat to dhal, to flavour sweets and in savoury snacks. In Western cooking they are a valuable ingredient in spiced vinegars, for making pickles and for flavouring sausages, tobacco and gin. Extracts from the seeds are often used in indigestion mixtures and to scent soaps, cosmetics and perfumes.

As a tea made from the seeds, coriander is used in domestic digestive remedies. The seeds have also been used externally as a warm paste to treat painful joints. An essential oil is distilled from the seeds and used as an aromatherapy remedy for muscular aches and pains, infections and digestive disturbances.

Cultivation

Cultivars available in the UK include 'Santo', a dwarf strain, and the taller 'Leisure', 'Salsa' and 'Cliantro', which produce broader, dark green leaves. All these varieties are claimed to be slow to bolt. A lemon-scented form is also available, and is particularly useful in Thai cooking, although this seems to be more tender in my garden.

Coriander can be sown at any time of year when the soil is warm enough, generally from late March onwards. August to early-autumn sowings often overwinter successfully, provided they are not too waterlogged. Overwintered plants are very useful to the home gardener as they provide the maximum amount of leaves for the space used before finally running to seed. Coriander is hardy to a few degrees below freezing – although I have known some plants survive at -7°C (20°F)!

Sowing coriander is sometimes not as successful as it might be. As with all umbellifers, the seed needs to be fresh to germinate readily, and quickly rots in cold wet soil. (Parsnip, another umbellifer, is renowned for being awkward to germinate.) Some seed merchants unashamedly sell coriander seed with very low viability. Germination temperatures for coriander are around 10–12°C (50–54°F) for sown seed – although self-set seedlings appear to be able to germinate well below this. Many of my Indian friends swear by soaking the seed before sowing, but I've never found I needed to.

The best rules for sowing seem to be: use fresh seed; sow no earlier than when you would normally plant potatoes, in late March to early April; sow in short drills half an inch deep; and continue sowing at three-weekly intervals until late August.

Thin the plants (using the thinnings in cooking) to 15cm (6in) apart. Plants can be cropped at any stage of growth, but ideally before the leaves have changed from broad to feathery and the plant has started to flower. Well-grown plants will sometimes respond positively to being snipped off to the first few leaf nodes at the earliest sign of bolting, and if well watered will resprout a fine new set of leaves. This is most likely to happen in a spell of damp summer weather, but abandon hope if you have hot dry conditions. If you do have bolting plants, keep them as a source of seed: saving your own seed is the best way to ensure good germination next year, and the hoverflies will enjoy the flowers in the meantime.

HALDI, TURMERIC

(Curcuma longa)

Family Zingiberaceae

The spice

Fresh haldi, or turmeric, is one of the traditional Indian signs of spring, as the roots come into season during the dark days of January to March. They are golden-grey to pale biscuit coloured, smaller and more oval in cross section than ginger, with many fine orange lines around the circumference. There may be little pointed buds nestling on the surface of the root, or a hairy network of roots below. Good turmeric should be plump, firm and look vibrantly alive.

When broken open, turmeric has a juicy, brilliant-orange flesh, with a spicy, penetrating smell and taste. The juice stains skin for a long time, and may stain clothes permanently.

Methods of preparation can alter the appearance of turmeric rhizomes – those from northern India are often air-dried after lifting, and any mud or debris round the roots is brushed off later, leaving a darker, slightly gritty skin with many little wounds from grit particles. Roots

originating from Pakistan are usually paler in colour, because they are washed immediately after harvesting, which removes the top layer of epidermis.

There are a number of related species: *Curcuma amada, C. zedoaria, C. zerumet* (see Amada, Mango Ginger for more information), and *C. aromatica*, a wild form of turmeric.

The plant

Turmeric grows throughout central Asia but may originally have been native to India: it has certainly been cultivated throughout most of the tropics for a long time. It is found in most gardens in tropical and subtropical Asia. Like other members of the Zingiberaceae family, it has big oblong-elliptic, pointed leaves, which can be 60cm (2ft) long. They look rather like aspidistra leaves, though not quite the same shade of dark green, with prominent veins either side of a deep midrib.

Turmeric plants grow up to 1m (3ft) tall and spread by creeping rhizomes, like mint.

The flowers are insignificant but heavily scented, carried at the base of the leaves in pairs, and have persistent bracts, pink at the top and paler green below.

The plant requires rich, well-drained yet well-watered soil, warmth and high humidity, as well as a period of dry weather to induce rhizome formation. It is often grown as an understorey crop among lines of young fruit trees, because it prefers semi-shaded conditions.

Normally turmeric is propagated by root division, but the plants can also be grown from seed. The best time to harvest them is when they are over two years old and the leaves have just withered. Rhizomes can be dried for at least three years without losing any of their goodness, but become very hard and difficult to process after about three months.

Nutritional value

In parts of the world where turmeric is native it is eaten raw as a snack, and I have watched

Turmeric Root - photograph by Peter Andrews

quite young Asian children devour fresh peeled haldi with as much relish as adults. However, it is not normally eaten in large enough quantities to be a major part of a daily diet. Taken in any quantity the medicinal properties of the root are more important than its mineral or vitamin content.

Other uses

Turmeric has a long tradition of use in the Chinese and Ayurvedic systems of medicine, particularly as an anti-inflammatory agent and for the treatment of flatulence, jaundice, menstrual difficulties, hematuria (blood in urine), haemorrhage and colic. It is a powerful antioxidant.

Turmeric is used as a natural dye for cloth, as well as a food colouring: it gives the golden-yellow colour to English piccalilli. The juice freshly squeezed from pounded roots is traditionally mixed with sandalwood powder and rubbed over the skin of an Indian bride before her wedding. It also acts as a mosquito repellent and has fungicidal, antibacterial and a generally healing effect on the skin.

Mixing fresh turmeric leaves with grain or using them to line village grain stores is proven to reduce insect attack, and spraying diseased pigeon peas with a solution of turmeric juice in water has been found to effectively cure fungal wilt disease.

Recently, compounds isolated from turmeric have been used in cancer treatments, as they appear to induce extra sensitivity to radiation in cancerous cells. Turmeric is a known anticoagulant and has been shown to reduce blood cholesterol levels.

Cultivation

Turmeric is easy to grow and, provided you have a reasonably warm place with good light – it doesn't even have to be on a windowsill – you can have your own personal spice plant! It has very handsome foliage, and looks rather like a leggy, brighter green aspidistra.

Look in your local Asian greengrocer's for the more shrivelled tubers, which tend to be discarded at the bottom of the box. Choose those that are maybe slightly wrinkled but still firm, with a little triangular bud protruding like a rhinoceros horn from the top. If you're lucky you may find one with a bud about to burst into growth.

To induce bud-burst in a budded root, plant the whole root, point upwards, about 4cm (1.5in) deep in a gritty, loam-based compost. Keep warm and moderately damp in full sun and at a temperature of around 18–20°C (65–68°F). Putting a plastic bag over the top of the pot often helps.

Turmeric, like ginger, is a greedy feeder, so once the first leaves appear, transfer plants to a bigger pot with richer compost. Leaf mould is beneficial for microflora – turmeric, being at home in a very active forest floor, likes its fungal partners – but if you don't have any, use well-composted bark chippings in your growing medium.

Once your turmeric gets going its leaves can reach 90cm (3ft) long as they reach for the light, so it will probably be happier on the floor than on a windowsill. Leaves that become too long to accommodate can be removed at the base and used to wrap little finger-sized portions of food – they go particularly well with large prawns – or added to flavour cooking as you would a bay leaf. In India, haldi plants are earthed up as soon as they have reached 20cm (8in) in height, which encourages rhizome production but also stabilises them when they grow tall.

Keep plants away from draughts, and mist with water occasionally. Turmeric is hardy to 13°C (55°F), with a minimum growing temperature of 16–18°C (60–65°F), but it will grow far better when hotter than this. If your plant is very happy it may reward you with flowers – this isn't a sign of stress but of well-being.

Sometimes a turmeric plant might turn yellowish or lose leaves in winter. This is a result of the lower light levels in the UK than in tropical India, although sometimes it is an effect of exposure to cold, but the plant should recover in spring. If it does suffer in this way, reduce watering and, if possible, move the plant to a warmer, lighter position during the winter. Move it away from a cold windowsill on frosty nights.

KARRI PATTI, CURRY LEAF

(Murraya koenigii)

Family Rutaceae

The herb

Curry leaves are often sold prepacked in small polythene bags, as this helps to keep them fresh. They are small, dark green and oval, a bit like rather tall, skinny privet leaves, growing opposite each other on green or dark grey twigs. Each leaf is about an inch long with a prominent midrib. When held up to the light it has many glands visible on the underside, like little pinpricks: these are what release the scent when handled.

When bruised, curry leaves have a strong scent that doesn't really smell like curry, more like a mixture of soot and crushed fresh citrus leaves. Fresh curry leaves will last about a week in their plastic bags in the salad tray of the fridge. They retain their scent when dried, but are better preserved by freezing, when they will last for six months.

The plant

The curry leaf tree is a fast-growing deciduous shrub or multi-stemmed small tree native to tropical parts of the Indian subcontinent. It is found in dry, open places and tolerates quite high altitudes. The tree has dark grey bark,

deep roots and deep green, finely divided aromatic leaves, often with nine leaflets. Murraya is related to Citrus and grows in a similar fashion, with a twiggy, scraggly habit. It suckers easily, which can be a problem in small gardens in the tropics. A fully grown tree can reach 6m (20ft) or so.

The flowers are small, starry-white, five petalled and very fragrant. They are carried on the tips of every branch in dense, flat-topped clusters and are popular with bees because of their rich nectar. They are followed by small, round, juicy berries, red at first then turning black, which are devoured by birds, bats and monkeys. The berries each contain a single seed, which tastes strong, hot and sour and is eaten in India but doesn't yet seem to have been introduced as a fruit to the UK.

There are a variety of cultivars of the curry leaf tree, including a dwarf form that is pale green and has a spreading habit, and the very slow-growing, thick-leaved, fragrant 'Ganthi' clone from Thailand. The tree is easily grown from seed or by stem cuttings.

A related species, kamini (M. paniculata), is widely grown as a garden tree in Asia: it has larger white heads of deliciously scented flowers and pungent leaves that are chewed to relieve toothache.

Nutritional value

Curry leaves are used only as a flavouring and aren't eaten in large enough quantities to make any nutritional difference to the diet.

Other uses

An old Punjab tradition was to scatter chopped curry leaves into the furrows when ploughing ground that would later grow rice, as this was believed to increase germination rates. Storing curry leaves among seeds, or using them to line a pit in which seed grain is stored, reduces insect attack and has been practised for generations by Asian farmers. The plant has been used as a rootstock for grafting lemon trees, as it is resistant to nematode attack.

An essential oil is extracted from curry leaves, and an infusion made from the leaves is recommended for stomach upsets. The dried seeds may be ground as an alternative to pepper.

Cultivation

The curry leaf tree will need the protection of a heated greenhouse or conservatory for most of the year in the UK, although it will enjoy full sunshine in a sheltered part of the garden during the hottest part of summer. It is hardy to around 12°C (54°F). As with most herbs, the most flavoursome leaves are produced when the plants are grown hot and dry.

Curry leaf plants are not widely available for sale in the UK, but are stocked by Poyntzfield and Old Hall Plants. Seed is offered for sale by a few suppliers, although this may take a bit of searching: Chiltern Seeds has sold it in previous years. The seeds require at least 20°C (68°F) to germinate and may take a long time – be patient! Chipping the seed or even sawing at it with a hacksaw blade can help, as can pre-germinating it by leaving it wrapped in a damp piece of kitchen towel in a warm place for two weeks before sowing. Don't cover the seeds too deeply. They will do best with a 50:50 mixture of grit and loam-based compost. Once germinated, the plants should be left until 10–12cm (4–5in) tall or a year old before repotting – they resent root disturbance and sulk after being moved. They grow very slowly for a couple of years, then suddenly gallop away like mad. They need good drainage and a sunny position.

If you've bought some very fresh curry leaves, you can try to root stem cuttings. Take twigs that are not very floppy and green nor very hard and woody, but somewhere in between (this stage is called semi-ripe), and remove most of their lower leaves. Cut the stem cleanly at a node and push the cutting a few centimetres into a 50:50 mix of potting compost and sharp grit, with about three leaves above the surface. Rooting hormone is not essential but may help if you have some handy. Place the cuttings in a propagator or covered pot, in a warm, light place out of direct sunlight. Rooting will take about three weeks

As the plants grow, trim them regularly to maintain a supply of young leaves for cooking. Water regularly but allow plants to dry out between waterings. Feed during the growing season with a general-purpose fertiliser.

Once the leaves start to dry and fall in the autumn, stop watering. Keep the pot in a warm, frost-free place – minimum temperature 12°C (54°F) without leaves; 16°C (60°F) with them. In early April, soak the pot, repot if necessary, and move the plant to a warm, light place at a temperature of around 18–20°C (64–68°F). Watch out for scale insects if you keep the same plants for a long time, as they seem particularly attracted to curry leaf trees.

MIRICH, CHILLI

(Capsicum annuum and related species)

Family Cucurbitacae

The spice

Chillies come in a great variety of shapes, sizes and colours, from tiny fiery slivers through larger broad conical shapes (sometimes called bull's horn or bullet chillis) to squashed or perfect spheres, and can be anything from bright green to brilliant yellow, red, black or blue in shade. They usually have a highly glossy finish to the smooth skin, which is sometimes oddly crumpled. Whatever they look like, they all taste hot. Some are much hotter than others – and don't believe the rule of thumb that says the smaller the pepper the bigger the punch, as big ones can be quite strong too! Chillies are measured on the Scoville scale, which gauges the amount of the alkaloid capsaicin present in the flesh.

Chillies have a thin skin and flesh, unlike their relatives the bell or sweet peppers, which are thick walled. Inside, clinging to a central membrane, are small, flat, circular seeds, which may be even hotter than the chilli flesh. Most have yellow or brown seeds but some are black.

There are thousands of different types of chilli, and many cultivars have been named, but it's worth remembering that 'Habanero' or 'Jalapeno' is really just the place where these types of peppers were first grown rather than true varieties.

All green chillies will eventually change to their ripe colour, which depends on the cultivar. They keep for a fortnight in the salad tray of the fridge, and can be dried by hanging them up on a cotton thread knotted between each pepper. They also freeze well, although they lose their aroma more from being frozen than from drying.

The plant

Chilli originates from the hotter regions of Central America and was cultivated in Mexico up to 7000 years ago, but was known to other parts of the world from only about 1500. Its unique taste, combined with

long-lived seeds that were easy to grow, meant that it rapidly spread across the globe. The largest growers and exporters of chilli peppers at present are Turkey and China.

A short-lived perennial or annual plant, chillis are a complex, closely related group of a few species. The most commonly cultivated chilli is Capsicum annuum, but other species that are cultivated worldwide include C. frutescens (syn. C. minimum), C. chinense and C. pubescens. For the non-botanist there is little difference between the species, except that some grow taller and live longer, forming small shrubs rather than herbaceous plants.

All chilli species grow more or less upright and have small, pointed, lanceolate to ovate leaves and small, white-to-greenish, dangling flowers that look vaguely potato-flower-like when upturned and examined closely.

Chilli peppers are usually divided into four groups, as follows.

- **Cherry peppers** – small, round peppers, from marble- to gobstopper-sized. Hot in flavour; red, yellow or purple.
- **Cone peppers** – these are carried upright on the bushes like little horns, up to 5cm (2in) long. They can be hot or sweet, and are white or green, turning red, crimson or purple when fully ripe.

- **Red cone peppers** – similar to cone peppers but slightly bigger – up to 7cm (3in) long – and carried in upright bunches. They are bright red, and hot.

- **Cayenne or chilli peppers** – these are the tiny, fiery, hot 'bird peppers': very thin, hanging fruits that are more or less conical and can be red, black or purple. Some cultivars have variegated leaves and a drooping habit.

Indian and Pakistani cultivars include 'Bharat', 'Early Bounty', 'Indira', 'Lario' and 'Hira'.

Nutritional value

Sweet peppers are rich in vitamin C but chilli peppers are used in such small amounts that any nutrient addition to the diet is negligible.

Other uses

Capsaicin is a powerful stimulant with carminative properties (it assists the release of trapped gas from the gut). It has been used in a variety of treatments, ranging from appetite stimulants and indigestion remedies to cold cures and ointments for rheumatism and related aches and pains.

Chilli powder is used in the processed food industry and in the making of alcoholic

drinks (where it can give a sensation of greater strength to weak solutions of spirits). Consuming chilli stimulates the release of endorphins in the brain, which may account for the existence of foods such as chilli-flavoured chocolate and phaal, a fiery curry invented in the UK by late-night Asian food outlets for macho Englishmen demanding ever-hotter food.

Dried chillis have been made into a tea or applied as a powder as a home-made pest repellent, for use on pests from aphids and slugs to mice, rats and rabbits.

Cultivation

If you can grow tomatoes successfully, you should be able to grow chillies. They are a little different in their needs but are just as easy to grow on a sunny patio, in a big pot on a windowsill or in an unheated greenhouse. They are hardy to around 7°C (45°F) when not in active growth, but 10°C (50°F) when growing. Chillies are best treated as half-hardy annuals, as they need a longer growing season than the UK climate allows.

There are hundreds of different cultivars of chilli pepper, and seed is widely available from seed suppliers – Simpson's Seeds do a wide range. Alternatively, you can save the seed from chillis you buy in the shops; they are quite likely to be true to type. Choose ripe fruits, which should be really soft and wrinkly before you remove the seeds. When extracting the seeds it's a good idea to wear rubber gloves to protect your skin.

Good varieties for heat include 'Scotch Bonnet' (cherry pepper type), with moderately hot orange or red crumpled pods; 'Ring of Fire' (red cone type), which is very hot, with thin, red hanging fruits; and 'Purple Tiger' and 'Trifetti' (chilli pepper type), with attractive marbled foliage and hot fruits that are blotched purple, green and cream. Note that growing chillies in a

cool climate doesn't make them any less fiery.

Sow seed in late February to mid-March. Either sow just a pinch in several 9cm (3in) pots and pull out all except the strongest seedling, or scatter seed thinly across a larger pot and transplant the seedlings. Cover the seed to its own depth in compost and keep at 21°C (70°F) for best germination. Pot on seedlings as they grow: if you're planning to keep the plants inside all summer they will need at least a 30cm (12in) pot when fully grown.

Harden off gradually from mid-May and plant out, if growing outdoors, by early June.

The plants will need a sheltered, well-drained site in full sun outside, but they don't require a very fertile soil. Unless you have a very warm sunny patio, plants growing north of Bristol will do better under cover.

Pinch out the growing tips occasionally to encourage the plants to bush out. They may need some support from twiggy branches pushed in around them, or they can be tied to a cane. If growing under glass, they prefer slightly hotter and more humid conditions than do tomatoes, with frequent misting or regular dampening down of the greenhouse floor to encourage fruiting. Aim for temperatures of 21–24°C (70–75°F). Although chillies are tropical plants they can be easily scorched by direct sunlight, so use some form of light shading if the sun is very bright.

When the plants are growing well, apply a balanced feed every ten days or so until the fruits begin to colour, then switch to one with a higher potash content. Pick the chillis when they are green or coloured as you need them.

Plants with unripe peppers at the end of the summer can be brought indoors to finish ripening, or you can ripen the green fruit off the plant. It is possible to overwinter chilli plants, especially the small bird-pepper types, by cutting them back to ground level and storing the pots somewhere cool but frost free and dry: the resulting plants will get away much quicker next season and give an early crop, but it's only worth it if you have a particularly good cultivar or lots of warm shed room. The requisite conditions are similar to those for dahlias, i.e. dark and cool but above 4°C (40°F), in a dry place but with sufficient moisture around the roots so they don't dry out completely – pack them

Photograph by Peter Andrews

in spent potting compost, for example.

Chilli plants are generally trouble free except for viruses, which occasionally show up in the form of marbled foliage and stunted plants. If you find this evidence in your crop, destroy the affected plants. Apart from the occasional red spider mite or aphid attack, you'll find that pests are deterred by the hot chilli taste. Chilli roots produce an exudate that repels Fusarium mould, although they occasionally develop other fungal diseases.

NIMBU GHAS, LEMONGRASS

(Cymbopogon species)

Family Poaceae

The herb

Lemongrass is becoming more mainstream as a foodie favourite in the UK, and is deservedly popular, with beautifully aromatic leaves. Specimens sold in Chinese and Thai outlets are often easier to recognise than those in Indian shops: neatly packaged, often cellophane-wrapped, they consist of short, trimmed lengths of the inner leaves of the grass, a bit like miniature spring onions with a tuft of green foliage at the top, and require only a rinse under the tap before use. Lemongrass sold in some large supermarkets is very similarly prepared.

Lemongrass from Indian stores looks quite different, naked and uncut. The very long, hard-textured leaves are folded over on themselves like daffodils tied up by an over-zealous park keeper, and the bulbous base is barely visible. Occasional fronds unfurl to snag the unwary, with surprisingly hard and paper-cut-sharp edges. This sort of lemongrass is likely to be Cymbopogon flexuosus, East Indian lemongrass, while the Chinese or Thai plants are probably mostly C. citratus, though may be a mixture of the two species.

When handled, both types emit a powerful aroma of sweet lemon, without the acid tang of a true citrus: depending on your memories, it may evoke cheap soap and candles or delicious Thai cooking. The smell can contaminate other delicate flavours in the fridge, so store carefully.

The plant

Lemongrass is one of a fragrant division of the grass family Poaceae. It is related to Poa annua, the small, annoying grass that pops up in the cracks between paving slabs whenever your back's turned – an all-too-common

British weed species.

In addition to Cymbopogon citratus and C. flexuosus, another species is C. nardus, citronella grass. The odour of citronella is familiar to most people who have ever had cause to use mosquito repellents.

Other relatives are rosha grass, C. martini, which has an odour like oil of geranium and is used in many rose perfumes; and ginger grass, C. martini var. sofia, which smells lemonish-peppery and has a distinctive, rather unpleasant air-freshener undertone. These are generally sold as medicine or incense ingredients. All forms of lemongrass are cultivated extensively in India for essential-oil production.

Cymbopogon citratus is native to southern India and Sri Lanka, and is a vigorous, clump-forming, spiky-leaved grass, with long, hard arching leaves with a prominent midrib. In India it reaches over 2m (6ft), though in the UK it grows to only about 1.4m (4ft 6in). Individual leaves can reach 1m (3ft) or more in length. Commercial strains of lemongrass rarely flower, although some strains are more ready to set seed.

Nutritional value

As with many of the other plants in this section, lemongrass is of little nutritional significance because it is eaten in such small quantities, but it is beneficial as an appetite stimulant and a tonic for the digestive system.

Other uses

Lemongrass has valuable medicinal properties, both in the form of the fresh plant or as the essential oil. Lemongrass tea is taken for upset stomachs, particularly for children, who enjoy the taste: it has antispasmodic and sedative properties. A stronger decoction is used to treat fungal infections of the skin, and to deter lice and scabies. Bathing aching joints with this extract is believed by many elderly Asians to soothe arthritis, especially if used regularly.

Essential oil of lemongrass is used commercially for all sorts of lemon scents, from cleaning fluids to bath preparations, shampoos and food flavourings. It has also, rather surprisingly, been used in synthesising the scent of violets in perfumes.

Cultivation

Lemongrass can be grown from seed but it's better to try to root your own from fresh stems. Select the freshest you can find, with a noticeable bulb left on at the base, rather than cut through at the lower section of stem. They are easily rooted from March onwards with a little bottom heat and a bright but not directly sunlit position. Use a shallow pan pot or deep tray filled with a 50:50 mix of gravel or vermiculite and potting compost. A

temperature of around 18°C (65°F) is ideal.

Move the plants into pots as soon as roots begin to form, and pot on as they grow. They are reassuringly unfussy, but appreciate some organic matter (finely composted bark or leaf mould) as well as grit in the potting mix. Sunlight and regular watering, so that the pot rarely dries out completely, will keep them happy. During the summer they can be planted out into the garden in a sheltered spot and make a nicely architectural feature in the border. Don't plant out before you'd put pelargoniums or other tender bedding outside. If growing on in pots, feed regularly with a balanced NPK feed or a comfrey-and-manure-water mix.

With a bit of tending, a single stem rooted in the spring will be large enough to divide into four or five clumps of stem by the late autumn. Reserve one to grow on through the winter on a sunny windowsill as a (rather untidy) houseplant, and use the rest to cook with. Lemongrass will survive near-frost conditions for short periods but can't usually be overwintered without heat in a greenhouse or polytunnel in the UK: it is hardy to only 7°C (45°F).

If you want to try sowing seed, a number of seed firms usually stock it (try Chiltern Seeds). Sow early in spring if you have sufficient heat – 21°C (70°F) – as it needs a longer growing season from seed than from cuttings to obtain a useful crop.

ORNAMENTALS

Am, mango

Amla and harfi, Indian and star gooseberry

Amrood, guava

Ber, jujube

Chikku, sapodilla

Imli, tamarind

Jackfruit

Nimbu, lime, and magrut, kaffir lime

Rambutan, lychee and longan

Sahijan, drumstick

Suran, kand and ratula, yam

AM, MANGO

(Mangifera indica)

Family Anacardiaceae

The fruit

Mangos are instantly recognisable, although to an Asian there are only a few varieties that truly deserve the name. They are large fruits, weighing up to 3kg (over 6lb) each, but the ones most often seen for sale in the UK are much smaller. The skin can be almost any shade of green, golden-yellow or orange, and may be brownish or tinted with red. Some cultivars are ripe when still green; others turn red or yellowish. Some have very fibrous and almost hairy-textured flesh; others, like the 'Alphonso', are barely stringy at all. There are said to be as many cultivars of mango as there are gods in India, or apple varieties in the UK.

When fully ripe the skin will feel slightly yielding to a squeeze but won't be too soft. Fruit that is brightly coloured but hard can be allowed to ripen at room temperature. Reject those with dark markings or dents on the skin.

The highest-quality mangos, sometimes called honey or sucking mangos, are small and golden, only as big as a small fist. They have thin skins; exquisite butter-textured, perfumed flesh with few fibres; and are in season from June to August.

The tree

Mangifera indica is native throughout most of subtropical Asia and has been grown in India for over 6000 years. The tree, which can be very large, is instantly recognisable in the tropics, with very dark foliage and spreading branches. It has rough, thick, dark grey bark and leathery, sharply pointed leaves. Young leaves are copper coloured, red or purple.

Mangos crop from about six years old and are very long-lived – some are said to be over 300 years old and still producing fruit. If wounded, the branches and trunk exude a sticky latex. The many tiny flowers, carried during late winter to spring, are pale yellowish and deliciously fragrant. They are pollinated by small flies as well as bees, and are followed in about four months by the large fruit.

Other uses

Mango roots are diuretic, and a decoction of boiled root is claimed to be helpful in cases of jaundice. The seed is vermifuge (used to treat parasitic worms), and the latex has been used to treat inflamed gums in Nepal.

Cultivation

Mangos can't be grown outside in the UK but make attractive (if rather large) pot plants, although they won't get big enough to flower or fruit. They need a minimum temperature of 20°C (68°F). They respond well to being kept confined and tolerate restricted growing conditions for a long time.

If you grow a mango from a stone, you may find many shoots developing from a single seed – this is called polyembryony. The strongest seedlings are likely to be the most similar to the parent tree and these should be selected. Most indigenous Indian cultivars are monoembryonic (with a single seedling emerging form the stone), but these are not always genetically identical to their parents. These cultivars are usually propagated by grafting on to seedlings of common mangos such as 'Alphonso', 'Bombay', 'Dashekai' or 'Muloga'. Polyembryonic cultivars include 'Peach', 'Carabao' and 'Kensington'.

Choose the ripest fruit you can find to select a stone from, and carefully remove all the pulp with a sharp knife and/or wire wool. Rub the seed with sandpaper or make a small cut in it using a chisel. Put it in a jar of water and keep in an airing cupboard or other warm place at about 21°C (70°F). Change the water every day for two weeks. If your seed starts to shoot, remove it from the jar and plant in a 9cm (3i)n pot of loam-based compost. If the seed hasn't sprouted, pot it up all the same: put the pot inside a plastic bag, seal it and return it to the cupboard for up to two months.

Pot on the seedling as it grows. After the first year, pinch out the top bud in the spring as the plant starts into growth, which will help keep it bushy, and repeat-pinch as needed. Keep in a bright place but not necessarily in bright sunlight.

Mangos prefer acidic conditions, so water with rainwater if possible and feed weekly during the summer with a high-potash liquid feed, as for tomatoes. Plants whose leaves go yellow (usually from lime-induced chlorosis) may benefit from being given a dose of sequestered iron, or seaweed feed. In winter, reduce the watering and keep warm but in a lighter place.

Every year, pot your plant up in a larger pot until you have reached the maximum size you can deal with. After that, remove an inch or two of compost from the top of the pot and replace it with a mixture of well-rotted garden compost and grit. As this sinks during the growing season, top-dress with more garden compost and a seaweed meal. Prune once growth has started again early in the season and pinch out the tips regularly. The tree will be happy in your living room for many years.

AMLA, INDIAN GOOSEBERRY

(Phyllanthus emblica)

STAR GOOSEBERRY

(P. acidus)

Family Euphorbiaceae

The fruit

A small and strikingly beautiful fruit, amla is a green or reddish-tinged, slightly flattened globe about the size of a conker, with a translucent glossy skin. On one side of the fruit, five to seven rays are visible gleaming through the smooth skin. The skin is quite tenaciously attached to the flesh, but will peel off with a sharp knife. The flesh is firm, translucent and quite juicy, and surrounds a small beige stone.

Amla flesh is refreshing and very sour-fruity tasting – not really like any other fruit flavour and remarkably sharp even when fully ripe. When unripe, amla are incredibly astringent and tongue-curling, like sloes. The fruits contain some of the highest levels of vitamin C found in nature.

For eating, select just-firm fruits with clear, unblemished skins that are golden or reddish tinged. If you want to try to grow one, select the softest and ripest, regardless of spots and bruises. To encourage one to ripen, just leave it in a sunny place for a few days.

Harfi look similar to amla but are more oval, with six deep ribs running down from the stem, and they don't taste quite as sharp.

The tree

Phyllanthus emblica comes from central and southern India and has been used there since around 1600 BC, while P. acidus is found throughout all the tropical regions of Asia. Small, dainty trees with graceful, finely divided foliage, looking very like some sort of acacia, they are semi-evergreen and shed their leaves a few at a time all the time, which makes them untidy as a garden tree. The new growth is pinkish-red and looks very attractive.

The Indian gooseberry tree normally grows to around 5m (16ft) but can reach up to 17m (55ft). Its bark is smooth and pale grey, overlaid on older growth with a brown peeling layer that flakes off in pale scrolls. Underneath, the new bark is a pale pinkish-buff. The star gooseberry tree reaches 11m (35ft) or so, and has bigger leaves.

In both species, male and female flowers are borne separately on the same tree but open at slightly different times, so another tree is required for cross-pollination. Flowering is stimulated by photoperiod (changes in day length). The flowers grow in little starry bunches at the base of the leaves – pale green in P. emblica and white in P. acidus; the male flowers in big tufts and the females in sparse ones – and the little clusters of fruit look very decorative as they ripen. The trees bear fruit from the age of about five or six years.

Cultivars of the Indian gooseberry include 'Barnasi', the sort most usually imported into the UK, which is large, early-season and ripens almost white; 'Chakiya', the heaviest-cropping variety, with large, fibrous fruits; 'Francis' and 'Hathijhool', which is principally used for medicines and cosmetics.

Other Uses

'Amalaki' means nurse – and amla is said to be everybody's nurse because it's so good for you. The fruit is very important in Ayurvedic medicine (it's one of the three fruits used in triphyla, 'the three myrobalans', which is a classic cooling and stomachic tonic). Considered to have a beneficial effect on the digestive system, it is held to prevent diabetes, reduce high blood pressure and improve the general body condition if taken regularly. Due to the high levels of Vitamin C it contains, it is a powerful diuretic. It is also renowned for its beneficial effects on the skin and hair, and is thought to be an aphrodisiac.

Cultivation

Amla and harfi are usually propagated by seed. Seed can be bought from tropicalfruitandveg.co.uk and it's always worth keeping your eyes on the latest seed catalogues (try Chilterns or Jungle Seeds). Greenwoood cuttings may be taken from established plants and propagated with misting or under a plastic cover with bottom heat, at 24°C (75°F) during late spring or summer.

The fruits as sold are not usually picked ripe enough to germinate, but look out for very ripe, squishy specimens. Otherwise, choose fruits that are very soft and ripen them further on a windowsill until they split open and begin to turn mouldy. Cut them in half and remove the seed. Wash away surplus flesh from the stone, and test the stones by seeing which will float or sink in a glass of water. Floaters can be discarded as being infertile.

Amla, photograph by Manji Kerai

Sow the sinkers immediately in a loam-based compost, kept moist and warm at around 24°C. Germination is erratic but can take as little as three weeks. Once the plants have two true leaves with the next one developing, transplant individually into large, deep pots to grow on, as the plants resent root disturbance. The growing medium should be rich but free-draining, and comprise up to a third composted bark or grit. Some old references mention adding a lump or two of charcoal to the pots to keep them 'sweet' (less likely to become waterlogged).

In summer, potted amla can be left outside, but they dislike direct sun all day. Harfi is slightly more susceptible to damage by cold winds. They won't produce flowers in northern Europe unless given supplementary lighting to give them the right day-length and wavelength type, but they make an attractive and interesting foliage plant. Misting with rainwater during the growing season is said to be helpful. If pruning is required, it's best to do it in January when the plants are almost dormant. In theory they are hardy to only 16°C (60°F), although established trees in the US have survived occasional frosts – so perhaps there is potential for trying them outside in Cornwall?

AMROOD, GUAVA

(Psidium guajava)

Family Myrtaceae

The fruit

Ripe guavas are instantly recognisable by their scent – once smelt, their sweet, slightly rank aroma is never forgotten and will beckon you through the doors of any shop offering them for sale. Guavas imported into the UK are generally pale green in colour, with a smooth skin and about the size of an apple, but they can be much larger than this. They are usually very under-ripe so have to kept in a warm place to ripen fully. A fully ripe guava becomes golden to pink-flushed and is as soft as a ripe peach. When it's cut open it reveals a thick skin with many seeds embedded in the central whitish or pink pulp.

Strawberry guavas (P. littorale var. longipes) are slightly larger, and an attractive dark red in colour. A close relative is the yellow strawberry guava or lemon guava (P. littorale var. littorale), which is bigger still, yellow to tawny gold and very sweet.

Guavas can be kept for a few days in the fridge once ripe but should be allowed to warm up before eating. Their enticing fragrance can be overpowering, sweet and exotic, but with a definite overtone of sweaty armpit, and tends to influence anything else kept next to it for even a short time. So if you don't want everything else to taste of guava, store them in a plastic container.

The tree

Native to tropical America, guavas are now widely grown throughout the tropics. They have naturalised in some areas but have never become a serious woody weed.

Guava makes a small tree or large bush, reaching about 10m (30ft) tall at most. The bark of young trees, and the branches of established ones, is a smooth and shiny red-brown: as the tree ages the bark flakes off in large shavings, in the same way as that of the paper-bark maple.

The leaves are oval and smooth, with deep central veins and short stalks, and grow opposite each other all along the angular twigs. Small flowers, about 2.5cm (1in) across, grow from between the leaf axils, usually singly or occasionally in pairs. They have four or five small white petals, masses of long stamens and look like tiny white fibre-optic lights among the leaves. Bees and other insects love them, and a flowering guava tree is a happy humming community. Guava honey is highly prized. The fruits are eaten by bats and monkeys as well as people, so are often harvested unripe and left to ripen in a sealed box or storeroom.

Guavas are usually propagated by seed, but some superior types are grafted. Cultivars include 'Cherry' and 'Thai White'.

Other uses

Guavas are a good source of vitamins A and B group, and contain about five times as much Vitamin C as an orange if the skin as well as the flesh is eaten.

The unripe fruit, bark and roots of guava are astringent and are used to treat dysentery. They are said to reduce blood sugar levels and to be antibacterial. Fresh leaves are brewed to make a tea for the treatment of malaria and other feverish infections.

Guava bark is used for tanning, and in Nepal it is used to make marcha, a fermenting sort of cake which is eventually distilled to produce a potent spirit.

Cultivation

Guavas were grown here by the Victorians, and fruited successfully in their glasshouses, although they were cultivated more as a curiosity and status symbol than a crop. If you have a large warm bathroom or kitchen and are willing to have a fairly big green friend sharing it with you, you too may, with some skill, grow your own guava.

Choose a ripe fruit that has become very soft and squishy, and extract the seeds from the pulp by washing them well in a sieve under a tap. This removes not only the pulp but also chemicals that inhibit germination. Sow several seeds in a 9cm (3in) pot of multi-purpose compost. Guava comes up very readily at

Guava flower - photograph by Manji Kerai

temperatures of no more than 18°C (65°F), usually in a few weeks, but you may find more seedlings appearing up to several months later. Beware of damping off at the early stage – fortunately, the plants appear to outgrow this tendency with age. Pot them on when big enough to handle if they're in an overcrowded pot, or at the two-leaf stage if sown only a couple to a pot.

Guava require a well-drained growing medium, not over-rich. A handbook from 1850 recommends using two parts of sandy loam to equal quantities of decayed cow dung and silver sand, but a good general-purpose loam-based compost should do, with a little extra grit added if you feel it isn't free-draining enough. Keep plants warm, at 20°C (68°F) or above during the growing season, and water well. Pinch out growing tips regularly to keep the plants bushy, and mist daily.

Feed with general-purpose fertiliser once a month while the plants are actively growing, and change to a high-potash fertiliser every three weeks once they are over 60cm (2ft) tall. In winter, reduce watering but keep misting the plants from time to time. They will tolerate a minimum temperature of 18°C (65°F).

If flowers do develop they will require hand-pollination, and fruits should ripen within four months. They always taste best off the tree but become very brittle-stalked as they ripen: if you knock one off don't worry, just leave it to mellow in the fruit bowl.

BER, JUJUBE

(Zizyphus species)

Family Rhamnaceae

The fruit

Ber, or jujube, are usually found in early spring in the shops, sold by the plastic bagful. Those generally seen in the UK are small, bright crimson fruits that look as if they might be related to cranberries, although some varieties can be yellow or brownish and oval shaped. They have a hard, papery outer skin and a thin, almost mealy flesh that surrounds a surprisingly big stone. Inside the stone are one or more seeds.

Fresh ber are shiny, round and plump, but with age they begin to shrivel and shrink into dull, angular blobs like little plastic beads. The fresh fruit taste pleasantly acidic, with a fizzy texture on the tongue like a sherbet sweet and a taste that lingers on the palate. As they age the flavour becomes sweeter, until they taste almost date-like. Ber are very popular as a nibble among Indian families.

There are a number of different species of ber sold in the UK for food – sometimes, confusingly, mixed up in the same batch. The fruits all look quite similar unless you are very familiar with them.

The plant

Depending on which botany book you read, there are between 20 and 30 species of Zizyphus and many different cultivars. All are prickly bushes or small trees, the tree versions looking rather like hawthorn, and are natives of hot climates from Africa and Egypt through Asia into China and the Americas. They have a long history as cultivated plants. Plants grown from seed take at least three years to flower, and often a lot longer in the UK. The trees all have spiny trunks and are distinguishable by the leaf colour,

shape and size, but this distinction shows up only once they are a couple of years old.

The common Jujube, *Z. jujube*, has been cultivated in China for over 4000 years and been known in the UK since around 1640, but never really caught on here, despite tolerating temperatures as low as -25°C (-12°F). The trees are fairly small, very drought tolerant and need hot, sunny conditions, but also have a chilling requirement before flower buds can form. The leaves are large, oval, leathery and shiny. Flowers appear in tiny yellowish clusters close to the leaf axils, and are self fertile; the fruits hang on long stems from the branches like solitary plums. The spineless variant (*var. inermis*) is said to have sweeter-tasting fruit than the thorned variety (*var. spinosa.*)

The Indian Jujube, *Z. mauritiana*, is a medium-sized tree with a textured foliage casting deep shade. It has large, dark green, oval, leathery, alternate leaves with three veins, closely spaced on long twigs. The plum-sized fruit taste crisply apple-like and are carried singly, each on a small stem from the leaf axils. The leaves are pale and downy beneath, and show up beautifully in the wind, making this an attractive garden plant.

Other species native to the Indian subcontinent include *Z. incurva*, a medium-sized tree that grows in the hills, and *Z. rugosa*, or wrinkled jujube, a small tree with scaly, dark grey bark and dark green, closely toothed leaves with a rusty or greyish felted underside. This has small, deeply ridged, pear-shaped fruits in long auxiliary or terminal clusters.

'Chania ber' has very tiny, yellowish-brown fruit and grows wild on small creeping plants that are found in dry waste places all over India. This may be Z. oenoplia, a thorny shrub native to tropical Asia, whose seeds are used to make rosaries.

Other uses

The inner bark of various species of Zizyphus has been used as a purgative, while the outer bark has astringent effects on the bowels due to the tannins it contains. An infusion of the leaves is said to promote hair growth and improve the health of the scalp. Betulinic acid, which some believe has beneficial properties in reducing tumours, has been isolated from Z. mauritiana fruit. The regular consumption of ber is claimed to be responsible for many beautiful Asian complexions.

Cultivation

Ber will grow quite easily from seed, but is rather lethal as a pot plant because of its inherently spiky nature. However, if you have a passion for prickles, or want to deter somebody from venturing in across a windowsill, it might be just the thing as a houseplant – provided you don't want to draw the curtains too often!

Several species of Zizyphus will grow in the Mediterranean, and may survive outside in very sheltered gardens in the UK. They might produce flowers but are unlikely to get to the full fruit stage. The difficulty is not the low temperatures in Britain, which are higher than the trees will happily withstand, but our uncertain spring conditions, with early warm weather being followed by sharp frosts.

If you fancy growing ber, select fresh, rounded fruit and split the stone (easily done with finger pressure) to extract the seeds before planting fingernail-deep in a gritty compost. The best time is perhaps November to February, when you can leave the pot outside to expose it to frost to break the seed's dormancy. If sowing your seed in summer, put the whole pot, with seed and compost, in a plastic bag in the bottom of the fridge for two to three weeks, then move it out into room temperature. Be warned, however, that germination may take up to 12 months.

Once the seed starts to grow, remove it to a deep 'long tom' pot (two or three times as deep as it is wide), as the plants resent root disturbance. If you intend to plant the tree outside, grow on for at least two seasons with protection before planting in a sunny spot, preferably by some sort of shelter, such as a wall. It will need to be several years old before there is a chance of flowering. Fruits are produced on new growth, so regular winter pruning may be beneficial.

Jujube Flower – photograph by Manji Kerai

CHIKKU, SAPODILLA

(Achras sapota syn. Manilkara zapota)

Family Sapotaceae

The fruit

Chikku resemble kiwi fruit at first glance, but are bigger, rounder and less fuzzy. On closer inspection a chikku seems more like an apple: smooth-skinned with a thin peel, and pale golden-brown to greyish in colour. The unripe fruit are hard to the touch, and if the skin is rubbed away a green inner skin is revealed. They ooze a white to grey sap if cut.

When fully ripe the slightly wrinkled skin gives slightly when pressed with a finger. The flesh is a soft, mealy, deep creamy-brown colour and encloses a few dark brown or black seeds in a casing similar to an apple core. The flavour is sweet, rich and toffee-like.

Chikku sold in the UK usually weigh no more than 75g (3oz), but the fruits can weigh up to 200g (half a pound) each. Unripe chikku will slowly become edible if kept at room temperature, while ripe chikku can be stored in the salad tray of a fridge for a few days. They also freeze successfully, and can be sliced and dried.

The plant

A native of South America, principally Venezuela, chikku is now grown throughout the tropics. Related to the gamboge tree (Garcinia cambogia), it is a dense evergreen with a broad spreading habit. It will tolerate brackish conditions and alkaline soils, so is often cultivated near the coast.

The smooth, untoothed leaves are dark green, oval to oblong, pointed at either end and at best as big as those of a loquat. The leaves at the very tips of branches tend to be curly edged, and young leaves and branches are covered in a light brownish fuzz. Standing underneath a chikku tree, one becomes aware that the leaves spiral round the branches in clusters at the ends, and that there are a lot of bare branches below, like the ribs of an opened umbrella.

Chikku flowers are small, less than 2.5cm (1in) long, and emerge individually from between the leaf axils. They have a thin orange-brown fur on their outer petals and open as white bells in the evening, with a slight scent, when they are pollinated by moths. The fruits, which ripen in about three months from flowering, are favourites with birds and monkeys as well as humans. They are picked young and allowed to ripen off the tree in a dark cupboard, like pears.

When wounded, all parts of the tree, but particularly the trunk, exude a sticky latex. Some clones grown for latex production can produce up to 3kg (over 6lb) per year.

Other uses

Most chikku in the world is grown for chewing gum production, and can be tapped regularly for latex without injury to the tree. Chewing gum is made by mixing the latex with sugar, glucose syrup and flavouring.

The sticky sap of chikku is boiled with bo tree (Ficus religiosa) latex and used to make bird lime. The seeds are laxative and diuretic, and the leaves contain tannins and may be used to cure leather. The dark red wood gives off a fragrance when burned and is used in religious ceremonies.

Cultivation

Chikku is not difficult to grow from seed. The fruit for sale in the shops is a good source of supply since, because most plants are grown for chewing-gum production rather than fruit, they are generally raised from seed rather than grafted and so are true to their parents.

Choose very ripe fruit and wash the seed well, then sow as soon as possible.

Germination temperature is 27°C (80°F). Seedlings emerge fairly quickly, usually within 28 days, but they grow on very slowly afterwards. Don't be tempted to transplant them as soon as the seed leaves are open, as germination happens in two stages and the central stem emerges before the root. By the time the first true leaves have opened fully, the roots should have developed enough to survive being moved.

Keep warm and moist, at a temperature of 18–30°C (65–86°F) during the growing season, misting daily with rainwater if possible. If necessary, repot and prune in February to March, although chikku tolerates being potbound quite well.

In the UK, chikku flowers in June, but you're not likely to get much of a fruit crop unless you're very lucky. Although it is supposedly hardy to only 16°C (60°F), mature trees in Israel have survived a few degrees of frost, so there is the potential to cultivate chikku in a cool greenhouse or conservatory. And you can always try making your own chewing gum while you're waiting for the plants to fruit.

Chikku flower and immature fruit – photograph by Manji Kerai

IMLI, TAMARIND

(Tamarindus indica)

Family Leguminosae

The fruit

Fresh tamarind fruits look like thin, furry brown sausages. Sometimes they're sold loose, and sometimes they appear in beautifully decorated red cardboard boxes like Turkish delight. They're about 7–12cm (3–5in) long and as thick as a man's thumb, surprisingly light but hard, with a finely furred outer shell. This is easily fractured, and splits off in irregular pieces to reveal a brown sticky pulp wrapped around several dark brown, almost oblong seeds. The seeds are linked to the pulp with dark red-brown strings, and may pull off when you remove the outer shell. The reddish sticky pulp is deliciously fruity, tangy and sour-sweet.

There are three types of tamarind: the sour; the sweet, which is the one usually imported to the UK; and the red-fleshed, which can be sweet or sour and has plentiful pulp, and is the best sort for making chutney or other preserves. The latter may be found here at the time of festivals such as Holi or Diwali.

In some parts of Asia and Africa you may come across 'white tamarind', a pod that looks similar but is filled with a white, sweet, fluffy pulp and dark seeds. This is the fruit of a distantly related but distinct tree, Prosopis juliflora, the mesquite or algoroba.

The tree

A tall, evergreen tree, tamarind is grown for shade and its nitrogen-fixing ability, as well for as its flowers and fruits. Most rural houses in India have a tamarind tree in their yard if they have enough space, and tamarinds are often planted as communal trees in schoolyards and other public buildings. The trees are drought tolerant, slow growing and long-lived.

Tamarind has pale green pinnate leaves with

many long narrow leaflets, which unfold a beautiful translucent green, like lime-tree leaves, and have a delicate texture with a pleasant taste. When very young they are eaten by Indian children, or occasionally added to salads. Tamarind bark is dark grey to black, and rough textured. The trees tend to have a large trunk but short branches.

The flowers are attractive, a bit like yellow sweet peas with pinky-red veins, or vaguely orchid-like, and are carried in long upright clusters. They have a sour taste and are used to make a traditional seasonal curry in Bangladesh and parts of northern India. Tamarind flowers are a favourite with bees, and honey from a tamarind tree has a slightly sharper flavour than that from other sources of nectar. Following the flowers, the long, dark brown pods hang in clusters from the branches and are often eaten by birds and fruit bats.

Other uses

Tamarind is a useful tree for the small grower: dyes are made from the bark (browns and dull reds) and leaves (red or yellow), an ink is produced from the burnt bark, and the seeds are crushed to produce starch.

All parts of tamarind contain tartaric acid, which is kinder on the stomach than oxalic acid and therefore better for people with dietary intolerances. They also contain a glutinous fluid which, along with the tartaric acid content, is responsible for the mildly laxative effect tamarinds have on stomachs that are not used to them. Tamarind preparations have been used for digestive problems throughout Asia for centuries.

Cultivation

Tamarinds can be easily grown on a windowsill. They make dainty, divided-leaved houseplants, thriving on sun, dry air and neglect, and are excellent subjects for bonsai.

The key to success is fresh seed, as with so many other warm-climate species. Eat some fresh tamarinds, save the seeds and wash them well. Sow as thickly as you like in a pot or a tray, covering with at least the seeds' own thickness of compost. A temperature of 20°C (68°F) is quite adequate to induce germination. They will take anything from six weeks to two months to emerge, but the germination rate can be as much as 100 per cent.

Once the seed leaves are through, pot on individually. If every seed germinates and you feel you have too many to accommodate, try the seedlings as salad ingredients. Tamarind leaves can be harvested when the plants are only a few inches high and taste refreshingly sour, something similar to sorrel. If you have lots of seed and want to use them for a crop during the summer, just sow in a row in a coldframe or polytunnel and snip off the foliage like cut-and-come again lettuce. You can transplant seedlings into a sheltered corner to grow as a salad source too.

A tamarind tree can live happily in a 27cm (10in) pot for over 40 years if pruned to keep within bounds – but the top few inches of growing medium should be removed and replaced annually. For a long-lived tree, choose a gritty, loam-based compost that isn't too rich, and a sunny position. Prune back in late spring and keep pinching back buds to make the plant small and bushy: the leaves shrink most gratifyingly after a few years of restricted roots, and a bonsai effect is easily achieved. Tamarinds are hardy to 10°C (50°F) and will happily live outdoors in summer, making an edible talking point on the patio.

JAK, JACKFRUIT

(Artocarpus heterophyllus)

The fruit

Jackfruit is sold mainly in Sri Lankan and Southern Indian or Tamil shops, as it's not popular all over India. It's usually easy to find by following your nose – like ripe guavas, ripe jackfruits have a characteristic and penetrating odour that is sweet and fruity, with a slight overtone of armpits. Jackfruit is oval shaped and looks like a vegetable armadillo, with a lumpy, leathery, intricately patterned greenish-yellow skin. Those imported into the UK are usually watermelon-sized and weigh 1.5–2kg (3–5lb), but in Asia they weigh up to 30kg (66lb); the biggest recorded fruit was 95kg (15 stone)!

The flesh is golden-yellow, coarse and very juicy. Each fruit segment or 'peg' usually contains a seed, and is separated from the next by stringy fibrous strips, which are inedible. The seeds are edible when roasted: I've found them to be a bland, rather oily but pleasant enough nut.

A jackfruit will start to become aromatic a day or two before it reaches full ripeness, and can be stored in the fridge for up to a week without losing condition. If you don't wrap it thoroughly in clingfilm, however, everything else in the fridge will also taste like jak.

The tree

Jak is found in most regions of India, but is more common in the south and grows wild in Kerala. It is a medium-sized, evergreen tree with smooth grey-brown or silvery bark, and forms a fairly dense crown. The leaves can vary a great deal on the same tree: a condition known as habitual heterophylly. Some are reminiscent of cherry laurel – elliptical in shape, dark green and leathery textured with glossy upper surfaces and a pronounced central vein; others are irregularly lobed, with three or four veins, pale green or mottled.

The pale flowers are a dull greenish-yellow to pale cream, varying with flower age and sex, and are spicily-sweet scented and nearly stalkless, emerging from the trunk or woody older branches. Male flowers are in spikes and female flowers form spherical heads a bit like a cauliflower floret. Each flower cluster gives rise to only a single fruit, which is carried on the tree's trunk or a branch rather than among the leaves – this phenomenon is called cauliflory. Fruits take four to six months to reach picking size, and a tree can produce up to 260 fruits per season. Unripe fruits can be eaten cooked as a vegetable.

Other uses

The young flowers and shoots of both species are made into a paste for women who have just given birth, to heal any internal damage and strengthen the womb. A similar preparation is made from the leaves crushed with palm sugar, used to treat boils and to increase the flow of milk in nursing mothers. Tests on leaf extracts have shown that they contain gamma-aminobuteryic acid, which causes a drop in blood pressure.

Jak is one of the fruits used by Hindu women in a nombu ceremony, where thanks are given for prayers that have been answered. Sixteen different fruits are given to other happily married women, a different fruit every year.

All parts of the plant produce a thick, sticky white latex when damaged. This is used to make bird lime, as it's incredibly awkward to remove.

Cultivation

Jak obviously can't be grown to fruiting size in the UK, but if you live in a warm house they will make a good houseplant for several years.

The seeds have no dormant period at all and can occasionally be found germinating within the fruit: they die if allowed to dry

out for even a few hours, but it is possible to keep them viable inside a damp, closed film canister at 20°C (68°F) for up to three months.

Germination is improved by thoroughly washing any flesh from the seeds, and carefully peeling off the hard, horny shell before planting them hilum side down. (The hilum is the small dark line on the seed, similar to that seen on broad beans. If you're not sure which side is the hilum, sow the seeds flat.) Use a large pot, as the seedlings resent disturbance.

A temperature of 27°C (80°F) is required for germination, which will take 10 to 40 days, though it can be 100-per-cent successful. The growing medium should contain some organic matter, such as leaf mould or composted bark, and be well drained.

Jak seedlings should be potted up into a 30cm (12in) or larger pot at the four-leaf stage. Repeated root disturbance can kill the seedlings, so don't move them into another pot until they're bursting out of their current one, and try to repot during late winter. Keep warm and humid, ideally at 26°C (79°F), and mist daily during summer. The plants make a very good choice for a steamy bathroom or kitchen, and don't need direct sunlight. Keep the pot standing on a saucer of damp pebbles to increase humidity further.

Water less during winter, and allow the pot to dry out between waterings. Top-dress pots with a good loam-based compost annually and feed occasionally with a general-purpose fertiliser. Prune sparingly in late spring to early summer, or pinch out buds – and wear disposable gloves, as the sap is very tenacious. It's best removed from secateurs using petrol or surgical spirit.

Jak Fruit is hardy to around 13.C (55.F) if grown hard – i.e. potbound, hungry and dry, so as to create a tougher, smaller plant.

NIMBU, LIME

(Citrus aurantifolia and C. latifolia)

MAGRUT, KAFFIR LIME

(Citrus hystrix)

Family Rutaceae

The fruit

Nimbu, or common lime, is of two types. The first is the West Indian, key lime or barkeeper's lime, Citrus aurantifolia, which is small, pale green ripening to golden, thin skinned and fragrant, with very sharp juice and up to twenty small seeds. The larger Tahitian, Bearss or Persian lime, C. latifolia, is pea-green ripening to lemon-yellow, slightly thicker skinned, seedless and has a milder flavour. Citrus latifolia in particular often goes rotten near the stalk end as it ripens. Both these limes are more or less egg-shaped and -sized.

Magrut, C. hystrix, also called kaffir or wild lime, is smaller, very round and sold brilliant green, ripening to bright yellow. Its extra-thick, deeply wrinkled skin is unlike any other citrus fruit in texture – the Malays compare it to a crocodile's eyebrows! The skin is highly scented when handled and leaves a perfumed twang on the fingers. Inside a magrut are many large seeds and white membranes, with little flesh, but what flesh there is should be very juicy.

Sometimes magrut leaves are sold, usually in small plastic bags to keep them fresh. They are long, pointed and oval in shape, but so pinched at the middle that it looks as if one leaf has grown out of another. The true leaf is the first or topmost portion, with a pointed tip, while the second, wider 'leaf' is in fact a peculiarly modified leafstalk. They have a delicious sweet fragrance, which makes them a unique cooking ingredient throughout South-east Asia. As they dry they lose scent, so the fresh leaves should either be stored in the fridge for quick use or frozen, when they will keep their fragrance for up to six months. When chopping magrut leaves, stack them one on top of the other and shave off slivers with a sharp knife.

Choose limes with a bright, oily-feeling skin that are heavy for their size, as they will be freshest and have the best flavour. If you are offered a small green fruit with a nipple-like end, it may be an unripe lemon. Discreetly rub the skin and sniff – the difference is real and distinctive.

The tree

Limes make small trees or large bushes and

Magrut or Kaffir Lime

come as both heavily thorned clones and spineless ones. Most cultivars are very thorny. Common limes are native to warmer areas of Asia, but magrut originally came from Thailand, Cambodia and parts of Malaysia.

Lime leaves are alternate and oval, with shallow-toothed edges and sometimes flattened stalks. Young leaves and the flower buds are pinkish. The flowers are white, cup shaped, five petalled and deliciously scented, appearing in small clusters between the leaves. The fruits take a long time, over ten months, to mature, and – given adequate light, warmth and water – flowers and fruit are carried on the tree almost all year round.

Citrus aurantifolia is a moderate-sized, bushy tree of medium vigour, with small thorny branches and pale green leaves that are blunt at both ends. It is widely grown in Asia, usually propagated from seed, and is very cold sensitive – hardy to only 10°C (50°F). Citrus latifolia may have been a spontaneous hybrid between a small acid lime and a citron: it is sterile and is propagated by grafting or air layering. It makes a larger tree than C. aurantifolia and is much hardier, to 3–5°C (37–41°F); the leaves are larger and darker green. Most clones are nearly thornless.

Citrus hystrix is a very thorny bush (individual thorns can be up to 2cm long), growing to only around 1.8–2m (5–6ft) tall. The tree is instantly recognisable by the distinctive 'double' shape of the pale green leaves. The young leaves can be purple on some bushes. Magrut is less hardy than either sort of common lime and will tolerate a minimum temperature of 12°C (54°F) for only a short time. It needs to be cross-pollinated by another, unrelated, bush to produce fruit. This isn't a problem in the tropics, but can be when it is grown under protection elsewhere.

Other uses

An essential oil is distilled from *Citrus aurantifolia*, which is used in aromatherapy to

treat a variety of conditions from acne to arthritis, chest infections and warts. The rind of all limes is said to improve the digestion, and the odour from freshly crushed lime leaves is sometimes inhaled to relieve headaches, dispel unpleasant odours and generally lift the spirits.

A whole lime, sliced thinly and put in the bottom of a kettle with a little water, will remove limescale if left overnight.

Cultivation

Limes are relatively easily grown from pips, although they don't often reach fruiting size indoors. There are a variety of virus diseases that affect all types of Citrus, but by growing from seed these are usually avoided. Obviously you won't be able to grow *C. latifolia* from seed, as it's seedless, but Cross Common Nursery, Ken Muir and Reads offer plants for sale. Note that there are restrictions on importing citrus plants into the UK unless they have an EU Plant Health certificate, but it is fine to bring in ripe fruits or seed from anywhere.

The plants grown from lime seed may not be the same as the parent, as Citrus is a very freely crossing genus and the species hybridise easily. Sometimes you may get a handful of seedlings coming up from a single pip (known as polyembryony). If this happens, select the strongest seedlings: the plants they produce often tend to be thorny and slow to crop, but are most likely to be true to the parent.

Citrus seeds have no dormancy and are damaged by becoming dry, so remove the seed

Lime flower - photograph by Manji Kerai

from the fruits, rinse well and sow immediately. Sow at 16°C (60°F) or warmer, in spring, preferably using a loam-based compost. Topping the seed with a 2cm (¾ in) layer of sharp sand will help prevent damping off. Keep moist at all times until seedlings emerge, but not humid or the seeds will rot. Germination may take up to three months.

Grow on in a loam-based compost. Top-dressings with pine needles or dried bracken can help to acidify the compost, and an annual feed with chelated iron may be beneficial. A Canadian grower I know has had great success with watering his magrut plants twice a year with Coca-Cola (full sugar version), diluted to beer colour with water. (I have tried this with lemon trees and it works – presumably the phosphoric acid acts as a chelate.) Citrus plants are especially prone to lime-induced chlorosis (leaf yellowing), so if you have hard tap water in your area use rainwater if possible. When growing indoors, mist daily with soft water during the growing season.

All citrus fruits benefit from being placed outside in summer and being quite cold and dry in winter, as this reduces problems with pests and sooty moulds. Common limes and magrut need plenty of light, but scorch easily

in full sun. Citrus latifolia will survive most winters in an unheated greenhouse if the pot is plunged in dry soil and the top wrapped in sacking during cold weather.

Limes seem to respond quite well to pollarding if grown in pots, although it reduces their flowering considerably. They also readily develop red spider mite, scale insects and mealybug, especially if kept indoors all year.

In some countries, though not at present in the UK, imports of C. hystrix leaf and fruits are controlled, as they have potential to carry citrus canker, *Xanthomonas axonopodis*.

RAMBUTAN

(Nephelium lappaceum)

LYCHEE

(Litchi chinensis)

LONGAN

(Dimocarpus longan)

Family Sapindaceae

Rambutan

The fruit

Rambutans are about the size of a small hen's egg and are covered with soft, rubbery spines with a slightly artificial feel. They are green when unripe, turning yellow and then fiery red as they mature. A pure golden-yellow strain is known, although this is rarely imported into the UK.

If the tips of the spines are black, it means the fruit is old or has been stored too cold or too dry, but the flesh inside is usually fit to eat. The spiny case peels easily away to reveal a pearly-white, unscented, glistening interior with a large central stone. This white edible part is an aril: it is very juicy, with a sweet-and-sour taste.

The rambutan is part of a wider family, which all taste quite similar. Lychees are more common in the UK, and look like small, pinkish-brown gobstoppers with a hammered finish, made of tiny crackly flakes that occasionally form soft, tiny spines. Very fresh lychees are bright pink when first picked, but they turn browner as they age. A lychee has perfumed, pearly-white flesh inside its skin, which cracks away rather than peels. Some people compare the scented taste to rose water.

Longans are the same size as lychees but are smoother skinned and tan-brown, with a creased or hammer-textured skin like worn leather. The white flesh contrasts with the striking single dark seed, hence their alternative name of 'dragon's eye'. The flesh is both juicier and chewier than that of a lychee, with a musky aftertaste that cuts through oily foods and freshens the palate.

A last relative, the pulasan, Nephelium mutabile, is a similar colour but is covered in small warty tubercles insted of spines. It's a little larger than a rambutan and is not widely found in the UK.

The tree

Native to the humid lowland forests of Malaysia, rambutans are large, spreading trees that are often cultivated for their shade. They look very attractive festooned with their miniature orange baubles, and are widely grown in orchards, as the fruits are popular throughout the Fast as a dessert.

The leaves are oval, dark green in colour and up to 25cm (10in) long, divided into many leaflets. Rambutan trees are normally dioecious (having separate sexes on different trees), although female trees sometimes produce a few male flowers. The flowers, greenish-brown tufted threads 15–20cm (6–8in) long, hang in clusters. Rambutans can be raised from seed, but these are usually very slow to fruit, and superior strains are propagated by budding or air layering of larger branches. Cultivars include 'Roningen', 'Classic Red' and P9.

Lychees make a similar but slightly smaller spreading tree, also often planted as a shade or street tree. They have a large crown and palmate leaves, which are like an evergreen version of a horse chestnut leaf and are bright coppery-red when young. The flowers are tiny yellow and red, held in fine, feathery upright tufts like seaweed fronds.

Lychees tolerate cooler conditions than rambutans, and are grown in areas with hot humid summers and cool, misty, frost-free winters. A lychee can crop for over 100 years. There are many cultivars – 'Salathiel' and 'Bengal' are common in India, and come fairly true from seed – but relatively few are available in the West.

Longans too can grow into very large trees. Natives of hot, humid mountain woodlands throughout eastern Asia, they are slightly more cold tolerant than rambutans or lychees. They make a dense, dark green tree, with deep red young growth, and provide a dense shade. The leaves are pinnate, with two to four pairs of leaflets and a smooth, glossy surface.

The flowers of longan, fragrant and beloved by butterflies, are much showier than those of rambutans or lychees, emerging in frothy, erect panicles in the upper leaf axils – from a distance a tree looks as if it's been covered with flowering rhubarb spikes wedged in the branches. The calyxes and young branches are covered in a brownish-grey woolly fur. The trees are notoriously erratic in fruiting, and so are often planted for their shade or for ornament rather than a crop. Cultivars include 'Kohala', which has large fruit; 'Chompoo' and 'Homestead'. Wild longan fruits are sometimes called cat's eyes, because they are smaller than the cultivated version.

Longan

Other uses

Unripe rambutan fruits are effective in treating parasitic worms, and an infusion of the bark is given to nursing mothers as well as used to treat piles and internal bruising. A decoction of the leaves may be used to treat fever. The young shoots are used to dye silk green, and the leaves, fruits and bark make a black silk dye. The seeds, which are very bitter, are sometimes crushed and rubbed on to granary doors to deter rats.

Eating longans is considered in folk medicine to improve brain function. Dried longan fruits have been used for centuries in Chinese medicine as a general tonic, and to treat insomnia.

Cultivation

You won't get a rambutan, lychee or longan to fruit in the UK, as they are just too large to house in the necessary conditions when at flowering size. Still, they're easy enough to grow from a stone, and will make a foliage plant that you can't buy just anywhere. They vary in hardiness: rambutans are strictly tropical and are hardy to around 18°C (65°F), although in general the warmer the better. Lychees have a chilling requirement to induce flowering, of about 100 days at around 3–7°C (38–45°F), down to 0°C (32°F) minimum, but will stand these low temperatures only once they're mature trees. Longans, which are native to higher altitudes, are a bit hardier and may cope with temperatures as low as 7°C (45°F) for a very short time.

As with many tropical plants, all the rambutan family's seeds have no dormant stage, so are very short-lived outside the ripe fruits. The seeds will remain viable inside the fruit, provided they don't dry out. Choose very ripe, squishy fruits for seed: for lychees, select those that are dull brown in colour. After extracting the seeds, wash well to remove germination-inhibiting chemicals, and sow in a loam-based compost at 21°C (70°F). Germination should occur within 20 days.

Lychees prefer a sunny, open position and a well-drained growing medium, which can be easily achieved by adding a little extra grit to the compost. They need an acidic growing medium, ideally pH 6.5 to 5.5, kept damp during the growing season. The seedlings grow very slowly – don't panic if they stop growing for as much as two years once they're about 18cm (7in) tall; this is normal. Don't overfeed them to try force them into growth, as the nutrients will just be wasted or will scorch the roots.

Rambutans and longans need high humidity and semi-shade, or at least subdued light, during the summer months. They will benefit from regular misting, but use rainwater to avoid the build-up of lime markings on the leaves. Being tropical woodland-edge dwellers, rambutans and longans appreciate having a little leaf mould or some finely chopped composted bark added to their compost, as well as an annual top-dressing with an organic material – bark, seaweed meal, leaf mould or garden compost. As mature trees they are greedy feeders, but the seedlings don't need much input, although chelated iron and/or seaweed may be useful in hard-water areas.

None of this family really enjoys being outside in the UK even in summer, although you might try giving them a short spell on a sheltered patio at the warmest times of year, where they will help create a tropical feel. All three will benefit from increased humidity during the growing season, and will respond to pruning quite well while young. You'll probably be able to keep one for five to ten years before it finally outgrows your home.

Lychees

SAHIJAN, DRUMSTICK

(Moringa oleifera syn. M. pterygosperma)

Family Moringaceae

The vegetable

The drumstick is not a member of the Leguminosae family, but to the uninitiated it does look like some relation of a runner bean. The pods come from a tropical tree and have a meaty texture – hence the name – although it's only the internal parts that are edible, not the outer skin, and those only after cooking.

Nothing else looks like these incredibly long, thin pods, with their distinctive skin texture, like plaited dark green beans. Inside, a drumstick has grey-green, soft-textured pith, with peculiar little pale green, three-winged seeds. Drumsticks are quite hard skinned, but should still feel crisp and fresh. If they look brownish and feel soft, they're too old. Shake one to test for freshness: if it undulates smoothly like a whip, buy it; if it droops like a limp rag, go elsewhere.

Drumsticks can be anything up to 60cm (2ft) long, although the ones that reach the UK are normally about 30–38cm (12–15in), and are usually sold wrapped in paper, as they're far too long to fit into a standard carrier bag.

The tree

A tall, sparse tree with feathery, divided leaves, the drumstick tree looks superficially like a robinia or acacia. The bark is silvery-grey to copper coloured, corky in texture and slightly furrowed. With age, the trunk thickens to become a very bulbous bole. The drumstick tree is resistant to salt and drought and is extensively cultivated for its fruits all over the southern half of Asia.

Drumstick leaves are bipinnate and short-lived, with fresh flushes of leaf produced throughout the year. From the leaf axils come large panicles of scented, creamy-white, five-petalled flowers, like a splayed-open wisteria flower. The pods follow the flowers, dangling down in large numbers and making the tree instantly recognisable from a distance.

Other uses

The leaves of the drumstick tree taste like a hotter version of mustard-and-cress when eaten young, are extremely high in protein (7–10 per cent) for a green vegetable, and contain many important amino acids. The

roots taste of horseradish, and were used by the British as a substitute for this condiment during its occupation of India. However, it was later discovered that the root bark is toxic in quantity, so the practice was discontinued.

A decoction of the drumstick tree roots root is given for asthma, gout and liver problems. The gum that exudes from cut branches is used to treat TB and septicaemia, and to relieve inflammation. Mature leaves are rubificant (warming) and counter-irritant as a topical application, and purgative when eaten. Crushed seeds pounded in a mortar and placed in a jug of drinking water will purify it if left to stand overnight.

Cultivation

The drumstick tree is hardy to 13°C (55°F), so is suitable only for a windowsill or a heated greenhouse in the UK, and is unlikely to produce flowers, let alone fruit, in this climate. However, with its delicate foliage the tree makes an attractive houseplant, and you can pick the young shoots, even from mature plants, for use in salads.

The drumsticks sold for food are unripe fruits, so are unlikely to contain viable seeds.

Seeds are available from a few specialist seed suppliers (e.g. Suffolk Herbs and tropicalfruitandveg.co.uk) and can be germinated fairly easily given a sufficiently high temperature – around 22°C (72°F). Once the seedlings are through, minimum temperatures of 15–18°C (59–65°C) are fine, but they will need plenty of light. The plants grow strongly and require pinching back to keep within bounds. You should have plenty of shoots to experiment with egg-and-drumstick sandwiches, stir-fries and salads during the summer months.

Use a loam-based compost, and add a little extra grit to improve drainage when potting up the plants. Allow to dry out between waterings, and keep on the dry side during winter.

When your tree finally outgrows its space, it will respond well to being pruned back hard and can be kept pollarded for some years. If you have a large enough plant you can grow more from semi-ripe cuttings in summer, using a propagator to enhance humidity.

SURAN, YELLOW GUINEA YAM

(D. rotundifolia group, syn. D. cayenensis)

Family Dioscoreaceae

KAND, CRIMSON YAM

(D. alata var. purpurea)

RATALU, GREATER OR WINGED YAM

(Dioscorea alata)

The vegetable

Ratalu, kand and **suran** are all members of the yam family and are eaten as root vegetables. The roots not only look different but also vary a great deal in texture and taste when cooked, in the same way that potato cultivars behave differently when boiled.

Yam flesh is white or creamy and exudes a milky sap when cut. Some yams have flesh that is slimy to the touch, while with others it is smooth and silky. Ask when buying: suppliers will usually be able to say which of their yams is best for a particular type of cooking.

You can sometimes find a yam with visible buds, especially during summer, which is ideal if you want to grow a plant but not so good if you want to cook it, as the root will have deteriorated and become soft once sprouting starts.

Ratalu are large, usually brown, elongated tubers with a thin, dry, sometimes wrinkled skin, often covered with fine hairs erupting from little dimples like the eyes of a potato, although they are never as hairy as arvi tubers (see page x). In the UK these weigh around 2–6kg (4–13lb), although some Indian yams can weigh as much as 60kg (130lb).

The word **kand** means simply 'root vegetable' rather than a specific type of vegetable, but

Yellow yam

Kand

certainly in the UK Midlands 'kand' is taken to mean the purple-fleshed yam. It is fairly large, some 25cm (10in) across or more, and usually weighs 1–2kg (2–4lb). Kand may be round or more irregular than ratalu, with mid-brown skin. The top of the tuber shows a series of irregular knobbles and small rootlets, rather like those on the base of a cyclamen corm. The skin is easily rubbed off to reveal a beetroot-coloured underlayer. Inside is a lilac-purple, slightly sticky flesh.

Suran look very similar to Ratalu but have pale brown, slightly hairy skins and yellow flesh. They are almost always long and oblong in shape. Suran juice is particularly sticky.

The plant

Members of the yam family have been cultivated for over 4000 years. They are grown worldwide as they are easy to cultivate, high in carbohydrates and will keep in good condition for a long time. In order for tuber formation to be induced, day and night must be of equal length, and production is therefore confined to the tropics. All the species described here need high temperatures, high humidity and plentiful rainfall.

Ratalu and kand probably originated in South-east Asia. They are vigorous, climbing perennial vines that can reach into tall trees. The stems twine to the right, are tinted purple or greenish according to cultivar, and develop four odd wing-like flanges or lobes as they age, although at the top of the plant they are usually round. In a few cultivars they may have a few widely spaced spines instead. Aerial tubers sometimes develop in the leaf axils, and these can form into new plants.

The simple, broadly heart-shaped leaves are strongly veined and resemble sweet-potato foliage. They are usually glossy mid-green but, depending on the cultivar, can be veined or blotched with purple. This is most often seen in kand, which is slightly less vigorous than ratalu and often has purple young foliage. The insignificant flowers are greenish, in minute tufts or clusters on long stalks: they look a bit like miniature potato flowers. Some cultivars, however, never flower.

Suran probably originated in Africa. Again the stems twine to the right but have four ridges or wings at the top of the plant. They are often spiny at the base, with short lateral branches. The leaves are more elongated than those of ratalu or kand and have a deeper indentation at the stalk end. Few or no aerial tubers are formed.

Other uses

Kand is recommended in folk and Ayurvedic medicine as a general tonic and a restorative food to stabilise the body's natural energies. Ratalu has been used as a diuretic.

After experimenting with various fabrics at

home, I found the purple colouring in the roots of kand, sadly, not to be a good dye source, although I don't know if the foliage may have any dyeing properties.

Cultivation

Yams won't crop in the UK, as the plants need a long period of high temperatures and 12-hour days to produce tubers. However, they make a handsome houseplant and a nice talking point. They are hardy to around 16°C (60°F) in leaf, slightly lower when dormant, but need temperatures of at least 20°C (68°F) to really grow.

Yam tubers have a natural dormancy for up to four months after harvesting. Sometimes you can see a cluster of dried-up roots visible at one end and a series of knobbly bumps above these. Commercially, the dormancy is broken using ethylene hydrochlorin: as ripe bananas release ethylene gas, it may be worth storing a yam you want to grow next to the fruit bowl. Yams will suffer cold injuries and start to rot if stored below about 10°C (50°F).

Select a tuber with buds visible if possible, and cut off most of the rest of it – eat this part and put the part with buds in a warm room to allow the cut flesh to dry. When a scab has formed, plant in a good general-purpose compost with bottom heat at 21°C (70°F), and keep moist. It will either rot or shoot quickly;

sniff the pot if in doubt which has happened. It might just be slow to emerge so be careful before grubbing at it with your fingers as the first shoots are very fragile.

As the plant starts to develop leaves, begin misting it daily and move into a larger pot as soon the first one seems to be at all small. By the time it is three months old you will need a 30cm (12in) pot as a minimum, and the bigger the better as Dioscorea hates being confined. The growing medium should be rich, with some organic matter – various authors recommend incorporating well-rotted compost, leaf mould, bark or decayed cow manure – but free draining. If using a standard multi-purpose potting compost, feed weekly with a general well-balanced fertiliser once the plants are growing.

Keep your yam in a warm, moist place – a bathroom or kitchen is fine – and give it something to climb up. Misting regularly will help, as will standing the pot on a tray of pebbles. You don't need to keep it in bright sunlight: so long as there is a source of natural light it will be happy to grow anywhere in a room. If kept very dark, however, it may grow leggy, so you will need to keep pinching back any long sprawling tips. During the winter, move it nearer to a source of light, keep it warm but reduce watering, and mist only occasionally.

If your yam develops mottled or marbled distorted leaves, it's probably suffering from a virus and should be destroyed, but otherwise the plants seem pretty resistant to pests. Slugs and snails are fond of them, although this isn't likely to be a problem indoors.

If you want to try growing a yam outside or in a polytunnel to eat in the UK, try the commercially available Chinese or cinnamon yam, D. batatas. This produces large and exceptionally deep-rooted tubers after about 18 months or longer, doesn't require 12-hour days, and is a bit hardier than the others, to around 7°C (45°F).

Sprouting yam

SUPPLIERS INDEX

Most of the plants listed in this book can be raised from seed, and for many of them seed may be easily obtained from UK suppliers. A list of these is given below. For some species, however, especially rare or unusual cultivars, seed is harder to come by. In these cases your best bet may be to try international sources. A number of US suppliers can be readily accessed via the Internet, and a few other international specialists are suggested in the list below.

Some overseas companies may require payment in foreign currency, which can sometimes be more awkward than the actual purchase of seed, but many are happy to receive payment in major currencies (i.e. pounds sterling, euros or US dollars). International Money Transfers come in handy for these transactions. Paypal is also increasingly accepted.

A list of mail-order plant suppliers is also given below. Buying a plant does of course give you a head start over growing one from seed, although isn't quite so rewarding in other ways. A few of the plants in this book can only be vegetatively propagated.

Importing even small quantities of seed from overseas, particularly from countries outside the European Union, is subject to regulations. There are few limitations on the importation of ornamental seeds for personal use, provided they are not from certain protected species, but vegetable seeds are subject to tighter rules. Those traded throughout Europe have to be approved for being true to variety and on a National Vegetable Cultivar List for each country. It costs about £400 a year to maintain a cultivar on the National List, so only big seed companies can afford to do so (hence organisations such as Association Kokopelli and the Heritage Seed Library, where you join a club, pay a subscription fee and get 'free' seeds

that are not on the National List). Some seeds are officially registered as ornamentals rather than vegetables.

From the point of view of the purchaser, the best advice is to buy your seed from a recognised seed supplier, since then the responsibility for complying with the relevant regulations will rest with that company. It is OK to import seeds from within the EU, although plants may need a Plant Health certificate – it is the seller's responsibility to obtain this, but the buyer's responsibility to make sure it has been issued and to produce it if requested by Customs. If, on the other hand, you receive seed from an informal supplier or personal contact from outside the EU, be aware that you may be liable for compliance with the legislation. You are allowed to import seeds of any kind from outside the EU for eating, but not necessarily for growing. Note also that certain rare plants are protected under the Convention on International Trade in Endangered Species (CITES), although these are usually not cultivated plants.

If in doubt, refer to the DEFRA web page www.defra.gov.uk/planth/ph.htm before sourcing seeds from abroad. You may need to register as an importer of seed if you intend to grow a lot. Registration is free to private individuals.

At the time of writing, travellers are allowed to bring back at least five retail packets of seed and up to 2kg of fruit and vegetables in their personal baggage when coming from outside the EU. The state of ripeness of the vegetables or fruits, of course, is a matter of personal preference.

Seed suppliers UK

Chase Organics

The Organic Gardening Catalogue, Riverdene, Mosley Road, Hersham, Surrey KT12 4RG

T   0845 130 1304

W   organiccatalog.com

Chiltern Seeds

Bortree Stile, Ulverston, Cumbria LA12 27B

T   01229 581137

W   chilternseeds.co.uk

Mr Fothergill's Seeds

Kentford, Suffolk, CB8 7QB

T   0845 1662511

W   mr-fothergills.co.uk

Jungle Seeds and Gardens – also supply plants

PO Box 45, Watlington SPDO, Oxon OX49 5YR

T   01491 614765

W   jungleseeds.co.uk

E W King and Co Ltd

Monk's Farm, Kelvedon, Colchester, Essex CO 5 9PG

T   01376 570000

W   kingsseeds.com

Association Kokopelli

(This is like the Heritage Seed Library in that you pay a membership fee to get a selection of free seeds)

c/o Chris Baur, Ripple farm, Crundale, Near Canterbury, Kent CT4 7EB

T   01227 731815

Real Seeds

Brithdir Mawr Farm, Newport near Fishguard, Pembrokeshire, SA42 0QJ

T   01239 821107

W   realseeds.co.uk

Seeds by Size

(good for Okra and Aubergine)

45 Crouchfield, Hemel Hempstead, Herts HP1 1PA

T   01442 251458

W   seeds-by-size.co.uk

Tropical Fruit and Veg

(excellent and informative site has several hard to find seeds)

W   tropicalfruitandveg.co.uk

Thomas Etty Esq

Seedsman's Cottage, Puddlebridge, Horton, Ilminster, Somerset TA19 9RL

T   01460 57934

W   www.thomasetty.co.uk

Thompson and Morgan Ltd

Poplar Lane, Ipswich, IP8 3BU

T   01473 695225.

W   thompson-morgan.com

Simpson's Seeds

The Walled Garden Nursery, Horningsham, Warminster, Wilts BA12 7NQ

T   01985 485004

W   simpsonsseeds.co.uk

Suffolk Herbs

Monk's Farm, Coggeshall Rd, Kelvedon, Essex CO5 9PG

T   01376 572456

W   suffolkherbs.com

Seed suppliers overseas

B & T World Seeds

Orders accepted by phone or email; minimum overseas order applies. Over 30,000 items listed in main catalogue, including tindora. Perpignan 34210 Aigues-Vives, France.

T   00 33 04689 12963

W   b-and-t-world-seeds.com

Solana Seeds
Minimum overseas order applies.
17 Place Leger, Repentignay, Quebec,
Canada J6A 5N7
W   solanaseeds.netfirms.com.
E   solana@aei.ca.

Tokita Seed Co Ltd
1069 Nakayawa, Omiya, Satiama 330, Japan.
W   tokitaseed.co.jp.
E   ike@tokitaseed.co.jp

Plant suppliers
(all supply by mail order)

Agroforestry Research Trust
46 Hunters Moon, Dartington, Totnes,
Devon TQ9 6JT
T   01803 840776
W   agroforestry.co.uk

Arne Herbs
Limeburn Nurseries, Limeburn Hill,
Chew Magna, Bristol BS40 8QW
T   01275 333 399
W   arneherbs.co.uk

Cross Common Nursery
The Lizard, Helston, Cornwall TR12 7PD
T   01326 290722 and 290668
W   crosscommonnursery.co.uk

Ken Muir Ltd
Honeypot Lane, Rectory Road, Weely Heath,
Essex C016 9BJ.
T   0870 7479111
W   www.kenmuir.co.uk

Old Hall Plants
1 The Old Hall, Barsham, Beccles,
Suffolk NR34 8HB.
T   01502 717475
W   oldhallplants.co.uk

Passiflora (National Collection)
Lampley Road, Kingston Seymour, Clevedon,
Somerset BS21 6XS
T   01934 838895
W   passionflow.co.uk

The Place for Plants
East Berholt Place, East Bergholt,
Suffolk CO7 6UP.
T   01206 299224
W   placeforplants.co.uk

Poyntzfield Herbs
nr Balbair, Black Isle, Dingwall, Ross-Shire.
T   01381 610352 (12.00–1300 and 18.00–
     19.00 only)
W   poyntzfieldherbs.co.uk

Reads Nurseries
Hales Hall, Lodden, Norfolk NR14 6QW
T   01508 548395
W   readsnursery.co.uk

Salley Gardens
32 Landsdowne Drive, West Bridgeford,
Nottingham NG2 7FJ
T   0115 923878 (evenings only)

Seeds of Italy, Franchi Sementi
(sometime seller of Jujube & other interesting
plants)
Unit 3 Phoenix Industrial Estate Rossylyn
Cresent, Harrow, Middx HA1 2 SP
T   020 8427 5020
W   seedsofitaly.com

Unusual Herbs and Edibles
23 Mill Lane, Wrentham, Beccles,
Suffolk NR34 71Q
T   01502 675364
W   www.unusualherbsandedibles.co.uk

APPENDIX I: PLANT NAMES

section	Primary name (and language if not Hindi)	Other names, and their language	English name	Latin name
leaves	chauli	bayam (Bangladeshi), callallo (Afro-Caribbean) lalshank (Bengali) sag (generic) tangerio (Gujerati)	amaranth	*Amaranthus gangeticus* and other *Amaranthus* spp.
leaves	haak	sarson (alt. Hindi) sag (generic) sharissashak (Bangladeshi)	mustard greens	*Brassica juncea*
leaves	kela na patti	kaluaa, hara kela (Bengali) kera (Gujerati)	banana leaf	*Musa* spp.
leaves	kela phulm	kela ka phool (Bengali) kela phuul (Gujerati)	banana flower	*Musa* spp.
leaves	methi		fenugreek	*Trigonella foenum-graecum*
leaves	pan	nagurwell (Gujerati)	betel leaf	*Piper betle*
beans	chairi, chori	barbati (Bangladeshi)	yard-long bean	*Vigna sesquipedalis*, syn. *V. unguiculata* subsp. *sesquipedalis*
beans	guar	goovar (Gujerati) matiggul mullangi (Tamil)	cluster bean	*Cyamopsis tetragonoloba*
beans	kacha channa	bataklaa, channabatalu, chotobata (Bengali) jingera (Gujerati)	green chick pea	*Cicer arietinum*
beans	liva (Gujerati)	sem (Hindi) sheem (Bangladeshi) val (Gujerati and English)	lablab bean, hyacinth bean bonavista bean	*Dolichos lablab* syn. *Lablab purpureus*
beans	papri (Gujerati)	sem (Hindi) sheem (Bangladeshi) val (Gujerati and English)	lablab bean, hyacinth bean bonavista bean	*Dolichos lablab* syn. *Lablab purpureus*

APPENDIX I: PLANT NAMES

section	Primary name (and language if not Hindi)	Other names, and their language	English name	Latin name
beans	valoor (Gujerati)	avaraikai (Tamil) sem (Hindi), sheem (Bangladeshi) val (Gujerati and English)	lablab bean, hyacinth bean bonavista bean	*Dolichos lablab* syn. *Lablab purpureus*
beans	toovar	(toovar also in Gujerati) gungo pea (Afro-Caribbean)	pigeon pea	*Cajanus cajan* syn. *Cajanus indicus*
roots	arvi, patra	dasheen, eddoe (Afro-Caribbean)	taro, elephant's ears	*Colocasia esculenta*
roots	garmar (Gujerati)	makkandi, maku beri, pashan bhedi, pattur chur (all Hindi) pashan bhedi also Sanskrit and Tamil)	Indian coleus	*Plectranthus barbatus* var. *barbatus*, syn. *P. forskohlii*, Coleus barbatus, C. forskohlii
roots	mooli	moola (Bengali) moora (Gujerati) mulaa (Bangladeshi)	white radish	*Raphanus sativus* 'Longipinnatus'
roots	sakurkund	misti alu, mitha (Bangladeshi) rataru (Gujerati) vel-kelenga (Tamil)	sweet potato	*Ipomoea batatas*
fruit	bhindi	binda (Gujerati) deodosh (Bangladeshi)	okra, lady's fingers	*Abelmoschus esculentus* syn. *Hibiscus esculentus*
fruit	brinjal	begoon (Bangladeshi) regona (Gujerati)	aubergine	*Solanum melongena*
fruit	chichingga	(chichingga also in Bangladeshi) gulka (Gujerati) lauki (alt. Hindi)	snake gourd	*Trichosanthes cucumerina* var. *anguina*
fruit	parwal	kotimra (Gujerati) patal (Bangladeshi)	pointed gourd	*Trichosanthes dioica*

APPENDIX I: PLANT NAMES

section	Primary name (and language if not Hindi)	Other names, and their language†	English name	Latin name
ruit	dudhi (Gujerati)	lau (Bangladeshi), lauki (Hindi), kaddu (Hindi, generic name for squash/pumpkin), surrakai (Tamil)	bottle gourd	Lagenaria siceraria
fruit	karella	karala (Gujerati), ucce (Bangladeshi)	bitter melon, bitter gourd	Momordica charantia
fruit	kali turai	jihinnga (Bangladeshi)	angled luffa	Luffa acutangula
fruit	ghia turai	dundhal (Bangladeshi)	smooth luffa	Luffa aegyptiaca syn. L. cylindrica
fruit	kontola	kakrol (Bangladeshi), kakur (alt. Hindi), kandola (Gujerati)	spiny cucumber	Momordica cochinchinensis
fruit	mandanmast	matunda (Gujerati)	passionfruit	Passiflora edulis
fruit	papeeta	penpe (Bengali), papay (Bangladeshi)	papaya, pawpaw	Carica papaya
fruit	babaco (English)		babaco	Carica x heilbornii
fruit	tinda	[tinda also in Gujerati], bimba (Bangladeshi)	Indian round melon	Praecitrullus fistulosus, syn. Citrullus vulgaris var. fistulosus
fruit	tindora (Gujerati)	kundru (Hindi), kovaiki (Tamil), tala kachi (Bangladeshi)	ivy gourd	Coccinia grandis
spices	adraku	(adraku also in Gujerati), aadaa (Bengali)	ginger	Zingiber officinale
spices	amada		mango ginger	Curcuma amada
spices	amb halad		zedoary	Curcuma zedoaria

APPENDIX I: PLANT NAMES

section	Primary name (and language if not Hindi)	Other names, and their languages	English name	Latin name
pices	dhania	(dhania also in Gujerati) dhoni pata (Bengali) kotamella (Tamil)	coriander	*Coriandrum sativum*
spices	haldi	holud (Bengali) hurda (Gujerati)	turmeric	*Curcuma longa*
spices	karri patti	limbra (Gujerati) karaparcha (Tamil)	curry leaf	*Murraya koenigii*
spices	mirich	(mirich in Gujerati & Bangladeshi) luka (Bengali)	chilli	*Capsicum annuum* and related spp.
spices	nimbu ghas	tea (generic) serai (Tamil)	lemongrass	*Cymbopogon* spp.
ornamental	am	ama (Bengali) keri (Gujerati)	mango	*Mangifera indica*
ornamental	amla	amalaki (alt. Hindi) amra (Gujerati) emblic (Bangladeshi)	Indian gooseberry	*Phyllanthus emblica*
ornamental	harfi	nuvee (alt. Hindi)	star gooseberry	*Phyllanthus acidus*
ornamental	amrood	mopera (Gujerati)	guava	*Psidium guajava*
ornamental	ber	beri, badaha (Hindi alt. names) bohr (Gujerati) llanti, iranti (Tamil)	jujube	*Zizyphus* spp.
ornamental	chikku		sapodilla	*Achras sapota* syn. *Manilkara zapota*
ornamental	imli	tetul, tintul (Bengali)	tamarind	*Tamarindus indica*

APPENDIX I: PLANT NAMES

section	Primary name (and language if not Hindi)	Other names, and their language	English name	Latin name
ornamental	jak (Malay)	katahal (Hindi) fonash (Gujerati) palapazham (Tamil)	jackfruit	*Artocarpus heterophyllus*
ornamental	chempedak (Malay)		chempedak	*Artocarpus champedensyn. A. integer*
ornamental	nimbu	lebu (Bengali) limbu (Gujerati)	lime	*Citrus aurantifolia and C. latifolia*
ornamental	magrut (Tamil)	badu limbu (Hindi) makrat (Malay)	kaffir lime, wild lime	*Citrus hystrix*
ornamental	rambutan		rambutan	*Nephelium lappaceum*
ornamental	lychee		lychee	*Litchi chinensis*
ornamental	longan		longan, dragon's eye	*Dimocarpus longan*
ornamental	sahijan	saraguaar (Gujerati) sajina (Bangladeshi) murrungaki (Tamil)	drumstick, horseradish tree	*Moringa oleifera syn. M. pterygosperma*
ornamental	ratalu	(ratalu also in Gujerati) matey alu (Bangladeshi)	greater yam, winged yam	*Dioscorea alata*
ornamental	kand	same in Gujerati	crimson yam	*Dioscorea alata var. pupurea*
ornamental	suran	same in Gujerati	yellow guinea yam	*Dioscorea rotundifolia group, syn. D. cayenensis*

APPENDIX II: BANANA VARIETIES

Please note that several of these species have been awarded RHS Awards of Garden Merit (AGM) for garden performance, although it is for their dramatic foliage rather than for flowering or fruiting potential.

Worth trying for leaf production

Ensete glaucum (syn. E. wilsonii, E. gigantea, Musa nepalensis) (snow banana).

Huge bluish leaves up to 3m (10ft) long, but may be a little thick in texture. Very fast growing under cover. Outside in the wind the leaves shred easily for an Ensete. Hates the wet, though plants have survived the odd UK winter outdoors in well-drained conditions. Try as a half-hardy annual because it reaches up to 2.4m (8ft) in a single season. Awarded AGM.

Musa acuminata 'Zebrina' (blood banana).

Handy almost-dwarf (for a banana) species, with shiny, smooth, mottled red-and-green leaves. Needs a sheltered site as leaves are susceptible to wind damage. Reaches only 2m (6ft) in its first year. Awarded AGM. Cultivars include 'Bordelon' and 'Williams'.

M. basjoo.

Almost hardy, or at least the roots and stem are, if carefully protected over winter. Grows to 2–2.2m (6–7ft) and is rapidly clump forming. Tricky to grow from seed, and has thinner leaves than some species so is particularly vulnerable to wind damage. The leaves I've tried don't taste quite as good as the commonly available commercial banana leaves. New cultivars with a reddish-purple colour, e.g. M. basjoo 'Rubra', are now available. Awarded AGM.

M. coccinea.

Indoor culivation only; prefers shade. Brilliant red flowers and relatively dwarf, reaching only 3m (10ft) or less. Easy to grow from seed. Awarded AGM.

M. sikkimensis (syn. M. hookeri).

Grows at altitudes of up to 2000m, so is a good try for growing outside with minimal protection to the roots. Claimed to withstand -10.C for short periods! Overwinters quite well if brought under cover – it even seems to tolerate being cut down to the roots. Leaves often open pinkish, later sometimes showing attractive red splashes and a red underside. Reaches 3m (10ft) or so in a single season.

M. velutina (pink banana).

Slender, dark green leaves; in the second year produces long-lived pink inflorescences followed by pinkish, velvet-textured fruits that are edible but full of seeds and not very nice! Best grown indoors. Easy to germinate but needs heat for it. Around 2m (6ft) when fruiting size. Awarded AGM for species.

Ensete ventricosum 'Maurelii'

A bit hardier than E. glaucum, it will overwinter with minimal shelter in a pot. Good strains have beautifully bronze foliage in cool conditions (especially when grown outside), though I don't know if this affects the taste. If conditions are warm enough the leaves turn green. Reaches 2.4–3m (8–10ft) in two years.

E. superbum (rock banana)

Originally from Thailand, this has large, bulbous trunks and big leaves. Easy to grow from seed, growing as a half-hardy annual or biennial. Two- or three-year-old plants grow to 3.5m (12ft) or more.

Musa cheesmanii

A close relative, possibly a subspecies, of M. sikkimensis, and may be as hardy. Pale green leaves; grows to around 3.5m (12ft). Easy to raise from seed.

M. itineran

From China: mature plants of this species are said to withstand light frosts. Leaves are whitish-coloured below. Good for outdoors in UK summers but tricky to overwinter as it seems prone to damping off – best used for bedding. Easy to grow from seed. Reaches 2.8m (9ft).

M. ornata (flowering banana)

For indoors only, a relatively small species with long grey-green leaves with red veins, followed in about three years from seed by a big spike of lilac-mauve bracts, showing the yellow flowers inside. If you hand-pollinate these you may get a crop of yellowish redsplashed fruit, which is sweet if seedy.
Reaches 2–2.4m (6–8ft). Awarded AGM

M. thomsonii (Thompson's banana)

Not at all a hardy sort, being a native of the subtropics. The young leaves are red flushed. Easy to grow from seed, it can reach 5m (16ft) rapidly.

Musella lasiocarpa (Chinese yellow banana)

Small growing and from high altitudes, this may be a good bet outside. The trunk reaches only 1–1.2m (3–4ft), and produces typical bright-green banana leaves. The roots will stand some cold provided they are kept dry, perhaps -5.C (23.F) for a short time; however the trunk is most definitely not frost hardy. At four years old the plants will produce weird, bright-yellow persistent inflorescences like water lilies on the top of the trunks, but unfortunately these are inedible. Relatively dwarf, for a banana, reaching only 2.6m (8ft). Seed may need chilling for germination.

Worth trying for edible flowers

Ensete ventricosum (Abyssinian banana)

Cultivated for its edible flowers for centuries although rarely seen for sale, it has strong foliage that withstands wind damage better than M. basjoo. Takes at least three to four years to flower from seed, and needs to come indoors for winter. Grows to 3–5m (10–16ft).

M. x paradisiaca

(Sometimes called the red or blood banana). Needs to be indoors at all times and grows even larger than M. cavendishii. Bright-red, delicious-but-tart flower bud, followed by sweet but very seedy fruits if grown from seed. Best selections are grown from offsets. Alternatively, almost-seedless clones are available, e.g. 'Goldfinger' and 'Rajapuri' (see below).

M. x paradisiaca 'Rajapuri'.

Said to be the hardiest fruiting banana, this is grown at high altitudes in India and reaches only 2m (6ft) tall. It is propagated only from offsets, and flowers in its second or third year but needs to be potted and brought indoors for winter. Stems have a white bloom; the flower buds are dark-purple to maroon and said to be delicious. This fruits well in pots too: it takes two years to come into production and then crops every year. The bananas are tiny – only about three to four inches long – but sweet.

Musa cavendishii (Canary Islands banana)

Propagated only by suckers or offsets, as this is the plant that produces the familiar banana normally sold for food, with no seeds. One for the (very) large office. A sucker will produce flowers and fruit after three years, when the plant will reach about 3.5m (12ft) high and 5m (16ft) across. To encourage it to flower, remove al the suckers except one. If you can, buy the extra-dwarf strain, M. acuminata 'Dwarf Cavendish' (awarded AGM), which is about a third smaller.

Also available from eco-logic books

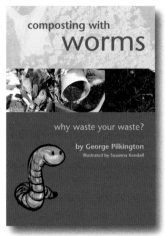

Composting with Worms

by George Pilkington

George Pilkington has been working with worms and preaching their benefits for over 20 years. During that time he has set up a company, Nurturing Nature that has won the coveted Green Apple 'Gold' Award for Best Environmental Practice. He advises councils and other organisations and gives lectures around the country on worm composting. This book is the collection of his many years' experience as an unashamed, worm composting fanatic.

In this book you will find out:
- How worms turn waste into compost
- Which worm bin is most suitable for your needs
- What to do when good bins turn bad
- Which worms to use
- The best uses for your worm compost
- Frequently asked questions

All this, together with a worm menu, will set you on your way to converting your waste, easily and efficiently to valuable, soil-enhancing compost

Britain's bestselling worm composting manual with more than 12,000 copies in print.

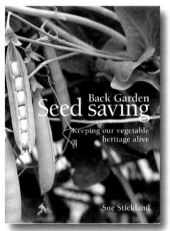

Back Garden Seed Saving

by Sue Stickland

First published in 2001 and updated in 2008 this is the classic seed saving manual giving easy to follow crop-by-crop guidelines to help you save seed for yourself

The latest strains of runner beans may give long stringless pods, but will they crop well on a cold windswept site? Dwarf peas may be the easiest to grow commercially, but you will still find the six-foot types in many gardens - they look attractive, crop for longer and taste 'like peas used to taste'. As such varieties have disappeared from the seed catalogues over the past few decades, dedicated gardeners have kept them in cultivation.

In this popular book you will also find out about some of the vegetable varieties no longer found in the seed catalogues, and others that are there now but may not be for much longer. It introduces you to some of the gardeners who grow such varieties, their tales and tips, and their infectious enthusiasm.

"Superb practical book… and one that will pay for itself in no time at all"
Allotment and Leisure Gardener

Also available from eco-logic books

Valuable Vegetables

by Mandy Pullen

When the author Mandy Pullen turned that a one and a half acre field into a successful, small scale market garden. She found she could grow not only enough produce to feed herself and her family, but have enough left over to run a thriving vegetable box scheme. This unique book is based on her own practical experience. In this book you can find out how to:

- Set up your garden and make it productive
- Use both simple and complex rotations to keep your soil healthy and productive
- Maintain the fertility of your plot without expensive fertilisers
- Save money by saving your own seed and propagating your own plants
- Erect and maintain a polytunnel
- Deal with weeds, pests and diseases without using chemicals
- Set up and run a successful, small business selling vegetables

All this, together with complete cultivation details for:

- 48 vegetables ● 21 herbs ● All the major soft fruits

"I'd certainly recommend it for beginners and small scale producers looking for sound practical advice"
Organic Way

Growing Unusual Vegetables

by Simon Hickmott

Author Simon Hickmott is a plantsman, seed saver and proprietor of the late lamented Future Foods, a company specialising in rare and unusual edible plants. In this book he has brought together over 90 unusual vegetables, all of them edible. Each plant comes complete with comprehensive cultivation instructions and fascinating notes on its origin, history and uses.

With this indispensable guide you can turn your garden or allotment into a unique storehouse of useful and unusual edible plants, many of which are surprisingly easy to grow. Then you can bring variety to the food on your plate that no supermarket or greengrocer will ever provide. An excellent companion title to Asian Vegetables.

"A unique fascinating book that broadens the kitchen gardner's horizon and genuinely says something new"
Kitchen Garden Magazine

eco-logic books ● Mulberry House ● 19 Maple Grove ● Bath ● BA2 3AF ● T: 01225 484472
For a complete list or to order visit **www.eco-logicbooks.com**